PERGAMON INTERNATIONAL LIBRARY
of Science, Technology, Engineering and Social Studies
The 1000-volume original paperback library in aid of education,
industrial training and the enjoyment of leisure
Publisher: Robert Maxwell, M.C.

HISTORY AND TRUTH

THE PERGAMON TEXTBOOK
INSPECTION COPY SERVICE

An inspection copy of any book published in the Pergamon International Library will gladly
be sent to academic staff without obligation for their consideration for course adoption or
recommendation. Copies may be retained for a period of 60 days from receipt and returned
if not suitable. When a particular title is adopted or recommended for adoption for class
use and the recommendation results in a sale of 12 or more copies, the inspection copy may
be retained with our compliments. If after examination the lecturer decides that the book
is not suitable for adoption but would like to retain it for his personal library, then a discount
of 10% is allowed on the invoiced price. The Publishers will be pleased to receive suggestions
for revised editions and new titles to be published in this important International Library.

Other Titles of Interest

JONES, F. C.
The Far East: A Concise History

MORRIS, A. J. A.
Parliamentary Democracy in the Nineteenth Century

RYDZEWSKI, P.
Art and Human Experience

SCHREIBER, S. M.
An Introduction to Literary Criticism

THIMANN, J. C.
A Short History of French Literature

WELLS, G. A.
The Plays of Grillparzer

International Journal of the Contemporary Artist
LEONARDO
Founder-Editor: Frank J. Malina

LEONARDO is a quarterly international professional archival journal for artists, art teachers and those interested in visual or plastic fine arts and in the impact upon them of science and technology.

In LEONARDO all tendencies in art are treated, ranging from figurative painting and sculpture to kinetic art and to the application in art of computers, lasers, magnetism, alpha brain waves, etc.

The importance and outstanding value of LEONARDO have become recognized by artists, scientists, art and design teachers, and by leading universities and art schools throughout the world.

The terms of our inspection copy service apply to all
the above books. Full details of all books listed will
gladly be sent upon request.

HISTORY AND TRUTH

by

ADAM SCHAFF

*Director, European Centre for Co-ordination
of Research into the Social Sciences, Vienna*

PERGAMON PRESS

Oxford   .   New York
Toronto   .   Sydney   .   Paris   .   Frankfurt

U. K.	Pergamon Press Ltd., Headington Hill Hall, Oxford OX3 0BW, England
U. S. A.	Pergamon Press Inc., Maxwell House, Fairview Park, Elmsford, New York 10523, U.S.A.
CANADA	Pergamon of Canada Ltd., P.O. Box 9600, Don Mills M3C 2T9, Ontario, Canada
AUSTRALIA	Pergamon Press (Aust.) Pty. Ltd., 19a Boundary Street, Rushcutters Bay, N.S.W. 2011, Australia
FRANCE	Pergamon Press SARL, 24 rue des Ecoles, 75240 Paris, Cedex 05, France
WEST GERMANY	Pergamon Press GmbH, 6242 Kronberg-Taunus, Pferdstrasse 1, Frankfurt-am-Main, West Germany

First Edition 1976

Library of Congress Cataloging in Publication Data

Schaff, Adam.
History and truth.

(Pergamon international library of science, technology, engineering, and social studies)
Translation of Historia i prawda.
Bibliography: p. 261
1. History—Philosophy. I. Title.
D16.8.S25413 1976   901   76-5469
ISBN 0-08-020579-8
ISBN 0-08-020595-X flexi

Printed in Great Britain by Wheaton & Co. Exeter

Contents

v

PART ONE
Epistemological Premises

In Place of an Introduction

Historians on the Causes of the French Revolution

"At a certain stage of their development, the material productive forces of society come in conflict with the existing relations of production. . . . Then begins an epoch of social revolution. . . . No social order ever perishes before all the productive forces for which there is room in it have developed; and new, higher relations of production never appear before the material conditions of their existence have matured in the womb of the old society itself. Therefore mankind always sets itself only such tasks as it can solve. . . ."

> K. Marx, "Preface to *A Contribution to the Critique of Political Economy. Selected Works,* English ed. Moscow, 1951, p. 392

Pour qu'une révolution éclate, il faut que les classes inférieres souffrent d'un terrible malaise ou d'une grande oppression. Mais il faut aussi qu'elles aient un commencement de force et par conséquent d'espoir.

> Jean Jaurès, *Histoire socialiste de la Révolution Française*

The French Revolution of 1789 is an historical fact of world significance. Among historians no one doubts this and no one will omit this fact when characterizing the historical process of the epoch. Difficulties and differences of opinion can, and do in fact, arise regarding a number of even the most fundamental problems connected with the presentation of this historical fact. The determination of the date of the event which constituted the beginning of the French Revolution, whether it was one or a number of revolutions, the character of this or the subsequent revolutions, and when the end of the revolution occurred are all problematic. Nevertheless, such conflicts and doubts do not alter the basic agreement of all historians as to the fundamental issue: the French Revolution was a significant event for the historical process.

Every historian of a given level who possesses his own individuality sees, represents and elucidates this event in his own fashion. The general agreement about the statement that the French Revolution did, in fact, take place and that it was a significant event conceals, in effect, an essential discord of views. This discord pertains not only to the explanation and interpretation of historical facts but also to the description and selection and even to the articulation of the historical process; that is, to the separation in the historian's perception of those events which, as partial facts, compose the entirety of the historical image of that great fact which was the French Revolution.

Thus, historians differ in their visions of the historical process and as a result we obtain different and sometimes even contradictory representations of one and the same fact. Why?

The present work is devoted to answering this question. To facilitate an analysis of the problem and to visualize it more vividly and tangibly it seems worthwhile to employ a specific example. Our choice of the French Revolution is based on several considerations. Firstly, this constitutes a truly significant historical fact. Secondly, its remoteness in time makes it possible to avoid an emotional impingement on the perception of the events. Thirdly, it is an event of the type in which not only those contemporary to it were socially involved but subsequent generations as well, so giving rise to a differentiation of the atttitudes of historians living in various periods. Fourthly and lastly, it is an event sufficiently remote and simultaneously so important that it entered the sphere of interest of a number of subsequent generations of historians. Thus it was possible to confront the vision of this same event in different historical periods.

In undertaking the decision to employ this example it was necessary to concretize the object of interest. The French Revolution is, of course, a subject so vast and many-sided that it cannot be taken as a whole within the framework of the exemplary analysis in which we are interested. We shall, therefore, limit the scope of our interest to the causes of the French Revolution and, in particular, to the problem of its economic causes.

One may postulate in a positivist vein a purely descriptive and facto-graphic history as purportedly the sole objective one; but no historian worthy of his salt is able to put such a postulate into effect. It is not only because of his historical cognition that he is unable to reject completely the influence of the subjective factor (this will be dealt with more than once in further considerations) but also because he will not be able to limit himself to answering the question of *what* happened. He must also engage in considerations of *why* did it happen in precisely such a fashion.

In circumscribing in this way the scope of our interests we have of our own free will imposed on ourselves one more rigour in order to avoid unnecessary complications and difficulties; we shall consider solely the works of French authors. The purpose is to avoid the introduction of an additional factor differentiating the attitudes of the historians; that linked with various cultural backgrounds, national interests and so forth.

We shall undertake the presentation of the views which are of interest to us in chronological order, beginning logically with the authors contemporary with the Revolution who wrote their work either on the spur of the moment or shortly after the events had taken place. The reading of works on the Revolution written during this period confirms the opinion that (in spite of appearances) it is extremely difficult to write current history. This is due not only to emotional involvement in the event, but also to the somewhat paradoxical fact that access to well-ordered sources is more difficult at the time than later on. In the case of the historical writing of the period of the Revolution an additional negative factor enters the picture; this was not history treated as a scientific discipline in accordance with the standards of a later age. Historical writing in the scientific model appears only later, dating from the period of the Restoration. The works of the authors contemporary with the Revolution are characterized by their authentic involvement in the current struggle and by their political nature. In at least one case—that of Barnave—the depth of theoretical grasp of a uniquely pioneering character is quite astonishing.

Among the many publications, memoirs, pamphlets, etc., of the period we have selected only a few works bearing in mind, above all, the representative nature of their involvement in the struggle for and against the Revolution. We have consciously selected those which, though they are not the works of professional historians, aspire to an historical presentation of the period and do not serve exclusively political aims (as, for example, the speeches and writings of the leaders of various parties and groups during the period of the Revolution). It is, of course, impossible to delineate a precise and clear boundary. Our aim, however, is the analysis of the works of historians, that is, of people who in writing the history of given events do so (seeing in this aspiration their professional mission) with the intention of transmitting the objective truth and in the conviction that they had really acquired it. What is interesting from the point of cognition and methodology is not the analysis of conscious lying (the occurrence is a banal issue from the scientific point of view), or of conscious tendentiousness for which the description of events is only the means for the achievement of some political aim, but an analysis of the cognitive deformation of an historian which takes place outside his consciousness and in spite of his different aims and aspirations.

We shall begin with the decided opponents of the Revolution. Among the foremost was Abbé Barruel who assumed the position of a fanatical opponent of the revolt. In 1798 he published his *Mémoires pour servir à l'histoire du jacobinisme* (new editions appeared in subsequent years). This is a work devoted to a single idea, but it is pursued with a consistency worthy of a maniac. According to him, the Revolution was the result of an internal conspiracy of the Jacobins. Among the key figures of the conspiracy were Voltaire, d'Alambert, Diderot and . . . King Frederick II. This was an example of a propaganda trick known to history before Barruel and since.

Here is a sample of Barruel's style:

> We have seen people blind to the causes of the French Revolution. We have also known those who wish to convince us that any revolutionary and conspiratory sect even before this Revolution was solely an illusion. According to them all the troubles of France and all the terrors of Europe succeeded each other and were connected with each other solely as a result of a coincidence of circumstances incapable of being foreseen. . . .
>
> On the basis of facts and armed with proofs which shall be presented in these Memoirs, we shall use a different language. We shall state and demonstrate that which the peoples and their leaders should know. We shall tell them everything that has occurred during this French Revolution including the most terrible crimes, all of which were foreseen, thought out, schemed, decided, determined; all was the result of the most profound criminality since all was prepared and brought about by people who kept in their hands the threads of a conspiracy hatched long ago in the secret societies . . . the cause of the Revolution, the cause of its great crimes, its cruelties . . . rests completely in the conspiracy hatched a long time ago.

If among our readers are those who will draw a conclusion from this that it is necessary to smash the rest of the Jacobins or all of society will perish . . . I shall answer this; Yes, one may await such a universal misfortune or smash this sect![1]

The above is, of course, only an historical curiosity, only an illustration of the intensity of the political struggle of the time and the emotional tensions connected with it, and not an example of an historian's work. One could put this matter away into the storeroom of factual proofs showing the blind hatred of the ruling classes towards a revolution were it not for the fact that a few decades later an historian of the Revolution, worthy of his keep, and, in addition, an adherent of socialism reverted to this subject. We have in mind Louis Blanc's *Histoire de la Révolution Française* which appeared in 1874. In the second volume of his work the third chapter entitled "Les Révolutionnaires Mystiques" is devoted to the influence of the Freemasons on the Revolution. Without hatred—on the contrary, in a factual fashion—Blanc attempts to show that the Revolution was the work of a conspiracy of a secret organization. Describing in detail the mechanism of its functioning, pertaining primarily to the "Illuminist" organization headed by Weishaupt, he refers to a number of sources, although their reliability is questionable (amongst others he refers also to Barruel). This is an interesting aside to the problem of historical "facts", in particular to the problem of those which should be acknowledged as such in one case and not in another.

In the specific instance which interests us, the matter probably rested on the fact of the stubborn maintenance of the conspiracy theory by the reactionaries and the total placement of responsibility on the Freemasons. As a result, Liberal historians, especially when the role of classes and the class struggle in the French Revolution began to be emphasized, omitted the role of Freemasons' organizations as lacking significance from the historical viewpoint. Thus, while one should not subscribe in the least to Barruel's primitive conception, one should not go to the other extreme which would lead to a negation of facts. If it is true, as Louis Blanc maintained, that the greatest figures of the Revolution were Freemasons, then one cannot simply dismiss the role of this organization in the origin and development of the Revolution. In any case, this is an issue worthy of serious study and, if

[1] Notes are at end of chapter on p.41.

research were to confirm this hypothesis, then it would not bring discredit to the Revolution nor reduce the problems of the Revolution exclusively to that of a conspiracy.

This marginal remark does not, by any means, change our view on Barruel's work nor modify our appraisal of it.

The work of Joseph de Maistre may be considered as a specific supplement to that of Barruel. His religious outlook, which led him to mysticism, is the reason why in his *Considérations sur la France* (1796) he grasped the causes of the Revolution in a particular fashion; there is, in fact, only one cause—divine dispensation or, more properly, divine chastisement. People are only instruments of Providence or the scourge of God. In the final analysis the Revolution leads to saving the monarchy which becomes stronger and purer than before. Only Robespierre could undertake the "dirty job" of conducting victorious external wars which added splendour to France; only he could overcome the centrifugal tendencies of the provinces, thus strengthening the state.

De Maistre also joins Barruel in his hatred of the Revolution, but he argues from opposite premises; where Barruel saw conscious human activity a conspiracy, de Maistre voiced the nullity of human will and aspirations, since man is but an instrument of Providence and, as a result, his acts differ from his intentions.

> The order of the world never comes forth more clearly in the light of day and never does Providence become more apparent than at the time when higher forces take the place of human ones; this is precisely what we are witnessing at present.
> What is most striking in the French Revolution is the turbulent force with which it smashes all obstacles. With its whirlwind it carries away everything that human force could counterpose to it like light chaff. . . .
> It has been correctly noted that the French Revolution tends more to guide people than to be guided by them. This is a most accurate observation. While it can, in fact, be said of all great upheavals it has never been more striking than in this period.
> Even the criminals who seemed to guide the fate of the Revolution are but simple instruments and the moment they aspire to dominate it—they fall ignominiously . . . they were forced to this by the course of events; a previously conceived plan would not have suceeded. [2]

As I have remarked above, these and similar works do not contribute very much to the problem of interest to us. Their value rests rather in reflecting the climate of the epoch. The matter is different when it comes to the testimonies of the liberals, although they likewise cannot claim to be scholarly historical works. I shall limit myself to the works of two characteristic figures of the period of the Revolution: Joseph Barnave, one of the eminent representatives of the initial revolutionary period, and Necker's daughter, Mme de Staël.

Joseph Barnave, an advocate of the constitutional monarchy, played an important role in the initial period of the Revolution and died on the scaffold during the Terror in 1793. Barnave, one of the greatest orators of the Constituent Assembly, was also a thinker and a writer. The notes left by him (among them also the *Introduction à la Revolution Française*) were published by his sister in 1843 in honour of her brother's memory. In spite of the outstanding value of the *Introduction* (in this work Barnave comes forth as a forerunner of the Restoration historians whom Marx considered to be pioneers in introducing the category of social classes into science, and even to a certain degree as the precursors of historical materialism[3]) it was only Jean Jaurès who evaluated it properly and introduced it into literature in his *Histoire Socialiste de la Révolution Française.*[4]

Jaurés employed the example of Barnave's ideas, as representative of the bourgeoisie of the Dauphiné, as proof of the fact that the growth of the bourgeoisie's economic strength brought about, as a consequence, a growth of its ideological consciousness. Had Paris failed, the provinces themselves could have initiated a revolution.[5] Reading the work of Barnave, a young politician at the time, does indeed give rise to admiration. It is an introduction to a study of the Revolution in the full meaning of the word; not simply its history but rather sociological reflections on history which make it possible to grasp properly historical events. Thus it stands on the borderline of the theory and methodology of history and in its concept is, as Jaurès emphasized, a precursor of Marxist historical materialism (Jaurès speaks of the economic interpretation of history).

Barnave began his considerations with an extremely important methodological postulate—to consider the French Revolution not in isolation but in the context of the social evolution of contemporary Europe; not as the outcome of fortuitous actions but as the result of a certain historical necessity.

> It would be an idle effort if in attempting to form a proper image of the great revolution now taking place in France one were to regard it in an isolated fashion,

detaching it from the history of the empires surrounding us from the centuries which have preceeded us in time . . . only by considering the general movement which, since feudalism to the present day, has caused the European governments to continue to change their forms can one clearly perceive the point which we have reached as well as the general causes which have led us to it.

There is no doubt that revolutions in the domain of forms of government just as all phenomena of nature dependent on human passions and will cannot be subordinated to such fixed and calculable laws as those which pertain to the motion of inanimate matter; nevertheless, among this mass of causes the combined influence of which gives rise to political events, there are also causes so closely connected with the nature of things, which act in such a constant and regular fashion and have such a preponderance in comparison with the influences of fortuitous cases that—in a given period of time—they lead in an almost inevitable fashion to a determined result. It is precisely they who almost always change the face of nations and all the petty events find their place within their general results; it is they who prepare the great epochs of history while the secondary causes to whose action this is ascribed only determined it as a rule.[6]

Barnave's further reasoning on the subject of the dependence of governmental forms on social conditions and on the changes of these forms as functions of changes of social conditions are even more strikingly of a precursory nature in relation to Marx. The importance of these considerations which constitute an introduction to the subject proper—the causes of the French Revolution—sanctions their being quoted *in extenso*. The more so that, although Jaurès had drawn attention to this work, it is still not appreciated properly up to the present.

Human will does not constitute laws; it has no or practically no influence on the form of governments. It is the nature of things—the social period reached by a given people, the land inhabited by it, its riches, needs, customs and habits—which distributes power; it bestows it in accord with time and place to an individual, to many, to all, and divides it between them in various proportions. Those who hold power thereby constitute laws so as to be able to exercise it and to stabilize their possession of it; empires are organized and constituted in this fashion. The progress of the social conditions creates, step by step, new sources of power, changes old and establishes new relations of forces. At such a time old laws cannot maintain themselves very long; since, in fact, new powers exist, then new laws must be shaped in order to have these powers function. In this fashion governments sometimes change their form by means of peaceful and insensible progress while at other times by means of violent commotions.[7]

Barnave then considers the subject of the origin of private property which he links with agriculture and sees inequality amongst people as arising from the emergence of private property. It is on this basis that aristocracy is born. A higher level of development, marked by industry and trade, leads to the new form of democracy.

With the moment that industry and trade become widespread among the people and form a new means of enrichment for the working class, a revolution in the sphere of political rights begins to take shape; a new distribution of riches prepares a new distribution of power. Just as the possession of land gave rise to the aristocracy, industrial property gives rise to the power of the people; it gains freedom, multiplies itself and begins to influence the course of affairs.[8]

Barnave employed the word "people" (peuple) as a synonym of the "Third Estate", that is, all those who did not belong to the privileged classes—the nobility and the clergy. Let us recall that the author met his death in 1937. What intellectual insight and social farsightedness was necessary to be able to write at that time the following words which clearly limit this apparent faith in the unity of the "people": "In small states the strength (of the people) will be so great that at times it would gain power. It is, however, true that this new kind of riches may give rise to a new aristocracy, to a certain type of bourgeois and commercial aristocracy."[9]

How did a man who was able to examine the mechanism of social development so profoundly and penetratingly pose the problem of the causes of the revolution?

Barnave took up this problem in the twelfth chapter of his work putting forth a hierarchy of causes which effected the Revolution.

Firstly, there was a change in the relations between social classes. This was occurring throughout Europe. The development of industry and trade enriches, on the one hand, the industrial part of the people ("la partie industrieuse du peuple") Barnave maintained, having the bourgeoisie clearly in mind, while on the other hand it leads to the downfall of the great landowners, thus bringing closer together social classes in respect of property. At the same time, science and education bring them closer together in respect of customs and enliven a spirit of equality among people. To these natural causes one should add the influence of royal authority, which combats the aristocracy by calling upon the help of the people. The people aid the royal authorities in this struggle, "but when it acquires sufficient strength in order not to be satisfied any longer with a subordinate role, it gives rise to an outburst and takes its place in the government". As a result: "When the unfortunate Louis XVI came to the throne everything in France was ready for a democratic revolution and the conduct of the government favoured it markedly."[10]

Secondly, following the conclusions of the previous point, the weakness of royal authority was a cause of the Revolution. In a society with a completely altered class situation only a ruler of great individuality could have saved the institution of the monarchy; Louis XVI was not such a man.

Thirdly, the false policy in respect of the growing bourgeoisie was closely linked with the problem of the monarch's personal traits. Instead of emphasizing it, as the only chance for overcoming the crisis of the system, it was cast aside, while the essentially powerless aristocracy was extalled.

> If a method of counteracting the gaining of power by the people did exist, it lay in having the people join the existing government and in opening to the Third Estate all the roads to a career; something quite the opposite was done. Since the corrupt government had smashed the aristocracy it was thought that a paternalistic government should restore its previous position. The Parliaments were revoked, all the privileges derived by right of birth were acknowledged anew, the road to a military career for the Third Estate was closed more than ever, a contradiction between laws and customs and the natural courses of events was created—everything was done to increase the envy of one class and the grudges of another. The Third Estate was made to regard the royal authority as a hostile force which it alone could maintain or abolish, the aristocracy was given back its feeling of smugness which subsequently, when it was desired to strike at it, led it to provoke a revolution of which it became the victim.[11]

Fourthly and lastly, America's war against her British rulers, a war supported by France, and in turn affecting France, considerably influenced the outbreak of the Revolution. The effect manifested itself in three ways: the American war helped to spread the ideas of revolution and freedom in France, it further brought out the dissemination of these ideas in the army and, through increased expenditures, led to a breakdown of France's financial system and, in consequence, to an economic crisis.

Barnave, in spite of all his insight and profound historical reflections, looked at the events through the eyes of the bourgeoisie, acting as its spokesman. As a result, while seeing and understanding a great deal in respect of the bourgeoisie's role in the Revolution, Barnave did not perceive any other social problems or conflicts apart from the collision of the bourgeoisie with the aristocracy and the monarchy. In particular, he did not note the importance of the other components of the "people" (i.e. the Third Estate), apart from the bourgeoisie—the peasantry and the industrial workers. This is probably why he did not concern himself with the problem of the misery of these social strata, caused by the crisis and in particular by crop failure. The problem of misery, especially among the peasantry, as one of the causes of the Revolution, a problem which was of such great concern to later historians was simply not noted by such a penetrating observer of the events which he had himself witnessed.

This does not in any way negate Barnave's significant role as a theorist of the Revolution. He considerably surpassed Barruel or de Maistre; he was a man who could perceive profoundly the mechanism of the bourgeoisie's class struggle against feudalism. In the field of theory he took a stand which was truly original. Simultaneously, his limitations were typical for a representative of the bourgeoisie; they closed his eyes to that which lay beyond the interests of the bourgeoisie and even more, to that which was opposed to it.

The matter does not, however, present itself in such a way as to make the mechanism of class influence on historical perception absolutely restrictive. As an illustration we shall refer to Mme de Staël's presentation of the causes of the Revolution.[12]

Mme de Staël was Necker's daughter and, understandably from a psychological point of view, she wrote her history of the Revolution to a great degree in honour of her father's memory; nonetheless, she presented it with exceptional insight and in respect to the problems of class analysis of society she may be ranked among the historians of the Restoration period.

Let us begin with the epigraph to the entire work which is characteristic of Mme de Staël's line of thought: "Revolutions which break out in great states are not the results of accident or the caprise of the peoples" (*Mémoires de Sully,* vol. I, p. 133). Such is the assumption which Mme de Staël acts upon in relation to the French Revolution; it was not a fortuitous event but a necessity.[13] Its causes should be sought in the dissatisfaction of all the classes of contemporary society—the aristocracy, the clergy and the people.[14] The profound cause of the Revolution rested, however, in the altered position of the bourgeoisie.

The daughter of the great financier Necker saw the source of the growing power of the bourgeoisie precisely in finances. Taxes and credit had become a necessity for France, especially when wars were waged by means of mercenary armies and not vassals. The parliaments which granted credits and established new taxes sought, just as in England, to take advantage of these circumstances for criticizing the administration while supporting themselves with public opinion. This also became a factor in the growth of the importance of the new class.

> This new power daily gained more strength and the nation liberated itself, one might say, by itself. As long as the privileged classes possessed great strength one could govern the state like the court, by manipulating deftly the passions or interests of a few individuals; but when another social class, the most numerous and most active, sensed its importance—the discovery and adoption of some broader way of conduct became indispensable.[15]

In Mme de Staël's view, the cause of the Revolution rested, however, not only in the altered social position of the new class but also in the misery of the peasantry and in the arbitrary nature of the authorities. A new element appeared in her reasoning, which will be of particular interest to us in further reflections: the element of the misery of the people as a cause of the revolutionary explosion and its severity.

> Young people and foreigners who did not know France before the Revolution and who today see a people enriched by the division of landed property and the abolishment of the dues of the feudal regime cannot imagine the situation of this country when the people bore the burdens of all the privileges. The advocates of slavery in the colonies often said that the French peasant was more wretched than the Negro . . . misery increases ignorance and ignorance in turn increases misery; when we ask why the French people were so cruel during the Revolution we cannot find another cause than the absence of happiness which led to an absence of morality.[16]
>
> The taxes which rested exclusively on the people have reduced it to hopeless poverty. Fifty years ago a certain French lawyer still called the Third Estate, in accord with custom, a people subject to Corvee and taxes at will and mercy.[17]

The views of Barruel and de Maistre, on the one hand, and those of Barnave and Mme de Staël, on the other, can be considered as representative of certain groups of people; contemporaries of the Revolution, who sought to reflect on its causes. It was a conspiracy or divine chastisement in the view of the opponents of the Revolution, while its liberal observers saw it as the explicit result of class relations and misery. The failure to include here the views of the radical advocates of the Revolution, expecially the respresentatives of the Jacobins, is explained by the fact that they did not leave behind writings in which the problems of the Revolution's causes had been directly dealt with and, in accordance with the assumption made, we are consciously restricting ourselves only to such works.

As may be seen above, the respresentatives of the liberals did already perceive the class sources of the Revolution while it was under way. Analysis of society and the class structure became characteristic traits and the strong point of the Restoration historians. It was taken up in the works of Thiers as well as Thierry and Guizot. The approach to the problem of the causes of the Revolution adopted in this period can be illustrated on the example of Laponneray.[18]

He was a professional historian belonging to a new epoch. He began with the characteristic declaration of faith; a desire to establish true facts, cleansing them from the deformations and ill-will of the majority of the historians. The theoretical premises on which his work was based are: firstly, the Revolution had its profound causes in the historical process and in the progress of ideas;[19] secondly, the sources of the Revolution should be sought in the class contradictions of French society.

> The French nation was divided into two classes one of which was the exploiter and the other the exploited and, to put the matter more precisely, the exploited class which was composed of the Third Estate and the common people, itself formed the nation since the exploiting class was only an imperceptible minority. The nobility and the clergy possessed all the privileges and all the prerogatives; they obtained all the honours, positions and dignities. The Third Estate and the people bore the burden of the taxes and a most degrading slavery. Such a state of affairs could not last long.[20]

Laponneray was not only aware of the concept of social classes but he also saw the class conflicts as based on exploitation; the "people" is not identified by him with the Third Estate but is outside of this Estate as the "multitude".

According to Laponneray relations between classes did not always take the same shape. In the past the nobility's position was sanctioned by its function of defending those who were dependent on it. The nobility later betrayed this function while the role of the Third Estate began to grow, favoured by the royal authority. It was in this situation that eighteenth-century philosophy arose and played an immense role in the undermining of the old order.

> Such was the state of affairs when the philosophy of the 18th century, the daughter of the religious reformation, appeared as a star shining in the deep night. Immense work was accomplished at this time not only in France but in all of Europe; a powerful, spiritual ferment arose. The method of free inquiry which Luther employed in order to shake the Roman Church to its foundations became a

terrible weapon with which philosophy undermined the rotten edifice of old beliefs
and prejudices. Everything became open to discussion and investigation; the severe
inquiries of rationalism showed no leniency towards any fault or abuse. A revolution became inevitable; not one of those revolutions which the history of fourteen
centuries of our monarchy provided so many examples, superficial revolutions
which limited themselves to replacing one form by another and substituting new
abuses in the place of old ones, but a profound, radical, egalitarian revolution
which was to enter deep into the innards of society so as to cause its complete
regeneration.[21]

Thus, in addition to the class conflict, its ideological expression—
Enlightenment philosophy—is seen to be one of the causes of the
Revolution. Today such a remark may appear banal but at that time an
idea formulated in this way was an innovation and, in effect, it
introduced both these factors as a permanent part of the arsenal of
arguments relating to the causes of the Revolution.

It may be worthwhile to refer here as a curiosity to two remarks by
Voltaire and Rousseau regarding the perspectives of the Revolution.
Laponneray used these views, and correctly so, as a proof of the
profound philosophical thought which prepared the upheaval. On
April 2, 1764, Voltaire wrote in one of his letters:

Everything that I see is sowing the seeds of the revolution which will come
inevitably, although I shall not have the pleasure of being its witness. The French
always arrive at everything too late but finally they do arrive. Knowledge has
become general on such a widespread scale that at the first chance an outburst will
take place and then there will be quite an uproar. The young are happy—they shall
see many things.

Four years earlier, in 1760, J. J. Rousseau wrote:

We are coming close to a critical stage and to the age of revolutions. I believe it is
impossible for the great monarchies of Europe to last much longer; they all
glittered and everything that glitters is already declining. I have in mind more
detailed reasons than this maxim but it would not be advantageous to expound
them here, anyhow everyone understands them well.[22]

It should be added that Laponneray pointed to the financial crisis as
the direct cause of the Revolution.

What we have quoted thus far is material of interest for characterizing the epoch but from the point of view of historical writing; with
the possible exception of Laponneray, it is still very crude and naïve. It
is only during the subsequent period after the 1848 revolutions that
qualitatively new phenomena appear in French historical writing and
along with them was initiated great controversy on the subject of the
economic causes of the Revolution which has lasted among French

historians to the present day. Of special importance were two great works devoted to the French Revolution, both considered as classics today: the first, Jules Michelet's many-volumed *Histoire de la Révolution,* began to appear in 1847, that is, on the eve of the 1848 Revolution, while the second, Alexis de Tocqueville's *L'Ancient Régime et la Révolution,* was being prepared at the same time. It appeared in 1856 but was not completed because of the author's death.

Jule Michelet was an ardent advocate of Danton and this emerges clearly from the pages of his very literary—as compared with the present-day style of scholarly works—*History of the Revolution.*[23]

This is, nevertheless, a work of erudition, based on considerable source material.

Michelet perceived a multitude of causes of the Revolution. He included in particular the influence of ideology and, especially, the views of Voltaire and Rousseau. This influence was far reaching, even to the court and the Queen herself. Apparently everyone wanted a revolution but drew back in the face of concrete, regenerative action. Michelet remarked humourously:

> Everyone appears to be converted and everyone wants the Revolution; everyone wants it not for himself but for others. The nobility would gladly direct it against the clergy, the clergy against the nobility.
>
> Turgot becomes a test for all of them; he impells them to pronounce whether they truly desire to improve themselves. Everyone answers unanimously: No . . . Let it happen what is to happen.[24]

Secondly, according to Michelet, the financial collapse of the state, in effect a complete bankruptcy caused by the pillaging of the treasury by the mighty, which the King was unable to resist, influenced the outbreak of the Revolution.[25]

Thirdly, the arbitrariness of royal authority and, in particular, the practice of removing importunate people by means of arrests without trial on the basis of *lettres de cachet* (sold and issued "in blanco") had a negative political influence on public opinion. This is precisely why the destruction of the Bastille—the prison into which people "disappeared" without trial (according to Michelet there were thirty such Bastilles in France, not to mention cloisters which often served this same purpose)—became the symbol of the French Revolution.[26]

Fourthly and lastly (Michelet puts this issue in the forefront), poverty was the cause of the Revolution. Michelet believed this although he complained of the lack of sources to confirm his hypothesis.

> If patience leads to Heaven then this people has truly surpassed during the past two centuries all the merits of the saints. But how can this be recounted? . . . the traces are very meager. Poverty is a general fact, patience in suffering is a virtue so common in France that the historians rarely perceive it. There was, as well, no history in the 18th century . . . up to the philosophical movement, the country was tacit. . . .
>
> It is the more difficult to relate the history of the poverty since it was not marked, as elsewhere, by revolts . . . there was no rebellion, nothing but the single Revolution.[27]

Nevertheless, Michelet sought support for his hypothesis regarding poverty as a cause of the Revolution in the various remarks made by people living in the period preceding the revolutionary events—Colbert in 1681, Boisguillebert in 1701, the Archbishop of Cambrai, the Duke of Orléans, the Bishop of Chartres, Fénélon, Mme de Châteauroux and others. On this basis he drew the conclusion:

> The evil rests in that it (French society) is organized from top to bottom in such a way as to produce ever less and pay ever more. . . .
>
> Since the times of Louis XIV taxes have become so burdensome that in Maules, Etampes and other localities the vines are being uprooted.
>
> Since the peasant does not have any furniture at all which could be sequestered, the Treasury takes his cattle; it destroys it slowly. There are no fertilizers. The cultivation of grain which had increased in the 17th century due to large-scale clearing of land began to contract in the 18th century. . . . Not only is the land producing less but less of it is being cultivated. In many localities it does not pay to continue cultivation.[28]

As we can see Michelet did not sustain the hypothesis of the Restoration historians regarding class conflict as the cause of the Revolution. In his writings this problem disappears, and with it the bourgeoisie's role in the overthrow of the feudal régime; different times, different concerns and needs. On the other hand, a new trend appeared (at least the sharpness of its expression was new) in the hypothesis of the poverty of the people as the prime cause of the Revolution.

Michelet published the first volume of his *History of the Revolution* in 1848 and completed his work in 1853. Alexis de Tocqueville worked on his book, which he published in 1856, at precisely the same period. But de Tocqueville put forth an idea contrary to that of Michelet: the Revolution's cause was not poverty but the country's economic development (in which the peasantry also participated) and the expansion of the sphere of political freedom. The idea was apparently paradoxical but, in contrast to Michelet, de Tocqueville was able to document and prove his hypothesis.

The antagonism between Michelet and de Tocqueville is the more interesting and important because it repeats itself in subsequent periods. Taine versus Jaurès at the end of the nineteenth century, Labrousse versus Lefebvre and Mathiez in the twentieth century provide examples. These arguments were increasingly documented as the problem still remained topical. All the more reason for looking at its beginnings.

De Tocqueville sharply opposed all those who wanted to see in the French Revolution only the results of haphazardness and the tendency to anarchy. On the contrary, he maintained:

> The Revolution was not in the slightest degree a fortuitous event. It is true that it surprised the world, but nonetheless, it was the completion of a long task, the abrupt and violent culmination of an act at which ten generations had toiled. Had it not taken place, the old edifice would in any case have collapsed everywhere, earlier here, somewhat later there; it would only have disintegrated piece by piece instead of foundering all at once.[29]

The Revolution was not only the result of an accident but it also constituted the outcome of a development on a scale broader than France; in fact, on a world scale. Its result was the downfall of feudalism.

"The effect of this revolution", de Tocqueville wrote, "was the abolition of political institutions which had ruled absolutely among the majority of the European peoples for many centuries, bearing usually the name of feudal institutions; they were replaced by a more uniform and simple social and political order which was based on the equality of estates."[30]

In the face of a general anti-feudal tendency the question arises of why did the Revolution break out precisely in France? De Tocqueville's answer is that this was so not because things in France were worse than elsewhere but because they were better, both economically and politically, thus causing the relics of feudalism to weigh more heavily. The entire trend of de Tocqueville's argument was original and new not only for his time. Some of the pages of his work reveal a profundity of thought which is remarkable even today.

To start with a general thesis:

> One thing which leads to amazement at the first glance: the Revolution whose proper aim was to abolish the remnants of medieval institutions, better preserved, were more burdensome and restrictive to the people but in those countries where their effect was felt the least; thus their burden appeared to be the heaviest there where, in fact, it was the lightest.[31]

De Tocqueville compared the situation of the peasantry in the petty German states and in France. In Germany the peasant was a serf and in the majority of cases "glebae adscriptus". In France the peasant had not only, with certain exceptions, gained his land a long time ago but also had become a landowner who continuously increased his property at the cost of large holdings; the Revolution only hastened the process which had been going on for a long time. The feudal lord had lost his administrative rights to royal authority and had preserved only judicial rights which were, in any case, being continually limited by the King. It is true that, in spite of these changes, burdensome contributions in money and in kind to the lord and the Church were still obligatory, and in the peasant's opinion they were the more burdensome in that he had already become to a large degree a landowner and thus had to contribute from his and not the lord's land. These same feudal laws and burdens, however, existed in a much more acute form throughout Europe. Why then, de Tocqueville asked, did they create an explosive situation in France, which was the most liberal in this respect?

> Why did the same feudal laws give rise in the hearts of the French people to a hatred so strong that it survived the object of this hatred and appears thusly to be inextinguishable? The cause of this phenomenon was that on the one hand, the French peasant had become a landowner and, on the other hand, that he had escaped totally from his lord's rule.[32]

De Tocqueville developed this trend of thought in the 12th chapter of the second part of his work.

In the eighteenth century, the French peasant was freer than before, his economic situation was also much better, but he was socially isolated. For the feudal lord and the noble "these people were no longer his subjects but they had not yet become his co-citizens".[33] Perhaps in individual cases it was different, de Tocqueville states, "but", he added, "I speak of classes for only they should be of interest to history".[34] This is undoubtedly a position worthy of note.

The lords abandoned the land when the fiscal system rendered its cultivation unprofitable. This made the main tax burden fall on the peasant, who did not develop cultivation or livestock breeding because of his fear of taxes. Military service, the construction and maintenance of roads; these were the burdens which in principal fell exclusively on the peasant. This was precisely the reason why, although his situation was better than before, he felt the burden of the system more painfully.

In conclusion, according to de Tocqueville, France of the second half of the eighteenth century underwent a rapid economic development.

Public prosperity developed with a heretofore unparalleled rapidity. Everything showed this to be so: the population increased, riches multiplied still more quickly. The war in America did nothing to hamper this development, the state fell into debt but individuals continued to enrich themselves, to become more industrious, enterprising and inventive. ". . . if one were to regard the difference of the periods one can become convinced that in no post-revolutionary period did public prosperity develop more rapidly than it had during the 20 years which preceded the Revolution." [35]

It was in step with this progress and growth of prosperity that dissatisfaction and hatred towards the old institutions grew. The revolution matured in this way and precisely in those parts of the country where the wellbeing was the most obvious. "One could say that the French felt their situation the more unbearable the better it became." [36]

Why was this so? The explanation given by de Tocqueville undoubtedly may be considered as one of the most beautiful pages of political thought.

> A revolution is not always the result of a deteriorating situation. It happens most often that a people which had borne without complaint the most burdensome laws, as if not sensing their weight, rejects them violently when their weight is decreased. The government destroyed by a revolution is almost always better than that which immediately preceded it and *experience teaches that the most dangerous moment for a bad government is usually the one in which it initiates reforms.* . . . The evil which was patiently endured as inevitable becomes insupportable when the idea of avoiding it is conceived. The abuses which are then done away with seem to reveal that what is left of them and cause the sensing of them to become more acute: *evil has diminished, it is true, but it is being sensed more sharply.* Feudalism never aroused as much hatred among the French when it was in full force as when it was dying. The smallest manifestation of arbitrariness on the part of Louis XVI seemed more difficult to bear than all the despotism of Louis XIV. [37]

This is a profound conclusion linking together into one harmonious whole the concept regarding France's economic development in the second half of the eighteenth century with that pertaining to the growth of revolutionary sentiments in this same period.

Thus, according to de Tocqueville the general trend of development in contemporary Europe, which was inclined against feudalism, was augmented in France by a particular cause of the Revolution; the country's rapid economic development and the broadening of the sphere of freedom which gave rise to a more acute consciousness of the limitations and burdens connected with the remnants of the feudal order.

In defending this viewpoint, de Tocqueville does not overlook the direct causes of the revolutionary outbreak: in the first place the government's financial difficulties connected with the growing budget deficit.

While, according to de Tocqueville, the financial system was no worse than that of Louis XVI's predecessors and the deficit was larger due to the government's positive action—public works, social aid, etc. (de Tocqueville leaves out with eloquent silence the questions of expenses in connection with the war in America and the accumulation of financial burdens resulting from the growing state debt, the interest which consumed over half of the annual income), it was true, nonetheless, that the state faced bankruptcy, so endangering the "sacred rights" of its creditors, and above all of the "rentiers". In this fashion the financial crises pushed the usually most conservative classes on to the road to revolution. They provided the revolutionary movement with an impetus unaware of where it would ultimately lead.

> The rentiers, merchants, industrialists and other men of money who usually formed the class most hostile to political innovations, most favourable to an existent government regardless of what it is like, the most subordinated to laws, even if it feels contempt for them and cannot bear them, proved this time to be the most impatient and the most decided in the cause of reform. Above all, it called loudly for a complete revolution in the entire system of finances, not thinking of the fact that, having shaken to the depths this part of the government, this would cause the fall of the restoration. [38]

We have here not only an outline of the causes of the Revolution but also a viewpoint clearly and decisively opposed to that of Michelet.

Two decades passed and then the events of the Paris Commune

marked a new epoch in the history of France. And not only of France. It was obvious that the problem of the French Revolution would be posed once more; this time as seen from the perspective of the events of the Paris Commune.

Thus, H. Taine in his many-volumed *Les Origines de la France contemporaine* (1875) returned to the conception of poverty, especially of the peasantry, as the cause of the Revolution. Hence, the conflict between Michelet and de Tocqueville was to be continued.

Poverty, dreadful poverty of the people: this is the picture which Taine painted in vivid colours making use of memoirs, declarations, administrative correspondence, descriptions, etc., from the reigns of Louis XIV, Louis XV and Louis XVI.

> Look through the administrative correspondences from the last thirty years preceding the Revolution; a hundred signs will reveal to you an excessive suffering, even if it did not transform itself into rage. For the man of the people, a peasant or an artisan who lived from the toil of his own hands life was precarious; he possessed exactly that minimum which is necessary in order not to die of starvation, and often even was lacking this.[39]

Taine noted the fact that the peasant had become an owner of land (in this case referring to de Tocqueville). On the one hand, he sought to explain this fact without infringing on his theory regarding poverty as the cause of the Revolution, while on the other hand he took up de Tocqueville's idea that the peasant-owner felt more acutely the burden of taxes and services than the peasant working on the seignorial lands. He regarded the fact that the peasantry possessed around two-thirds of the land before the Revolution as a phenomenon derived from the decline of the nobility and the determination of the peasantry who bought the land for a song but, in spite of their sacrifices, had no profits from it. In this fashion, Taine salvaged his theory regarding poverty as a general and constant phenomenon. On the other hand, he emphasized strongly that the peasant-owner opposed the system more vigorously than his predecessor.

> When a man lives in poverty [Taine wrote] he is embittered, but if he is simultaneously an owner and lives in poverty—he is embittered still more. One may reconcile oneself to poverty but not to spoliation; and such was the situation of the peasantry in 1789, since during the entire 18th century it has been acquiring land....
> In acquiring land the small farmer took upon himself the burdens connected with it. As long as he was a day labourer and possessed only his own hands for toil, the taxes effected him only partially: "where nothing exists, the King loses his rights".

At present, although he is poor and considers himself poorer than he really is, the treasury has him in its grasp to the entire extent of his new property.[40]

In referring to this aspect of Taine's views of the causes of the Revolution, to his theory of the people's poverty, we do not in the least want to create the impression that Taine did not see other causes and other aspects of the problem. His work is not only gigantic in size, full of erudition and richly documented on the basis of extremely varied sources but also many-faceted in its grasp of the historical process. Nevertheless, it is a highly controversial grasp. Precisely because the work is so rich, we are forced to limit ourselves consciously only to the problem which directly interests us here primarily—the economic causes of the Revolution. In another case one could engage in a discussion (of which Jean Jaurès gave an example) of the fact that Taine, in analysing the structure of French society in the eighteenth century, in effect bypassed the development and role of the bourgeoisie as a class as well as that, in analysing eighteenth-century French philosophy, he counterposed it to science and deprived it of a concrete revolutionary content. This would lead us too far astray, however, from the task facing us.

We are interested here in only one matter—the answer to the question regarding the economic causes of the Revolution. Taine's answer is the poverty of the people. As in the case of Michelet this answer met with opposition; this time it was expressed by Jean Jaurès in his fundamental work *Histoire socialiste de la révolution française* (1901). The cause of the Revolution was not poverty, Jaurès maintained, but the growth of the strength of the Third Estate resulting from rapid economic development.

Let us begin with Jaurès' important initial hypothesis, later taken up by Mathiez, that a precondition for revolution is not only oppression of the classes which undertake a revolutionary struggle but also a certain minimum of forces and means which make its conduct possible. Precisely such a situation existed in France in the eighteenth century.

For a revolution to break out [Jaurès maintained], it is necessary for the lower classes to suffer either a terrible discomfort or a great oppression. But it is also necessary that they possess some minimum of strength and thus also of hope. Such was precisely the state of French society at the end of the 18th century. The nobility and the clergy who possessed over one-third of the land were free from all taxes and services. They cast all the burdens on the rural people and the urban bourgeoisie, taking for themselves all the resources of a budget supplied by the poorest, wounded the feelings and greatly damaged the peasant class and the bourgeois class.

Nonetheless, there were simultaneously sufficient small peasant holdings, there was also, in spite of the Treasury's severity, sufficient savings hidden in the country-side to have all the small rural landowners hope for liberation and even for buying one day a bit of church land.

The bourgeoisie, on the other hand, exalted by two centuries of industrial, mercantile and financial power, had penetrated the rural world through purchases to a sufficient degree to feel able to struggle against the nobility and church even in the domain of agriculture. It felt sufficiently strong to be able—if one may express it thusly—to cover the entire surface of society.[41]

According to Jaurès the cause of the Revolution was, above all, the growth of the forces of the bourgeoisie as a class who therefore sought power. Other phenomena, such as, for example, the budget deficit and the financial crisis of the state, were the occasion for the Revolution's outbreak, but its cause lay deeper in the class conflict of contemporary society. In polemizing with Taine, whom he criticized sharply for failure to understand the role of the bourgeoisie in the revolutionary movement of the eighteenth century, Jaurès opposed the idea that the sole cause of the growth of revolutionary sentiments among the bourgeoisie was its interest in the works of the philosophers. Jaurès continued:

> Monsieur Taine does not even suspect how immense was the development of interests which imposed on the bourgeoisie its revolutionary role and gave it the strength to fulfill this role.
>
> He reasons as if abstract philosophical theories could arouse and set an entire nation on its feet. . . . This alleged "realist" limited himself to the reading of philosophical works. He does not perceive life itself: he has ignored the immense effort of production, labour, savings, industrial and commercial progress which turned the bourgeoisie into a first-rate power and forced it to take into its own hands the management of a society in which its interests already played such a significant role and could encounter so many risks. Truly, Taine has suffered much from not having read Marx and not having reflected a bit on Augustin Thierry.[42]

Jaurès did not by any means negate the revolutionary role of ideology, but he interpreted it differently from Taine. While for the latter Enlightenment philosophy had an abstract character deriving its ideas from antiquity, Jaurès saw the strength of its influence in the fact that it constituted an instrument of the bourgeoisie's class-conscious-ness. The role of Enlightenment thought can be understood solely in close connection with the development of the bourgeoisie.

Two large forces, two revolutionary forces at the end of the 18th century impassioned the minds and affairs and by a powerful coefficient increased the intensity of events.

On the one hand, the French nation had achieved intellectual maturity. On the other hand, the French bourgeoisie became conscious of its strength, its richness, its rights, its almost unlimited possibilities for development. In a word, the bourgeoisie had attained class consciousness while thought had attained a consciousness of the universe. Herein rest the two sources, the two points of combustion of the Revolution. Due to them it became possible, due to them it became dazzling.[43]

The power of the bourgeoisie was derived, first, from its industrial, commercial and financial activity and, secondly, from its role as the state's creditor which was carried out by the mass of rentiers. It was precisely the latter who, threatened by the spectre of the state's financial bankruptcy, favoured the search for a new social order which would guarantee their rights. "But the French bourgeoisie was powerful in 1789 also due to its industrial and commercial activity", states Jaurès.[44] He devoted a large chapter (around 60 pages) of his work entitled *La Vie économique* to showing on the basis of source material and statistical data the rapid growth of the bourgeoisie in the eighteenth century in the field of trade, finances and industry. It seems that even the costly war with England over the American colonies which led state finances to ruination was a source for the amassing of immense fortunes by the bourgeoisie. In Bordeaux, which grew rich on the war, even the working class raised its standard of living and there were no sharp conflicts there between the bourgeoisie and the proletariat during the Revolution as well.[45]

The situation was similar in Marseilles. This made possible the unity of the Third Estate in the struggle against the nobility.

It was the bourgeoisie, supported by the strength and enthusiasm of the people, which went forth to conquer power. In Marseilles and the Provence this ardent unanimity of the Third Estate, of the bourgeoisie and the workers, of the rich and the poor could be seen in the course of the tumultuous and radiant days preceding the Revolution, when Mirabeau began his struggle with the nobility which excluded him from its midst. The flower girls embraced the tribune and the bankers acclaimed him. He himself, when during his magnificent speech to the States of Provence he had counterposed the power and rights of the producers to the privileged sterility of the nobility, understood by these words both the great leaders of trade and industry as well as the common labourers.[46]

On the other hand, the situation in Lyon was completely different. Here an alliance existed between the bourgeoisie and the aristocracy which participated in industrial activity; simultaneously, a conflict arose between the bourgeoisie and the proletariat from the outset of the Revolution. This difference in the situation, as compared with Bordeaux and Marseilles, was derived from the varying levels of industrial development and the different types of commercial and industrial activity in Lyon and these cities.

It is characteristic that Jaurès, in defending the thesis regarding the prosperity of the prerevolutionary period, bypassed in silence the problem of the working class' standard of living—unemployment, the rise in grain prices in connection with the crop failure, etc. In the chapter "Le prolétariat" (pp. 157-169) he was interested in only one thing; to show that the working class was not, and could not yet, be an independent class at this time, that it did not possess either class consciousness or proper organization. This may be the reason why, in concentrating on the bourgeoisie as the main force of the Revolution, Jaurès saw the question of prosperity from its viewpoint. On the other hand, the standard of living of the peasantry, who did play an important role in the Revolution, did nevertheless draw his attention.

In accord with his general line of reasoning, Jaurès demonstrated, above all, that agriculture in the pre-revolutionary period had made considerable progress. French agriculture in 1789 should be compared, if one wants to resolve the dispute regarding its development, with the conditions twenty or thirty years earlier and not with contemporary English agriculture which was indubitably on a higher level. Employing a proper system of reference there can be no doubt, according to Jaurès, that progress had been made in this field as well.

> We cannot deny, he wrote, that in the years 1760-1789 considerable progress in agriculture had taken place: a large-scale renovation of methods, buildings, tools. . . .
> I know that Arthur Young spoke many times in his work on his trip through France about the insufficiency of agriculture; and it is certain that French agriculture was much inferior to the English. But Arthur Young was unable to compare the state of French agriculture in 1789 with its state in 1760.
> A number of trustworthy testimonies and a number of significant economic facts show that during the twenty-five years considerable progress in the direction of intensive cultivation had been made.[47]

According to Jaurès the cause of this development was, above all, the participation of capital in agriculture. A considerable part of the land passed into the hands of the bourgeoisie who could not tolerate the stagnation which, heretofore, had prevailed in this area. A class of rich farmers also appeared who rented lands and based their economy on the principle of capitalist profit. Income from the land increased rapidly; according to Galonne this was in fact a revolution which caused income from agriculture to increase during twenty years.[48] In 1785 the "Société Royale d'Agriculture" was founded in Paris whose task was to raise the level of agricultural technology among the peasants. This concept of Jaurès is supported by copious and convincing source material.

What was the situation of the working peasantry? It should be admitted that Jaurès concerned himself less with this problem, treating it rather on the margin of the effects of capitalism's progress in agriculture in the shape of the liquidation of old institutions of communal rights, of benefits for the poor such as the rights of pasture, and as the result of the progressing concentration of land ownership, in particular, the direct and indirect expropriation of the peasantry as shown by the numerous complaints contained in the peasants' "cahiers de doléances" from various provinces.[49]

Let us add to this the notoriously unjust system of taxes and services (in particular the salt tax) which irritated the peasantry and also found an acute expression in the peasant "cahiers", in order to understand the final conclusion of Jaurès' considerations on the peasantry.

> Thus, all the parts of rural France will respond with a vibrant passion to the first acts of the Revolution. And not only will the revolutionary bourgeoisie, so powerful due to its economic strength and the strength of its ideas, not be disavowed by the vast rural population but this population, possessed as if of an excess of rage, is ready to exceed the limits marked out by the urban Third Estate.[50]

It should be admitted that this ultimate conclusion is astounding against the background of all of Jaurès' deduction on the subject of French agriculture in the second half of the eighteenth century; it simply does not follow from these deductions, which consistently aimed at emphasizing one factor—the rapid development of agriculture in this period. One may, of course, reason like de Tocqueville and Jaurès; the remnants of feudalism are still more irritating and arouse still more opposition, the less they suit rapidly developing capitalist relations. This is undoubtedly the truth but it is, however, too generalized since there are not data regarding the economic causes of the discontent of the working peasantry (this does not negate the hypothesis about the simultaneous development of capitalist agriculture; on the contrary, it forms one totality with it); such data were drawn from source materials by later students of the problem and will be subsequently discussed.

Jaurès was clearly under the influence of his primary hypothesis that it was not poverty but economic development connected with the bourgeoisie's development which lay at the foundations of the Revolution. This idea found its advocates and continuators among the great majority of eminent twentieth-century historians. We shall illustrate their views by referring to the synthesizing works on the French Revolution of Albert Mathiez and Georges Lefebvre. Before we proceed to this, however, we shall take up the work of Franz Brentano's *L'Ancien Régime* which dealt in detail with the peasant problem in France at the end of the eighteenth century and especially with its economic aspect. This study fills a gap in Jaurès' reflections and is simultaneously a good introduction for discussing the great synthesis of the history of the Revolution, created by the above-mentioned authors.

Brentano's principal idea is as follows: not only did agriculture develop in the eighteenth century but the economic situation of the working peasantry was good and the picture of its poverty as sketched by historians is due to their exaggeration or to the failure to understand the true historical nature of the rural relations of the time. What a contrast in comparison with the works of Mme de Staël, Michelet and, in particular, Hippolyte Taine, bemoaning the peasants' poverty!

Brentano began the chapter devoted to the village with an adroit polemical trick. Hippolyte Taine, in order to add colour to his concept about poverty in pre-revolutionary France, quoted La Bruyère describing the peasant of that time as a man degraded by poverty to the condition of an animal. Brentano repeated this quote at the outset of the chapter but then quoted right afterwards another writer of the period, Sebastien Mercier who in describing a rural wedding painted a pastel picture of an idyll.[51]   The intention of this juxtaposition is clear: in order to pass judgement on facts one should not be influenced by a literary description.

Brentano thus rejected literature and sought the testimony of those who themselves came from the countryside of that period, who had lived in it for a longer time and had left descriptions of this life. These included the Burgundian peasant, Restif de la Bretonne, Marmontel, a peasant from Limousin and Mistral, and a peasant from Provence (the latter represented a later period, the beginning of the nineteenth century).[52] All of them presented a picture of a prosperous and staid village, quite unlike the picture by La Bruyère.

The conclusions which Brentano drew from his studies are clear: the French village experienced a period of development during the second half of the eighteenth century:

> Regardless of the opinion of Arthur Young about French agriculture at the end of the Ancien Régime, it could not be denied that from the middle of the 18th century it was in great motion which, through progress effected in all the fields of national activity, impelled all of France towards a new future. The peasants are buying land in all parts of the country. It is a true passion of possessing. Land is being bought for more than it is worth.
> Under the influence of agricultural societies . . . many processes are being perfected, agricultural machinery imported from England; expensive barns were replaced by haystacks in the fields; the number of cultivated pastures is increased. Arthur Young states that the cultivation of lucerne was on such a high level in France that his countrymen came to our country in order to acquire knowledge in this respect. The introduction of the cultivation of corn, the potato, the raising of silkworms . . . of the Spanish merinos, acclimatized to new conditions . . . marked in France at the end of the "Ancien Régime" achievements of such significance that the 19th century cannot show anything comparable.[53]

Does it follow from this that there were no conflicts in the village and no poverty to inspire sentiments of rebellion? Of course not.

Firstly, the years of serious crop failure (drought or heavy winter) 1709, 1740, 1767, 1771, 1775, 1784 and 1789 were a true scourge. The inability to import larger quantities of grain due to the limited possibilities of maritime transport, the system of internal tariffs, which in fact isolated particular parts of the country from each other and finally, the prohibition against accumulation of reserves—all this increased even more the difficulties caused by crop failure.

Secondly, progress in agriculture was hampered by the parcelling of landed property; the peasant was too poor and his sphere of activity was too limited to be able to improve his farming.

Thirdly, the traditional rural communes did not provide any

possibility for the development of individual initiative and were also another hampering factor.

What general conclusions did Brentano draw from these reflections? He maintained that the village was developing and living tolerably. The descriptions of peasant dwellings, clothing, food, etc., which he quoted brought him to these conclusions. It is true that among them were also alarming reports speaking of poverty, particularly in the years of crop failure, but Brentano always neutralized then by quite opposing testimonies. One thing remains unclear: Brentano admitted that in this period the phenomenon of vagabondage and banditry, which became a plague of the rural areas, appeared on a mass scale. Where did these people come from? What was the origin of this phenomenon if we reject the hypothesis of poverty as the stimulus? What was the influence of the years of crop failure, especially of 1784 and 1789?

In spite of these reservations and questions, which the reading of Brentano's work gives rise to, its fundamental idea seems to be borne out; two decades before the Revolution the rural areas were not in a period of decline but, on the contrary, of development. This was so, even if economically negative phenomena appeared simultaneously.

Henri See, in his work on economic and social conditions in France in the eighteenth century, seems to confirm this position. He maintained that, with the exception of the period directly preceding the Revolution, there were no peasant revolts; they broke out only after July 14 and in particular after August 4, 1789, when the peasants demanded the abolition of the services originating in feudalism, which were imposed on the villages. The position is likewise not negated by Georges Lefebvre. In his study of the peasant question during the Revolution he defended the idea of the autonomous character of the peasant revolution which resulted from the contradiction of interests of the peasantry, not only with the interests of the nobility, but with those of the bourgeoisie as well.[54] Pierre Gaxotte supports this standpoint and adds his own interesting argument: the descriptions of the peasant's poverty are based on appearances which the peasant had to maintain in defending himself against the existing tax system.[55]

After this digression on the peasant question during the Revolution, let us return to the more general controversy which in most recent times was continued, on the one hand, by Mathiez and Lefebvre, and by Labrousse on the other.

Albert Mathiez was clearly influenced by Jaurès' position.

> The Revolution [he maintained] did not break out in an exhausted country but, on the contrary, in a flourishing and fully developing country. Misery which sometimes gives rise to disturbances cannot be the cause of great social upheavals. These arise always as a result of an imbalance between classes.
>
> The bourgeoisie already possessed the major part of France's national wealth. The bourgeoisie progressed while the privileged estates ruined themselves. Its very growth made it sense the legal discriminations to which it was condemned even more vividly.[56]

Mathiez developed this idea both in analysing the class conflict between the bourgeoisie and the aristocracy and in seeking the ideological reflection of this conflict. For the bourgeoisie not only "controlled the money but had taken moral power into its hands as well".[57]

The writers and philosophers who represented the bourgeoisie's interests waged the struggle with their pens, imbuing the masses with class consciousness. This interesting and important concept clearly inspired by Lenin's works on the role of the intelligentsia, which brings class consciousness in "from the outside" to the spontaneous working-class movement.

> The Revolution had taken place in the minds a long time before it became apparent in action and it is correct to include among its responsible authors those who were to become its first victims.
>
> The Revolution could come only from above. The working people, whose narrow horizons did not exceed their occupation were incapable of undertaking the initiative and, even more so, of taking into their hands the course of events.[58]

The growing wealth and increased power of the bourgeoisie lay at the foundations of this phenomenon. After quoting facts and figures relating to the development of industry, trade, banking, etc., Mathiez concluded:

> The bourgeoisie manifested immense economic activity. The price paid for a position of stockbroker had doubled during a single year. Necker wrote that France possessed almost half of the currency in circulation in Europe. The merchants were acquiring the properties of the indebted nobility and were building luxurious palaces for themselves . . . the cities were being rebuilt and embellished.
>
> The infallible sign of the growth of national wealth was the rapid increase in population and the constant rise of the price of food, land and real estate. . . . Prosperity gradually embraced not only the large but also the middle and ultimately the petty-bourgeoisie. In general, clothing and food was better than before. Above all, education became more widespread.[59]

Thus, it was not poverty which gave rise to the Revolution. Neither is this negated by the budget deficit nor by the financial crisis connected with it, which after all, led to the calling of the Estates General and to the outbreak of the first phase of the Revolution—the revolution of the nobility. The deficit arose as a result of the malfunctioning of the state but in a society which was enjoying prosperity.

> . . . The financial problem dominated all the other issues. In order to carry out reforms, money was necessary. In conditions of general prosperity the Treasury became emptier day by day. It could be filled only at the expense of the privileged and with the approval of the parliaments, little inclined to sacrifice the private interests of its members on the altar of public welfare. The longer the hesitation lasted, the deeper became the abyss of the deficit, the more marked became the resistance.[60]

Mathiez spoke clearly about the economic crisis and the unemployment connected with it, he referred to the crop failure of 1788 and the rise in bread prices, linking these events with the Revolution's outbreak. It should be admitted, nonetheless, that these facts of a transitional nature also do not negate the general concept regarding the country's economic development and relative prosperity. They should be noted, however, both because of their importance and in view of the polemics with Labrousse.

> The election campaign (to the Estates General) coincided with a serious economic crisis. The trade treaty concluded with England in 1788, having lowered the tariff rates, opened the doors to English goods. Textile manufacturers were forced to limit production. Unemployment in Abbeville rose to 12,000 workers, in Lyon to 20,000 and it appeared in other localities proportionately as well. At the outset of winter, which was particularly severe that year, it was necessary to organize welfare workshops in the larger towns especially because the price of bread was increasing continuously. The 1788 harvest was much worse than usual. The lack of fodder was so great that peasants were forced to dispose of a part of their cattle and to leave their fields either untilled or to sow them without fertilizer. The market places were empty. Bread was not only very expensive but it was feared that it would be lacking. . . . In March, when the election campaign began, "riots" broke out. . . . This movement was directed not only against the speculators who were hoarding food products, against the old tax system, the octroi and feudalism, but also against all those who exploited the people and lived at its expense. This movement was closely linked with the political disturbances.[61]

These are undoubtedly new emphases against the setting of the general concept regarding the prosperity and economic development of contemporary France, although, as we have already remarked, they do not negate this concept; nevertheless, they do clearly impose the need for an additional interpretation of this idea as borne out by the discussion on this subject, in particular Labrousse.

George Lefebvre in his *La Révolution Française* takes a similar, although more shaded position. In reference to the problem interesting us, Lefebvre takes a decided stand: the cause of the Revolution was not poverty but the class struggle connected with the country's economic development which had brought about the growth in the strength of a new class. The eighteenth century was a century of the enrichment of Europe in general and of France in particular:

> The fact is that Europe became enriched, above all, in the West which is in itself understandable. It is not precisely known to what degree. The national income of France and England more than doubled, it would seem, during the 18th century. . . . The improvement of the material situation and the growing flexibility of inter-human relations advance, although it was, of course, primarily the ruling classes which benefited from this.
> . . . The artisans, merchants and rich peasants did gain certain advantages from this enrichment: the continuing growth of the consumption of certain food articles seems to confirm this. . . . The dimunition of famine and the resources which industrial progress created decreased mortality. . . .
> It should be added that the enrichment explains the optimism, the intellectual expression of which was the idea of progress, which stimulated the contemporaries to a courageous undertaking of reforms, dictated, in their opinion, by the social and intellectual transformations which had taken place.[62]

The concept regarding progress in the eighteenth century pertains also to the French peasantry in spite of the fact that it suffered from the burden of greater taxes and services than any other social class. Nonetheless, the economic and political situation of the peasantry in the eighteenth century had improved and it was, in any case, much better than in the countries of Central and Eastern Europe.[63]

On the other hand, the situation of the proletariat was completely different. Lefebvre clearly distinguished the proletariat as a social group deprived of class-consciousness and treats its fate separately. The urban and rural proletariat were on the margin of society: dispersed, devoid of any class-consciousness as yet, having only the beginnings of organization, it constituted a social group discriminated against economically as well. In the years 1730-1789 wages in France rose around 22%, while prices increased by 60%. This meant a growth of poverty further enhanced by years of crop failures and unemployment.

In France one-fifth of the population was composed of the poor and each economic crisis considerably enlarged their number. Social assistance did not exist as a rule. . . . Spreading mendicity began to be almost a characteristic trait of the country; it was sought in vain to prevent this by interning the beggars. Vagabondage was becoming widespread, which in turn was transformed into banditry on a large scale. In addition, the number of homeless wanderers seeking work increased, as did the smugglers giving trouble to the internal customs offices. A crop failure and the industrial crisis it inevitably brought on, increased the evils. . . .[64]

Thus an important correction has been added to the general concept which pertains to the not insignificant figure of 20% of the country's population.

As far as the causes of the Revolution are concerned, Lefebvre saw a number of them. It is, nonetheless, the class conflict which comes to the forefront in the mutual counterposition of royal authority, the nobility and the bourgeoisie.

On the greater part of the continent absolutism still existed although it had been more or less transformed. The philosophers praised the "enlightened absolutism" of the rulers whom they thought to be under the influence of their propaganda. Nonetheless . . . the aristocracy accused the royal authority of having subjugated it, while the bourgeoisie was irritated at being pushed aside from the government and, simultaneously, the rivalry between these two classes became more acute. France was not the first to resolve this triple conflict by means of a revolution.[65]

According to Lefebvre, class interests caused not only the bourgeoisie but the nobility as well to be concerned to limit royal authority and to sympathize with libertarian aspirations both in the economic and in the political sphere. Whereas aspirations of this type brought the nobility and bourgeoisie together, the opposition of the former with respect to the postulate of equality of rights gave rise to a conflict between them. In defending its interest the bourgeoisie had to place an emphasis on equality of rights; this distinguished the French Revolution, for example, from the English. As a result the revolution initiated on the basis of the financial crisis by the nobility became transformed into a bourgeois revolution and already in January 1789 Mallet du Pan wrote the following words: "The public debate has changed its character. The issues of the king, of despotism, of the constitution are becoming marginal: this is a struggle between the Third Estate and the other two."[66]

The direct cause of the Revolution was, nevertheless, the economic crisis which led to an unusual rise in the price of bread and to unemployment. Here is Lefebvre's conclusion which is of interest from the point of view of our reflections:

> *One should have no illusions as to the social significance of the enrichment caused by economic progress;* the prosperity of the kingdom had already been brought out into the light of day a half a century ago, above all by Jaurès, in order to explain the growing might of the bourgeoisie and in this sense it is correct to counterpose to Michelet's opinions the idea that the Revolution broke out in a society in full development and not in a decrepit society, fated as if to catastrophe by the providential parsimony of nature. It should be remarked that the profits derived from the exploitation of the colonies were realized, above all, by re-export and that the national economy did not benefit from this to such an extent as it might seem; moreover, the long-lasting boom increased the incomes of the large owners and the bourgeoisie without giving rise to a proportional increase of wages. Since we know at present that in the decade preceding the Revolution production had lost its balance and became considerably weakened, it remains true that the *situation of the masses became worse and that ultimately they faced famine.*[67]

This, however, is not any longer a full support for de Tocqueville's and Jaurès' conceptions of prosperity in pre-revolutionary France. Although Lefebvre accepted this concept in principle his reservations and restrictions were so far-reaching that, in effect, he occupied an intermediate position between that of Jaurès and Labrousse.

The uniqueness of C. E. Labrousse's position as an historian of the Revolution lies, above all, in the fact that, in considering the problem of its causes, he took as his starting-point two specific and concrete economic problems: he analysed the movement of prices and incomes in eighteenth-century France as well as the crisis which preceded the Revolution. His two fundamental works were devoted to these problems.[68] The analyses, unusually important for understanding the origin of the Revolution, were undertaken for the first time with such vigour and in such a profound fashion and so became a new significant historical fact (in the meaning of a scientific fact).

Labrousse's first work *Esquisse du mouvement des prix et des revenues en France au XVIII siècle* devoted to this problem, created in fact the basis for his negative attitude towards the concept that pre-revolutionary France was an economically flourishing country. In picturing the violent rise of prices in the years 1785-1789 (pp. 229, 304, 361-364, etc.) and the influence of this factor on the lowering of the population's standard of living (pp. 306, 590, 595, 597-604, etc.) the author solidly prepared his final conclusion. The work has 690 pages, filled to the brim with factual, pertinent material. We shall note only, inasmuch as reporting this rich factual material is impossible and unnecessary, that Labrousse arrived at the following figures: prices rose by 63% in the years 1726-1789 while wages by not quite 26% (pp. 588-590).

What were Labrousse's final conclusions? Above all, that the sharp economic crisis of 1788-1789 and the high prices and unemployment caused by it, were the direct cause of the outbreak of the Revolution.

> There is no need to demonstrate the influence of the movement of prices and incomes on the bringing into being and course of the Revolution. The economic boom to a large degree favoured the Revolution. . . .
>
> It has been known for a time already that 1789 was a year of very dear bread, that the 1786 trade treaty had caused the breakdown of the textile industry and considerable unemployment among the workers. . . .
>
> We have already remarked several times that the revolutionary explosion in July 1789 in the towns and in the countryside falls not only on the same years but approximately even at the same time of the year when grain prices reached the highest level, taking into consideration the period from the beginning of the movement and even from the second decade of the century. . . . The sudden, virulent and general agricultural crisis of under-production burst out in a country which had already experienced a severe industrial crisis which was the result of a normal event—the Franco-English trade treaty of 1786. But the agricultural crisis will effect as usually happens, industrial activity.[69]

This is a synthesis-like summing up of the data pertaining to the movement of prices and incomes in pre-revolutionary France. What is the connection of this phenomenon with political events?

> The accumulating difficulties of the monarchy, brought about by the financial crisis, rendered still more profound by the economic crisis, found greater repercussions in this situation. The Paris revolt became general in the towns and in the countryside during July and August. There are hunger riots. The peasants burn the archives and refuse to render seignorial services. . . . Riots caused by the market situation and the taxes on bread. This is a conflict between wages falling to the minimum and ground rent rising to the maximum. The burning down of urban customs offices and those of tax farmers, the plunder of salt warehouses. This is a contradiction between decreasing wages and the increasing consumption tax. Plunder of the castles. This is again a contradiction between decreasing wages, between the total income of the owner-purchaser drawn from various sources and falling to a minimum and feudal rights whose significance grows progressively in relation to ever poorer years, ever poorer land and ever poorer farmers.[70]

This picture of the causes of the Revolution differs from that of Mathiez as well as that of Lefebvre. Politics has been radically reduced here to economics and economics is faced with a great crisis. In the period immediately preceding the Revolution's outbreak prices were, in any case, rising, incomes decreasing and unemployment growing. This is not a picture of prosperity but, on the contrary, a picture of the poverty of the masses of the people.

This was precisely the conclusion, formulated clearly and distinctly, which Labrousse reached in his subsequent work, devoted to the problem of the economic crisis during the decline of the "Ancien Régime". In the methodological introduction to this work Labrousse wrote:

> In certain respects the Revolution—as Michelet had felt in contrast to Jaurès' concept taken up by Mathiez—was really a revolution of poverty. Not that Jaurès and Mathiez denied the existence and effect of poverty, but—if one is to believe them poverty played a relatively limited and fortuitous role. This could be true had the crisis in 1789 been really what it appeared to be at first glance; a usual "food crisis", caused by the hailstorms of 1788 to which the propitious heavens either immediately or shortly thereafter put an end to. . . . Poverty is thus reduced to a meteorological accident. Unfortunately, the economic breakdown of 1788-1790 has another dimension. It struck at the entire French economy. . . . The factor which favoured the Revolution was undoubtedly a cyclical revolutionary crisis but it was also the regression in the pre-revolutionary period and this to a degree which much surpassed that what Jaurès and Mathiez had thought on the subject. The crisis and the regression profoundly effected the events of 1789 and 1790 . . . and this is why they are their cause.[71]

Labrousse does not deny the fact that in the eighteenth century a development of the French economy had taken place on the basis of a growth in prices of agricultural products, but only up to 1778. At that time a breakdown of the prices of agricultural products took place which rested at the foundations of the cyclical crisis. The population growth increased the difficulties of the labour market and unemployment grew. To this were added the natural disasters of 1787, and the regression caused by the convergence of various circumstances: the 1786 trade treaty with England, the natural disasters and, in particular, the disruption of state finances under the burden of the expenses of the war in America, were linked with the cyclical crisis during the years 1778-1787. The financial crisis was the direct cause made more profound by the economic regression which made it impossible to remedy the evil. As a result, according to Labrousse, a poverty of the masses of the people which lay at the foundations of the revolutionary outburst. As we can see from the above, Labrousse decidedly took the stand of Michelet and Taine against their opponents but, simultaneously, he put forth certain reservations which throw an additional light on his position on this question and on the problem itself.

> Economic anemia in the 18th century? Some protest against this. After all, prosperity of this epoch is an article of faith. One shall counterpose perhaps to this concept the other sayings of the author. Did he not write ten years ago, did he not maintain only recently that the inflow of prosperity embraced not only the entire 18th century but the beginning of the 19th as well? Assuredly, but the inflow rose very irregularly. . . . After a cyclical outflow which is a normal thing and—let us add—does not interest us here, an abnormal outflow of inter-cyclical dimensions began around 1778 which culminated around 1787. The progress represented then begins anew and continues, in spite of crises of different characters, to the last years of the century, to the consular and imperial epoch during which its tempo was increased.[72]

The mental reservation at the end of Labrousse's methodological reflections is even more eloquent.

> Revolutionary events, great revolutionary institutions are thus born to a large degree from the lowering of profits and wages, from the troubles of the industrialist, artisan, farmer, from the poverty of the worker and farm labourer. An unfavourable· conjuncture of circumstances linked the bourgeoisie and proletariat in common opposition. *From this point of view the Revolution looks much more like a Revolution of poverty than Jaurès and Mathiez had imagined.* Nonetheless, one may entertain doubts as to whether the end of the 18th century explained everything whether it was exclusively the final years, years of stoppage in periods between cycles or years of crisis which effected institutions. Economic difficulties during the reign of Louis XVI, no matter how accutely sensed by the contemporaries, constitute only an episode in the epoch between the Regency and the Republic. *The 18th century remains basically a century of great economic expansion, of an increase of capital income, of progress of the bourgeoisie's wealth and power.* And one may doubt whether the long period of progress had a lesser influence on the Revolution than the relatively short period of regression, although this period is very close to the events and hence very dynamic.[73]

In the light of these two statements, and in particular the last one, it can be seen clearly that both of the apparently contradictory concepts (in a certain interpretation if, in pointing to a given cause of events, the word "solely" were to be added, they would be really contradictory) may be considered as complementary concepts; while economic development was characteristic of the entire eighteenth century, the period directly preceding the Revolution was marked by crisis and the concomitant poverty. Thus, both those who point to the economic development and the strengthening of the bourgeoisie's class position as the cause of the Revolution and those who speak of poverty as the direct revolutionary stimulus are correct. Of course, everything depends on how they perceive their concepts. Nonetheless, historical truth in this case is clearly much more complicated than a simple reduction of the causes of the Revolution either to poverty or to prosperity. It is not surprising, therefore, that the process of coming to know these causes is far from finished; in its course, through the collision of opposite views historical truth forms itself as a whole, as an ever more complex and many-faceted entity composed of partial and, in this sense, relative truths.

Nonetheless, we shall not undertake here the task which can be only carried out by a historian, that is, the evaluation of who was correct in this debate and to what degree and measure this correctness may be acknowledged. What interests us—for this is precisely the object of our reflection—is the very fact of variability, diversity and even incompatibility of the positions of historians who, in theory, have the same source material at their disposal and who, in their subjective inclinations, strive, after all, for the truth and only the truth, even believing that they have truly attained it. It is precisely due to the object of our interests, that our own role had to be limited to the selection of authors and to permitting them to present their views by quoting from their works.

The confrontation of these quotations is so eloquent that it speaks for itself, even without a commentary, and gives rise to the question which is the central object of our reflections in this study—is objective truth in history possible?

This apparently simple question entails, obviously, a whole series of others. Why do the positions of historians differ so much even in concrete problems? Does this mean that historians, striving towards some non-scholarly aims, consciously falsify truth? If not, then what does objective knowledge and subjective truth signify in history? How are they to be attained? Why do various historians on the basis of the same source material create different, sometime contradictory pictures of the historical process? Are these different pictures, different objective truths?

These are some of the questions which the confrontation of the quotations cited gives rise to, questions which constitute the starting-point for further reflections to which the present work is devoted.

Notes

1. A. Barruel, *Mémoires pour servir à l'histoire du Jacobinismee,* vol. I, pp. viii-xii, Hamburg, chez P. Fauche, 1803.
2. J. de Maistre, *Considérations sur la France,* pp. 5-6, Paris, 1821.
3. Fernand Rude in his introduction to a new edition of the *Introduction* . . . (*Cahiers des Annales,* p. xviii, Paris, Armand Colin, 1960) puts forth the supposition that Karl Marx may have known this work and had been inspired by it.
4. J. Jaurès, *Histoire Socialiste de la Révolution Française,* vol. I, pp. 119-130, Paris, éd. de l'Humanité, 1922.
5. *Ibid.,* p. 130.
6. J Barnave, *Introduction à la Révolution Française,* ed. Armand Colin, p. 1, Paris, 1960.
7. *Ibid.,* p. 3.
8. *Ibid.,* p. 9.
9. *Ibid.,* p. 10.
10. *Ibid.,* pp. 51-52.
11. *Ibid.,* p. 53.
12. Mme de Staël Hostein, *Considérations sur les principaux événements de la Révolution Française,* vol. I, Liège, J. A. Latour, 1818.
13. *Ibid.,* pp. 1-2.
14. *Ibid.,* pp. 43-44.
15. *Ibid.,* p. 48.
16. *Ibid.,* p. 71.
17. *Ibid.,* p. 118.
18. Laponneray, *Histoire de la Révolution Française depuis 1789 jusqu'en 1814,* vol. I, Paris, 1838.
19. *Ibid.,* pp. 5-6.
20. *Ibid.,* p. 6.
21. *Ibid.,* p. 7.
22. *Ibid.,* pp. 7-8.
23. J. Michelet, *Histoire de la Révolution Française,* vol. I, Paris, Bibl. de la Pléiade, 1952.
24. *Ibid.,* p. 61.
25. *Ibid.,* pp. 64-67.
26. *Ibid.,* pp. 67-76.
27. *Ibid.,* p. 46.
28. *Ibid.,* pp. 48-49.
29. A. de Tocqueville, *L'Ancien Régime et la Révolution,* 3rd ed., p. 55, Paris, 1857.
30. *Ibid.,* p. 54.
31. *Ibid.,* p. 57.
32. *Ibid.,* p. 69.
33. *Ibid.,* p. 208.
34. *Ibid.,* p. 209.
35. *Ibid.,* pp. 286-288.
36. *Ibid.,* p. 291.
37. *Ibid.,* pp. 291-292. (Emphasis—A.S.)
38. *Ibid.,* pp. 295-296.

39. H. Taine, *Les Origines de la France contemporaine,* vol. II, p. 209, Paris, Libr. Hachette, 1875.
40. *Ibid.,* pp. 226-230.
41. J. Jaurès, *Histoire Socialiste de la Révolution Française,* vol. I, pp. 44-46, Paris, ed. de l'Humanité, 1922.
42. *Ibid.,* p. 56.
43. *Ibid.,* p. 49.
44. *Ibid.,* p. 62.
45. *Ibid.,* p. 73.
46. *Ibid.,* p. 77.
47. *Ibid.,* p. 209.
48. *Ibid.,* p. 211.
49. *Ibid.,* p. 248.
50. *Ibid.,* p. 264.
51. F. Brentano, *L'Ancien Régime,* pp. 393-395, Paris, éd. Fayard, 1929.
52. *Ibid.,* pp. 395-409.
53. *Ibid.,* pp. 432-435.
54. G. Lefebvre, *Etudes sur la Révolution Française,* Paris, 1954.
55. P. Gaxotte, *La Révolution Française,* p. 32, Fayard, 1962.
56. A. Mathiez, *La Révolution Française,* vol. I, p. 13, Paris, éd. Armand Colin, 1937.
57. *Ibid.,* p. 13.
58. *Ibid.,* p. 15.
59. *Ibid.,* pp. 12-13.
60. *Ibid.,* pp. 21-22.
61. *Ibid.,* pp. 40-42.
62. G. Lefebvre, *La Révolution Française,* pp. 40-41, Paris, Presses Universitaires de France.
63. *Ibid.,* pp. 52-55.
64. *Ibid.,* pp. 58-59.
65. *Ibid.,* p. 82.
66. As quoted by G. Lefebvre, *op. cit.,* p. 113.
67. *Ibid.,* pp. 128-129. (Emphasis—A.S.)
68. C. E. Labrousse, *Esquisse du mouvement des prix et des revenus en France au XVIII siècle,* Libr. Dalloz. Paris, 1932: *La Crise de l'économie française à la fin de l'ancien Régime et au début de la Revolution,* Paris, Presses Universitaires, 1944.
69. C. E. Labrousse, *Esquisse du mouvement des prix . . . , ed. cit.,* pp. 640-641.
70. *Ibid.,* pp. 641-642.
71. C. E. Labrousse, *La Crise de l'économie française . . . ed. cit.,* p. xlii.
72. *Ibid.,* p. xxiii.
73. *Ibid.,* p. xlviii. (Emphasis—A.S.)

CHAPTER 1

Cognitive Narration—The Process of Cognition—Truth

... when grand philosophy is ostentatiously put out at the front door of the mind, then narrow, class, provincial and regional prejudices come in at the back door and dominate, perhaps only half consciously, the thinking of the historian.

Charles A. Beard, *Written History as an Act of Faith,* p. 18

The ancients maintained that the source of philosophy was the astonishment (*taumadzein*) which man feels when faced with the mysteries of the world around him. From this point of view, history (not in the meaning of "res gestae" but in the meaning of "rerum gestarum") is assuredly a fertile source of philosophical thought and is closely connected, in spite of the current opinions of positivistically inclined historians, with philosophy.

It is sufficient in this respect to point to the example of divergences among historians who present the same event differently, seen by them either from the perspective of various periods and generations or from the same period of time but based on different value systems and criteria of evaluation: emanations of divergent class and group interests, world outlooks and so on. We began our exposition by presenting a sample of this type of situation. Nevertheless, this was only an exemplary illustration of a much broader and more profound issue which, in fact, extends to all of history and, literally, to all the most important works in this field. There are the ones we are concerned with, not propaganda history but strictly scholarly history maintained on the level of the highest professional competence of a given period.

Here, too, begins the field of that "astonishment" which impregnates philosophical thought. For questions arise insistently, the

43

answer to which calls for metatheoretical reflection, philosophical reflection.

Are the historians, in spite of perfected methods and research techniques, present in reference to the same issues and events not only different evaluations and interpretations but also a different selection of facts and even often perceive and present the same facts differently, not simply engaged in camouflaged propaganda instead of science?

And if this is not so, if we assume the subjective honesty of the scholars and the probity of their intellectual effort, then is Clio perhaps the muse of an art and not of a science and should history writing, therefore, be included among the arts and scientific measuring standards not be applied to it?

And if, as a result of a long-lasting dispute which has been waged on the subject, we were inclined, together with all the professional historians who in solidarity wax indignant at these "artistic insinuations", to uphold firmly the scientific nature of historical writing, then it is capable (in the face of the incontrovertable fact of the existence of divergences in the interpretation of the same events by historians representing different periods or various classes in the same period, etc. due to the necessity of rewriting history in almost every generation) of formulating and transmitting the objective truth about the subject under examination?

If the subjective element in historical cognition is so evident at present that it can be denied only by the guardians of the positivist museum and not by scholars on the level of contemporary knowledge, does this not stand in contradiction to the postulate of the objectivity of scientific cognition and, hence, of the scientific nature of historical writing?

This, together with these questions and the theoretical "astonishment" connected with them leaves us in the embraces of philosophy; in spite of the objections in this respect and the assurances regarding the philosophical "innocence" of history, which up to the present day the positivistically inclined—and there are still many of them—representatives of this field of knowledge do not spare us.

Engels once warned the representatives of the natural sciences that the attempts to deny the role of philosophy in the natural sciences or even the elimination of philosophy from this field of research, in accord with the postulates of positivism, lead to falling into the embrace of the worse possible philosophy; a mixture of bits and pieces of school knowledge together with views current and fashionable in a given period on this subject. In fact, one cannot eliminate philosophy from these reflections and thus when expelled through the door it returns through the window. *A fortiori*, and for a variety of reasons, this warning pertains to historians.

Philosophers who concern themselves with metatheoretical reflection in history generally complain of the failure to appreciate philosophy in this field. This is understandable, above all, from the psychological point of view. On the other hand, it is rarer, much rarer, to come across an understanding of these issues among professional historians. This enhances such statements as the following made by E. H. Carr, the well-known English historian and theorist of history.

> The liberal nineteenth century view of history had a close affinity with the economic doctrine of *laissez-faire*—as the product of a serene and self-confident outlook on the world. Let everyone get on with his particular job, and the hidden hand would take care of the universal harmony. The facts of history were themselves a demonstration of the supreme fact of a beneficient and apparently infinite progress towards higher things. This was the age of innocence, and the historians walked in the Garden of Eden, without a scrap of philosophy to cover them, naked and unashamed before the god of history. Since then, we have known Sin and experienced a Fall; and those historians who today pretend to dispense with the philosophy of history are merely trying, vainly and self-consciously, like members of a nudist colony to recreate the Garden of Eden in the garden suburb.[1]

The same thought is expressed in different words, in a sharper and stronger fashion, by H. J. Marrou, a French historian and theorist:

> It is time to end with these old reflections and to tear oneself out of the lethargy in which positivism has retained the historians for too long a time (just as their colleagues in the "exact" sciences as well). Our profession is a difficult one, burdened with technical servitudes; in the long run it tends to develop in the practitioner the talent of a specialized insect. Instead of helping him to react against this professional deformation, positivism provided the scholar with a clear conscience ("I am only a historian and not a philosopher"). One should denounce energetically such a spiritual stance, which is one of the most serious threats to the future of our Western civilization, i.e., the bogging down in atrocious, technical barbarity.
>
> Parodying the Platonian maxim we write on the pediment of our Propylaea . . .: "No one who is not a philosopher can enter here", who has not previously reflected on the nature of history and the historian's condition. The health of a scientific discipline requires from the scholar a certain methodological disquiet, a concern for awarement of the mechanism of his conduct, some effort of reflection on the problems derived from the "theory of cognition" which are implied thereby.[2]

This idea was perhaps expressed most forcefully by Charles A. Beard, the American historian and theorist who was a follower of the school of presentism. The words of Benedetto Croce quoted by him coincide with Engels' warning addressed to the natural scientists:

> . . . any selection and arrangement of facts pertaining to any large area of history, either local or world, race or class, is controlled inexorably by the frame of reference in the mind of the selector and arranger. This frame of reference includes things deemed necessary, and things deemed desirable. It may be large, informed by deep knowledge, and illuminated by wide experiences; or it may be small, uninformed, and unilluminated. It may be a grand conception of history or a mere aggregation of confusions. But it is there in the mind, inexorably. To borrow from Croce, when grand philosophy is ostentatiously put out at the front door of the mind, then narrow, class, provincial and regional prejudices come in at the back door and dominate, perhaps only half-consciously, the thinking of the historian.[3]

These few examples taken from non-Marxist historical literature (Marxist literature consciously based on historical materialism presents a different picture) suffice to illustrate the concept of interest to us. Of course, as we have already mentioned, it is the philosophers who engage in theoretical reflection on history and consider much more often the problem concerning us, nonetheless, for the reasons already outlined, their statements are less characteristic, although no less interesting or instructive. We shall quote as an example only the statement of one of them, Ernest Nagel. This is a statement of particular interest for us since it leads directly into the core of the principal subject of our considerations in the present book, the objectivity of historical cognition.

> Like other intellectual workers, professional historians are rarely self-conscious about the organizing concepts or the principles for assessing evidence which they habitually employ in their discipline. To be sure, historians have written extensively on the specialized techniques of their craft as well as on the general problems that arise in the external and internal criticism of documents and other remains of the past. Nevertheless, serious discussions of such broad questions as the structure of historical explanations, the ground upon which they are warranted, and in particular the logic of causal imputation in historical research, have in the main been carried out by professional philosophers or philosophically minded students or in other branches of social inquiry. When historians do express themselves on such issues (usually on ceremonial occasions) they are therefore likely to voice philosophical ideals imbibed by chance during their school days or in their desultory reading, but which they have seldom subjected to rigorous criticism in the light of their own professional experience. At any rate, this hypothesis helps to explain the radical skepticism (or "relativism") professed by many contemporary historians concerning the possibility of objective knowledge in their discipline, despite the fact that in their substantive historical analyses they do not practice what they preach.[4]

Thus, this situation may be summed up briefly in the following fashion: theoretical and methodological problems (which should be distinguished from research techniques) in history had been the concern mainly of philosophers and only exceptionally of historians; most often, when positivist connections were present, the latter consciously ignored these problems. As a result, in spite of the current opinions and desires of many historians, the significance and responsibility of the work of the philosophers in this field has risen immensely. If philosophy cannot be eliminated from history, if on the contrary (as Raymond Aron maintains and, given a certain interpretation of his statement, I agree with him completely) "theory precedes history"[5] if historians satisfy themselves with bits and pieces of current philosophical theories, then it is precisely philosophy which is primarily responsible for the historians' theoretical muddleheadedness, especially with regard to those problems which rest on the borderline of history and philosophy. A classical example of this is the problem which interests us of the objectivity of cognition and truth in history; a problem *philosophical par excellence* which has been obfuscated mainly by the traditional theory of cognition. Conscious and critical philosophical reflection is an indispensable premise for the resolving of the complex theoretical and methodological problems in history. We shall begin with this.

Three Models of the Process of Cognition

Regardless of whether historians, just as representatives of other sciences as well, are aware of this fact or not, whether they recognize the function of philosophy in their research or not, their views regarding the process of cognition and, in consequence, the problem of truth are derived from philosophy. We will go further; they are imposed by the philosophical views prevailing in this sphere and responsibility for them (as already mentioned above) is borne, above all, by philosophy.

The philosophical analysis of the process of cognition and its product which constitutes the content of the so-called theory of cognition has, at present, such a copious literature (taking into account the fact that in philosophy the process of a natural selection of works due to their outdatedness does not take place) that, in effect, during the span of a lifetime it cannot be perused and utilized to the full. It is also sensible to assume that various so-called new ideas had already been expressed in this literature in a developed or embryonic form. In such a situation one can act in a two-fold fashion: either seek to delve into this ocean of erudition and show off one's knowledge to the broad public, which creates a beautiful decorum of scholarliness but, in truth, does not contribute anything except a staidness of exposition and boredom, or ignore the consideration of a superficial scholarliness and state simply what one has to say on a given subject. Of course, in doing so one risks not only the loss of decorum, of importance in a certain milieu but also, which is more painful, the loss of the possibility of paying a scholarly debt of gratitude to all those to whom one is indebted intellectually, in one way or another. Since we have consciously chosen the second of the above-mentioned courses, I shall begin with the declaration that the elements of what I have to say on the subject of the process of cognition and its products, which I regard as the indispensable premise for further reasoning pertaining to the subjects of interest to us in this book, have been expounded many times and from various points of view in the literature of the subject. Since this is so well known, the burdening of the exposition with an eruditional apparatus and footnotes becomes additionally super-fluous. In such a context the only originality to which an author may lay claim lies in the joining together of previously known elements into a given totality and in the use which he makes of this totality in his reasoning.

Let us begin then with the traditional trinity which appears in every analysis of the process of cognition (of course, in various terminological forms): the cognitive subject, the object of cognition, and knowledge as the product of the process of cognition. We shall refrain consciously here from taking up the psychological aspect of the problem and thus leave the act of cognition outside the sphere of our interest, concentrating only on gnoseological problems.

It is only pedantry that impells us to add that each of the terms mentioned by us—"subject", "object", and "knowledge"—implies content and philosophical problems of immense complexity. We are freed from developing them by the context of our considerations. This makes it possible to limit ourselves to the acceptance, where known, of certain intuitive meanings of these terms. We shall return to only one of these in our further consideration, that is, to the term "cognitive subject", not for the purpose of semantic elucidation but for reasons of merit. "Hic et nunc." We shall interest ourselves with this trinity of the cognitive process only from the point of view of the typology of the relations between its elements. In this respect, I distinguish three basic models of the process of cognition (theoretically, as we shall see further on, their number is greater, due to the possible combinations of their component elements).

If we understand by the process of cognition a specific mutual interaction of the cognizing subject and the object of cognition which gives rise to the intellectual products, which we call knowledge, then the interpretation of this relation can be placed within the framework of a number of theoretical models. This is not speculative typology, for each one of the models finds its concrete illustration in historically existing philosophical trends.

The first model lay at the foundations of a mechanistically interpreted theory of reflection. The conception here was as follows: the conceived object acts on the perceptual apparatus of the subject who appears, in this conception, as a passive, contemplative-receptive element. The product of this process—cognition, knowledge—is to be a reflection, a copy of the object of cognition, while the origin of this reflection is connected with the mechanical acting of the object on the subject. This is why this model may be classified as mechanistic.

As we have already stated, this is a model which was, in fact, represented in the history of philosophical thought and which radiated from philosophy to other fields of thought. In one sense it is a classical model, both due to the frequency of its appearance as well as to the long history of its functioning; at least from Democrates' theory of "Ejdola" up to modern sensualism and transcendental empiricism. It is a classical model also because it was historically linked with a so-called classical definition of truth, creating the necessary theoretical background for the concept that a judgement which states something regarding the object of cognition is true, if what the judgement maintains corresponds to reality. Without the theory of reflection (although not necessarily interpreted in a mechanistic and simplified fashion) one cannot, after all, consistently defend the classical definition of truth

The first model is thus a model in which the subject, as mentioned, is a passive, contemplative-receptive element in the cognitive relation; it plays the role of an instrument registering external stimuli; in the extreme view, the role of a mirror (when dealing with visual perceptions). The differences in the picture of reality in the case of different cognizing subjects are reduced to the individual or genetic divergences of their perceptual apparatus. Popper refers to this theory of the process of cognition by the colourful phrase "a bucket theory of consciousness" ("eine Kübeltheorie des Bewusstseins").[6] It was connected historically, above all, with diverse schools of materialist thought, since the prerequisite for its existence was the recognition of the reality of the object of cognition and a sensualist-empiricist interpretation of the cognitive relation. If a materialist vision of the world facilitates the grasping and understanding in the theory of cognition of the objective element in the cognitive relation, then due to the accentuating of this objective element it renders difficult (though not impossible by any means!) the extraction and understanding of the subjective elements of this relation. Marx noted only an obvious fact when he wrote in the "Theses on Feuerbach" that all past materialism had interpreted the subject in the form of an object, and not as human practice, while the active aspect was developed by idealism, although it was done, due to its abstractness, in an imperfect fashion.

If, in the first model, the passive contemplative one, it is the object which gains the upper hand in the subject-object relation, then the opposite is true of the second model, let it be called idealist-activist, in which the upper hand, if not exclusiveness, is gained by the cognizing subject. In accord with the model the subject creates the object as its product. It takes on its historical shape in various subjective-idealist philosophies and, in pure form, in solipsism.

As mentioned above, Marx recognized the superiority of idealism in relation to pre-Marxian materialism in that idealism developed the active aspect which pertained also, of course, to human cognition. This is understandable in the light of the second model of cognitive relationship; after all, it concentrates attention on the subject, attributing to it even the role of a creator of reality. It is true that in this model the object of cognition disappears in a way which is contrary with human experience. But the role of the subject in the process of cognition emerges still more clearly. The psychological concept, that the theoretical foundation employed as a starting-point for observation and reflection determines a concentration of attention on a given aspect of reality, is thus, once more, confirmed.

A splendid analysis of this turn towards the subject and thereby towards the subjective factor in the process of cognition (which is a characteristic trait of the second model) can be found in K. Mannheim's epistemological expositions contained in his *Ideology and Utopia.* Clearly influenced by Marx and Marxism, Mannheim stresses the role of two factors in this respect; first, the disintegration of a traditional social order and, along with it, of a world outlook, and secondly, opposition during the end of the Middle Ages and the beginning of modern times to the principle of authority, on the basis of the human individual and his experiences, taken as a starting-point.[7] The question, however, is how this individual is to be understood and interpreted.[8]

With the problem of the human individual to which we shall refer below, we enter into the realm of the third model. What is characteristic of it is that it counterposes to the principle of the preponderance of one of the elements of the cognitive relation—the object (first model) or the subject (second model)—the principle of their mutual interaction. Thus, it rejects the mechanistic model of cognition in which the subject is reduced to a role of a passively contemplating register; it emphasizes the active role of the subject who is conditioned in many ways, but always socially, thus bringing into cognition his socially transmitted mode of perceiving reality. No less energetically it rejects the "a rebours" mechanistic model of cognition of subjective idealism, in which the objectively existing object of cognition disappears in a mystical fashion, while only the cognizing subject and its products remain on the field of battle. On the other hand, it accepts, within the framework of an activistically modified theory of reflection, a model of cognitive relationship in which both the subject and the object retain an objective and real existence and, simultaneously, interact upon each other. This takes place within the framework of the subject's social practice, as it recognizes the object in the course of activity. This model of a process of cognition, which we personally favour, finds its specific form in the properly interpreted theory of reflection as developed by Marxist philosophy.

It is obvious that the choice of one of these models implies important and far-reaching consequences for the ensemble of one's scientific approach and, in particular, for one's concept of truth. Up to this point we have been concerned only with an enumerative typology. The moment has now come to justify the selection undertaken and thus to develop the categories which come to the fore. However, before we engage on this positive exposition of our views in this field, the foreground should be cleared by explaining, even briefly, why we have limited our horizon to a certain selected category of models and why we have rejected some of them "a limine".

Let us, above all, answer the question of whether other models of cognitive relationship, apart from those we have named above, exist and are possible? The answer to this question is, of course, in the affirmative. Different variants of a dualist model may serve as an example, such as a model based on Leibnitz's concept of pre-established harmony, on the concept of occasionalism, etc. Why are these models of no interest to us? Simply because of their anti-scientific or even mystical character, which at present not only deprives them of any heuristic value, but also of the ability to appeal to the minds of contemporary scholars.

Let us return, however, to the basic issue, to the analysis and development of the model selected by us; an activistically interpreted theory of reflection.

Cognitive relationship remains in this model, as well, obviously as a relationship between the subject and the object. By removing one of these elements we remove the relationship itself. For materialists (and the selection of a model of the process of cognition is indissolubly linked with the world outlook on the basis and within the framework of which this selection takes place), it is obvious and indubitable that the object of cognition being the external stimulus of sensory impressions of the cognizing subject exists objectively, that is, outside of any cognizing mind and independently of it. According to the materialist who accepts the third model of the cognitive relationship, the ontological concept regarding the mode of existence of an object of cognition can be denied only by someone who has galloped into a blind alley of philosophical speculation, who also necessarily negates by his actual practice the views voiced in theory. Nonetheless, by stressing with full force the importance of the objective element in the cognitive relationship (for this purpose I have repeated certain concepts which, although banal from the point of view of materialism, being out this emphasis), the adherent of the third model of the cognitive relationship sees the subject as its main element. This is closely linked with a consistent introduction of the anthropological factor into the theory of cognition. It is this which calls for a broader explanation and interpretation.

It is the concept of the human individual which here comes to the forefront and constitutes, as is borne out, a problem not only of an autonomously understood philosophy of man, but also of all inquiries in which man, as a concrete acting individual, plays a foremost role.

It is understandable that when we speak of the cognitive relationship as a relationship between the cognizing subject and the object of cognition, that very much, if not everything, depends on how the expression "cognizing subject" is understood. The individualist-subjectivist concept on the one hand and the social-objective on the other come forth in this respect as two struggling rivals.

The first is linked in modern times, as far as its origin is concerned, with the disintegration of the former socio-economic order which, during the transition from formation to formation, brings about a loss of ties between the individual and society in the shaping of the individual. As already mentioned, Karl Mannheim speaks of this in an interesting fashion; he is influenced by Marx not only in connection with the problem of the social conditioning of human views and attitudes, but also, perhaps above all (although this is usually not noticed in the literature of the subject), in respect to the interpretation of the individual as a social animal. Neither is it fortuitous, as Mannheim himself notes, that a new conception of the human individual and an understanding of his conditioning by society appeared at the time when the social effect of an individualistic social order, bordering on anarchy, began to be clearly felt.[9]

In interpreting the individual in the light of the individualist-subjectivist concept we interpret him detached from society and his influences or, in other words, in detachment from culture, and thus reduce him to biological existence which in a natural fashion determines his traits and properties. In spite of appearances, such an interpretation does not raise the rank of the individual or the subject in the process of cognition but, on the contrary, lowers this rank. It is only with such an interpretation that one may also arrive at the construction of a mechanistic passive-contemplative model of the cognitive relationship. The individual is biologically determined and brings this determination into the process of cognition in his perceptual apparatus. Apart from this, he is only a being, registering and transforming in a given fashion the stimuli which emanate from the external world.

The error lies, first, in this singular construction of the human individual and, secondly, in interpreting cognition as contemplation and not as action. Thus, erroneous premises not only determine the construction of the model of the cognitive relationship but also predetermine the solution of the problem which is, after all, the object of inquiry: how is the process of cognition, as a relation between the subject and the object, accomplished?

Both of these erroneous assumptions have been attacked in recent times both often and from different sides. Nonetheless, not only priority in time, in comparison with competing trends, but also superiority in respect to the systematic nature of the interpretation of the problem and consistency in the carrying out of the new concept, undoubtedly must be ascribed to Karl Marx. As a source of knowledge regarding Marx's views in this field we should like to point, above all, to the *Theses on Feuerbach*, although these views are to be found in a developed form in *The German Ideology* and other earlier or later works. We do so because we consider the *Theses on Feuerbach* to be a brilliant work (one should add, the work of a young, barely 27 years old, author) which, in the condensed form of theses for a critical appraisal of Feuerbach's philosophy, contained an outline of his own new philosophy. An understanding and appreciation of the *Theses* calls also, even if due to their conciseness and compactness, for considerable knowledge of philosophy in general, and Marx's philosophy in particular. Thus it is not easy reading, but this does not change the high estimation of the work's value, as a contemporary professional philosopher knows exceedingly well even if on the basis of the example of the interpretation and meaning of L. Wittgenstein's *Tractatus Logico-philosophicus*.

In the Sixth Thesis Marx expresses certain thoughts on the subject of the concept of the human individual which are truly revolutionary; both in a sense that they constitute a profound critique of L. Feuerbach's philosophical anthropology, typical for that period, as well as in the sense that they laid the foundations for a new Marxian anthropology, which has preserved its value and topicality to the present day, and this not only within the framework of a Marxist philosophy. We have accepted these thoughts as the basis and the starting-point of our own conception of the human individual, which we consider to be Marxist both from the point of view of its origin (it is after all, derived directly from Marx's own views stated "expressis verbis") and its agreement with other theses of the Marxist world outlook. Here, then, are the thoughts referred to:

Man is, in his reality, an ensemble of social relations; if one disregards this social content of the human individual, then only the ties of nature will remain as a link between people, which is an erroneous view.

This is precisely the question: Is the human individual solely a specimen of a natural species, linked with other similar ones only by a biological, natural bond? In the light of contemporary knowledge we shall answer this question in the negative: the human individual is, of course, a biological individual, as a specimen of the *Homo sapiens* species, but this does not suffice to characterize him since, in addition to biological determinates, social determinates also exert a moulding influence on him, and this is precisely why he is a social individual. Marx emphasizes this vividly stating that man is "the ensemble of social relations".

I do not intend to disregard in the least the natural, biological determining of the human individual and his personality, that is, the complex of views, attitudes and psychic dispositions which form the real human individual. Man is a part of the animal world, both genetically and factually. It would be a mistake not to perceive, what, for example, Feuerbach had already clearly seen in his anthropology, that man as a part of nature is subject to its general laws. At present this would be even more of an error than previously, since we know incomparably more on the subject of the biological or bio-chemical conditionings of an individual. We speak of the genetic code; we come ever closer to the core of this matter by explaining the role of the ribonucleic acids (DNA and RNA) in the mechanism of heredity, veering perilously close to the moment when bio-chemical intervention would make it possible to interfere in the realm of human personality. We have said "perilously" since the deciphering of the secret of the genetic code, in the sense of the possibility of practical interference with its structure, signifies such a power in inter-human relations that, in one sense, its significance is superior to the deciphering of the secret of atomic energy, both in its positive as well as its negative results for humanity. In any case, no serious student of the problems of man can today belittle the nature aspect of the problem; quite on the contrary, the weight and significance of this aspect continue to grow.

This does not, however, decrease the meaningfulness of our concern with the social determinants of the human individual. Regardless of the appreciation of natural determinants and our knowledge about them, it is still a fact that man, in a qualitatively different way from the entire rest of the animal world, is receptive to the process of aculturation and that he is the product both of the development of nature and of society. What is more, without this social-cultural context neither can he be understood on the basis of the natural determinants, since these are the products of development on which the social factor exerts influence. The day is not far when, after having mastered the structural laws of the genetic code, humanity will set itself the task of mastering its dynamic laws as well, posing the question as to the origin of the genetic code. At that time the social-cultural factor will also enter into the domain of nature.

In any case, it is only the taking into consideration of this aspect of the issue which makes it possible for us to pose the problem of "man", not in an abstract fashion, that is, not solely as a biological specimen, but in a concrete-social way, that is, by drawing attention to his historic, group- and individual-specific traits.[10] Only the human individual thus interpreted as a concrete individual, both in respect of his natural and of his social conditioning, is a concrete subject in the cognitive relation. Given such an interpretation it becomes clear that this relation does not and cannot have a passive character, that the subject in this relation is always active, that he contributes, and must contribute, something of himself to the process of cognition which is always negative-objective.

What is this subject in the cognitive relation? Assuredly not only a perceptual apparatus, conditioned by nature, which registers solely external stimuli, although the subject cannot exist without some perceptual apparatus. What is decisive is precisely that which differentiates man from animals, and which is manifest in his acculturation; that he is both the creator and the product of culture. We are not interested here with what determines the ability for acculturation, with which it is primarily connected. We take this process for granted; we are concerned, above all, with its results in the realm of the process of cognition.

Varied results, also in the field of cognition, are derived from the fact that man, the subject, is the "ensemble of social relations". Beginning with the fact that the given articulation of the world, that is, the mode of perceiving it, delimiting its specific parts, the dynamics of observations, etc., are connected with language and its conceptual apparatus which we obtain from society: including education, as the transmission of social experience and accumulated phylogenetically; including the social conditioning of our appraisals due to the class or group character of the systems of value accepted by us (which Marxism in particular developed strongly and consistently and sociology of knowledge continued); up to and including all those biological and social factors which in the ontogenesis of the individual shape his psychical being, consciousness and subconsciousness, explained and developed by modern psychology by so-called depth psychology in particular. These are the principals, though by no means all, of the directions of research on the social determinants of the cognizing subject and his behaviour, research impels a radical rejection of the passive, mechanistic model of the cognitive relationship. The cognizing subject is not a mirror, nor an apparatus passively registering external stimuli. On the contrary, it is precisely the force which directs this apparatus, sets it up accordingly and then, in a particular fashion, transforms the data it has obtained. Someone has correctly remarked that those who compare cognition with the photographing of reality forget, apart from everything else, that the camera takes that which the photographer's eye and hand have directed it, thus one photograph is not the same as another.

The cognizing subject "photographs" reality while possessing a specific socially created mechanism which guides the "lens" of this apparatus. In addition it "transforms" the information obtained on the basis of a complicated code of social conditionings which enter his psychical make-up by means of the language with which he thinks, through his class position and the group interest connected with it, through conscious and subconscious motivation and, above all, through his social activity without which cognition is a speculative fiction.

It is here that the second revolutionary thought of Marxism in regards to cognition and the cognizing subject comes to the fore. It pertains to the category of practice in human cognition.

In the *Theses* already quoted by us, Marx wrote:

> The chief defect of all heretofore existing material—that of Feuerbach included—is that the object, reality, sensuousness, is conceived only in the form of the *object* or *contemplation* (Anschauung) but not as *human sensuous activity, practice,* not subjectively. . . . (First Thesis.)
>
> Feuerbach, not satisfied with *abstract thinking,* appeals to *sensuous contemplation,* but he does not conceive sensuousness as a practical, human-sensuousness activity. (Fifth Thesis.)

(Text of theses in F. Engels, *Ludwig Feuerbach,* N.Y., 1935, pp. 73-74.)

Out of the great abundance of problems connected with "praxis" in the works of Marx, even as they appear in the *Theses on Feuerbach,* we shall select a certain segment which, nevertheless, in the given context plays a decisive role. What we have in mind is the role of practice in the process of cognition and the meaning of this category in the interpretation of the cognizing subject.

In the above we have sought to demonstrate the active role of the subject in the process of cognition by referring to the social conditioning of the subject, to the subject as the "ensemble of social relations". The aim was to show that the subject is not a passive registering apparatus, but that it brings into cognition the subjective factor bound up with its social moulding. This explains the difference not only in evaluation and interpretation, but also in the perception (articulation) and description of reality, a difference which characterizes the cognition of subjects appearing in different historical era, or even in the same period, although in various social milieu (ethnic, class, etc.). Nevertheless, the *par excellence* active character of the subject of cognition is linked with the fact, most often overlooked and passed by in silence in abstract considerations of cognition, that man comes to cognition by action. This is precisely what Marx had in mind when he reproached Feuerbach for not interpreting sensual cognition as practical activity, that is, as activity which transforms cognized reality. It is characteristic that Marx called such an interpretation of sensual cognition as practical activity "human-sensual", clearly seeing in this some distinguishing, specific trait (Thesis 5). This also lay at the foundations of his critique of "past materialism", as not having interpreted reality, taking the object as human mental activity, that is, as practice, and thus, not having interpreted it from the position of the active role of the subject and hence subjectively.

These two elements, a special concept of the human individual as a social individual, and of cognition as sensual activity and practice, are necessary for deciphering and understanding the third, activist model of cognitive relationship. As we have stated already, it is organically linked with an activistically interpreted theory of reflection, the only interpretation of this theory which can form a coherent part of the system of Marxist philosophy.

The theory of reflection may be interpreted in a twofold fashion: in the spirit of a mechanistic model (the first in our typology) of the cognitive relationship, that is, taking the process of cognition as passive-contemplative, or in the spirit of an objective-activist model (the third in our typology) of the cognitive relationship, that is, taking cognition as sensual reality.

In spite of all the differences between these two models of the cognitive relationship they can be embraced by a broadly conceived theory of reflection, although, of course, interpreted differently in both cases. There exist, in both cases, elements which constitute the basis for a certain interpretation of cognition, as opposed to the second model (idealist-activist), and in connection with this make it possible to use the name "theory of reflection", common to both. These elements are as follows:

Firstly, the recognition of the objective existence of the object of cognition, that is, its existence outside of any perceiving mind and independently of it. This is a materialist standpoint in ontology and a realist one in the theory of cognition, which clearly counterposes the theory of reflection, in its manifold interpretations, to any subjective-idealist concept of the process of cognition.

Secondly, the recognition that the objectively existing object of cognition is the external source of sensual impressions without which the process of cognition would be impossible. This is a consistent continuation of realism in the theory of cognition and of materialism in ontology.

Thirdly, the recognition that the process of cognition is a particular relationship between the objectively existing subject and the objectively existing object and is, therefore, a subjective-objective relationship.

Fourthly and lastly, the recognition that the object is knowable and, therefore, the recognition, as opposed to all agnosticism, that in the process of cognition "The thing in itself" becomes "The thing for us".

Even if we limit ourselves to these four points we can see the significance of the common elements of the different variants of the theory of reflection which, in spite of internal differences, are solidly opposed to idealism and agnosticism. The third and the fourth points, in particular, explain the appearance of the word "reflection" in the theory's name which, historically speaking, was engendered to the same degree by the struggle against agnosticism (especially Kantian) as that against idealism.

This unity of attitudes does not exclude differences in the interpretation of the theory of reflection. On the contrary, as we have already stated, such differences do, in fact, appear in the historically known presentations of this theory. Let us try to present these differences in the following points.

Firstly, this pertains to the interpretation of the cognizing subject which, while it is understood by all the representatives of the theory of reflection as an objective existence, has, nonetheless, according to some, a passive-receptive character while, according to others—as we have tried to show above—an active character.

Secondly, the cognizing subject is interpreted by some individualistically, and by others socially, as the product of social conditioning.

Thirdly, the theories of reflection, while in accord on the concept that the process of cognition is subjective-objective, may differ in their interpretation of this subjectiveness of the process which is closely linked up not only with the understanding of the subject but also with a different understanding of cognition itself; by some, as a passive-contemplative process, by others, as an active-practical process.

Fourthly and lastly, the agreement of all the theories of reflection with the concept that the object of cognition is knowable does not negate the possibility of differences arising in the interpretation of this knowability as a unique act or as an infinite process. Nor does it negate the possibility of the existence of differences of opinion in respect to the products of the process of cognition: interpreted by some literally as a copy, as a duplicate and thus a faithful image (naïve realism: the object is such as it appears in sensual cognition and the corresponding qualities rest in the objects themselves), and by others as the mental reproduction of reality (critical realism: the image of reality in the mind is not fortuitous, it is the reproduction of this reality, and this is why it makes effective action possible, but it is not a perfect copy, the concept regarding the process-like character of cognition would in any case negate this).

As we have stated above, the activist version of the theory of reflection connected with the third model of the cognitive relationship is the only one which can be a coherent part of the entire system of Marxist philosophy. We understand this in a two-fold fashion: firstly, in the direct sense, that is, that only such an interpretation can be linked with the system of other fundamental concepts of Marxist philosophy in a non-contradictory fashion; secondly, that precisely such an interpretation of the theory of reflection can be reconstructed from the corresponding statements of Marx, Engels and Lenin. Since a study of the Marxist theory of reflection is outside the scope of our present interests and possibilities while, on the other hand, some of the elements will be necessary for our further reflections, we shall not present this matter in any detail. Simultaneously, we should like to note that Marxist works on this subject also show occasionally a primitivization of the problem by interpreting it in the spirit of a mechanistic model of the cognitive relationship. As far as a more detailed interpretation of this problem is concerned, of course, for a viewpoint which we ourselves maintain, we must refer the reader to our earlier works on this subject.[11]

Three factors, three component elements of Marxist philosophy argue, above all, in favour of accepting an activistic variant of the model of the cognitive relationship and the rejection of the mechanistic model.

Firstly, the Marxist concept of the human individual as an "ensemble of social relations".

Secondly, the interpretation of cognition by Marx as practical activity, that is, sensuous activity.

Thirdly, the interpretation of cognition as an infinite process of striving towards an absolute truth through the accumulation of relative truths.

If one desires to respect these concepts of Marxist philosophy, and each one of them plays a fundamental role in this philosophy's system, then to be consistent, one must accept the objective-activistic model of the cognitive relationship which joins together with them in one organic whole.

How does the problem of the objectivity of cognition present itself in the light of the above?

Let us establish at the outset in what sense we understand the word "objective" here, appearing, as it does, as an adjective defining the word "cognition".

A glance at any philosophical dictionary will show that we are dealing with a world of manifold meanings, differently employed by various authors and, in addition, possessing divergent and even contrary meanings in various historical periods. In such a situation the way out is to employ a projective definition which should, if possible, respect the sense of the word as it exists at present; not infringe unnecessarily the current intuitions in the literature of the subject, but, in ones own fashion and upon ones own responsibility, specify precisely the sense of the words employed. In accord with these postulates we shall distinguish three meanings of the word "objective" which will concern us in further analysis.

Firstly, "objective", as coming or derived from the object. In this sense "objective cognition" is to be understood as a cognition which reflects in the mind (in some special meaning of the word "to reflect") an object which exists outside of the perceiving mind and independently of it. Subjective cognition, as opposed to objective, would then provide the possibility of a cognition which creates its own object, instead of reflecting it, as maintained by certain philosophical trends (subjective idealism).

Secondly, the word "objective", in relation to the cognition and the mind of the perceiving person, shall be taken in the sense "cognitively significant for all", "Objective cognition", therefore, equals cognition possessed of general and not only individual value (as opposed to the "subjective").

Thirdly and lastly, "objective" will mean "free of emotional coloration and partiality connected therewith". In this sense, the word "subjective" is tantamount to the expression "emotionally colored" or "partial".

After this attempt to define precisely the meaning of the words "objective" and "subjective" in relation to cognition, we shall pose the question: what is the situation of the postulate of objectivity of cognition in the context of the different models of the cognitive relationship? And in particular: may one speak of objective cognition within the framework of the objective-activistic model (the third)?

The answer to this question is as follows:

Within the framework of each variant of the theory of reflection (thus, both within the framework of the first, as well as of the third) one may speak of the objectivity of cognition, in the first of the above meanings of the word "objective".

This, however, is but a banal statement. What interests us here, above all, is "objectivity" in the second and third of the above meanings. We assume, also, that what matters is scientific cognition, undertaken competently and with the intention of discovering the objective truth.

Can we speak about the objectivity of cognition in the sense of its value, its significance, not only of an individual but of a general nature? Can we speak about the objectivity of cognition in the sense of its emotional colourlessness and impartiality when one assumes, simultaneously, that the cognizing subject, as the product of social relations, plays an active role in the process of cognition, and thus will always contribute something particularly linked with the subject, hence something subjective?

Both yes and no! Everything depends on a more precise definition of the meaning in which the expression "objective cognition" is employed here: Yes, if it is not absolutized, no if it is interpreted in absolute categories.

Let us begin with objectivity understood as the elimination of partiality and emotional coloration. If the active role of the subject in cognition is not eliminated by taking on a corresponding assumption, then, of course, this cognition is neither emotionally colorless, nor completely impartial. In that case, what does "objectivity" signify here? What it means is the postulate of the maximum elimination of the emotional coloration and partiality, which deform true cognition, from the process of cognition. "Objectivity", in this sense, is thus always tinged subjectively, since it is always not an absolute objectivity, but a human, relative one. "Objectivity" in this sense is always relative (*this* cognition is more objective than *that*) and not something absolute. It is always in the process of becoming.

If one recognizes the active role of the subject in the process of cognition, and thus also that he must, of necessity, introduce the subjective factor into cognition, then it is clear that "objectivity"—in the meaning of the property of the universal value of this cognition, and not an individual or group value—cannot signify that this is the same value for all, that all differences of cognizing subjects disappear, and that we have obtained absolute truth. Here again, what matters is a certain tendency, a certain process and not a state. What matters again is a relative trait (*this* cognition is more generally accepted than *that,* which in any case does not coincide with the criteria of its truth) and not an absolute one.

Taking into consideration the active role of the subject in the process of cognition, "objectivity" in the second and third meaning—in accord with the table of meaning established by us earlier—is only relatively a property of cognition: both in the sense that this is a property which can be spoken of solely by comparing the products of various processes of cognition, and in the sense that it is always only the process which is involved, and not a ready and ultimate state. Thus the process of scientific cognition and its products always have an objective-subjective character. Objective both due to its reference to the object which is in a given way reflected in cognition, and to the relative universality of the value of this cognition and the relative elimination of its emotional coloring. It is subjective, in the most general meaning, due to the active role of the subject in the process of cognition.

Having ascertained that a subjective factor always appears in cognition, one should consider its relation to the objective-social factor. We have already dealt with this problem in another work.[12] Thus we shall repeat here, in a condensed form, only the principal ideas of my previous reflections.

It can be stated generally that we understand the subjective factor to be that which the cognizing subject brings into the process of cognition. This differs from the traditional understanding of the expression "subjective factor". What matters here is not an element of cognition which is not connected with the object, as a type of its reflection, since subjectivism of this kind we consider to be a speculative fiction. It is also not individual views, as distinct from generally accepted ones, which are of concern here since—apart from conscious falsification for purposes of propaganda—the borderline between these views is, as we have seen above, fluid. What does matter is the active role of the subject in the process of cognition, his influence on the shaping of this process and its results through factors which determine the psychical make-up and attitude of the subject. What does matter are such factors as: the structure of the subject's perceptual apparatus; the language in which he expresses his thoughts, obtaining thereby a conceptual apparatus which conditions a given articulation and perception of reality; class and group interests which jointly decide the selection of a system of values by the individuals belonging to these classes and groups, etc.

That which we call here "the subjective factor" because, metaphorically speaking, it is the emanation of the subject in the process of cognition, does not have an individual-subjective character, as one customarily assumes in traditional reflections on the subject, but—on the contrary—an objective, social character. All the exemplifications of the "subjective factor" which we have enumerated above have, after all, a social origin and a social character. The issue is clear when we speak of language which we receive from society by means of education as a ready product and a ready apparatus for our thinking. It is also clear when we speak of the determinants (social, ethnic, class, group) of the psychical make-up and attitudes of the subject, particularly in the domain of systems of values and judgements, that is, when we speak of determinants which are the object of study in cultural anthropology, the sociology of knowledge, and so on. The issue is, however, not all that clear when we speak of the structure of the perceptual apparatus, which undoubtedly affects the entire process of cognition to an immense degree (although the functions of thinking do not coincide completely with the function of sensory perception) and which is something highly individual; but, after all, this structure is, genetically speaking, also derived from social sources and, therefore, possesses an objective-social character.

Why then do we speak of a "subjective factor"? Because it is organically connected with the cognizing subject taken as an "ensemble of social relations". On the other hand, a "subjective factor", interpreted in this way, has an objective-social and not an idealist-subjective character. This, however, is already a matter of concepts and interpretation.

In this fashion we have completed our considerations on the subject of the model of the cognitive relationship, which lead us in turn to the problem of truth and to true cognition.

Truth as a Process

The problem we are concerned with, the objectivity of historical truth, impels us necessarily to take up in the initial epistemological reflections; not only the problem of the model of the cognitive relationship, but the problem of truth as well. We shall have to speak about this in the context of historical cognition, and this is a typical philosophical problem. Once again the fraility of the foundations of the historians' distaste for philosophy becomes apparent; the actual state of affairs shows that in history, just as in all the sciences, we encounter problems which are *par excellence* philosophical and which cannot be truly resolved without availing oneself of the achievements of philosophy. We cannot, after all, eradicate from our language such words as "truth", and it is sufficient to reflect on the problem of truth to see that it is undubitably a philosophical problem. Of course, one can solve it on one's own, without seeking the aid of philosophy as a scientific discipline, but then one replaces the philosophy without changing, in the least, the nature of the problem; ignoring, in addition, the work already accomplished and hence risking either a rediscovery of America or—which is much worse—the commission of ordinary stupidities.

In speaking of the problem of truth we shall introduce certain definitions and precisions of viewpoint in order to make it clear what positions we assume in interpreting this problem. We aim here only to repeat briefly matters which we have already treated more broadly elsewhere,[13] taking up in a new way, in specific references to the tasks facing us, the problem of absolute and relative truth and of full and partial truth.

Let us begin with an elucidation: when the word "truth" appears in the text it should be understood as a "true judgement" or a "true proposition". Without entering here into discussions on truthfulness of norms and evaluations, on the subject of other types of statements which are not predicative propositions, we are limiting clearly the scope of significance of the word "truth".

On the other hand, in reference to the definition of the expression "true judgement", we take our stand on the basis of the so-called classical definition of truth, according to which that judgement is true, which voices something that corresponds to reality. It is not difficult to note that the classical theory of truth constitutes a "pendant" to the theory of reflection, or, at least, that both these positions are organically linked; in accepting the stand of the classical theory of truth one cannot reject the theory of reflection and vice versa. What is more, both these positions complement each other and, theoretically, imply each other's existence.

The classical definition of truth is well known as one of the many that exist in the literature of the subject. A departure from the classical definition, which is, after all, a common-sense one, brings with it certain theoretical difficulties, even those who, for a given set of reasons, chose some different definition most often preserved this first one in their repertoire. Starting with the explanation of what one understands by "reality", and going on to the elucidation of the relationship between what one believes and that which really exists ("adaequatio", according to some, correspondence, reflection, conformity, similarity, reproduction, etc., for others), a relationship which is characteristic of "truth", everything here is problematical and constitutes an arena of fierce dispute among various philosophical schools. Thus, not only doctrinal considerations, although they, of course, play a role, but also the desire to avoid certain theoretical difficulties, have given rise to various attempts to define truth in a simpler and more tangible fashion, for example, as universal consent, coherence with a system, practical utility, economy of thought, etc., that is, in accordance with a certain accepted criterion of truth. None of these definitions can be accepted without rejecting, as a result, the theory of reflection and all the philosophical implications connected therewith. In addition, one can easily become convinced that none of the criteria mentioned above, for example, universal agreement, coherence, etc., guarantees the truthfulness of cognition in the sense that, if we voice something on the basis of these criteria, we can be assured that reality corresponds to what we are saying.

Thus, if in any science, and in history in particular, we maintain that the judgement we have stated is true, we understand this statement to mean that we are convinced (and thus also possess scientific proof of this) that reality corresponds to what we believe. This is the stand of the classical definition of truth, which everyone of us accepts almost intuitively in his activities. Thereby, we reject the claims of other rival definitions of truth. However, it does not follow that we shall not avail ourselves, in an auxilliary fashion, of the criteria proposed by them in the attaining of truth. Universal consent, coherence with a system, practical utility, etc.: all of these have some significance in our considerations, and may serve as arguments which can give rise to additional reflections on specific proposals. But the matter rests there.

What does the problem of the objectivity of truth look like from this point of view?

In accepting the position of the classical definition of truth, to define it more closely, as objective truth, is a pleonasm. After all, there is no other truth than the objective, both in the sense that what matters is a judgement referring to objective reality, and in the sense that the cognitive relationship is itself objective, in the meaning expounded by us above (the first and third model of this relationship). The opposite of objective truth would have to be subjective truth, but, in accordance with the classical definition of truth, the expression, "subjective truth", contains a "contradictio in adiecto"; subjective truth, in this interpretation is tantamount to falsehood. It follows from this that every truth is objective, and thus to speak about an objective truth, in order to distinguish it from other truths, is devoid of any sense. The expression, "objective truth", although it does contain a pleonasm, may, however, retain a value of emphasizing the objectivity of the cognitive relationship; the matter is still more understandable and permissible, since this expression is traditional in the literature of the subject.

On the other hand, the distinguishing of absolute and relative truths, and the problem of the consequences derived from this for an understanding of the process of cognition, are much more complicated.

The old dispute of absolutism and relativism disguises two different, although closely linked, problems: the first assumes the shape of the dispute of the advocates of absolute truth, interpreted in the sense that a given judgement is true or false, regardless of the circumstances (regardless of when and where it was pronounced and who pronounced it), with the advocates of the opposite stand, who defend the concept that the truth or falsehood of a judgement (proposition) depends on the circumstances in which it is voiced; the second assumes the shape of the dispute about whether the truths appearing in human cognition have a complete (full) or partial character.

In the case of the first manifestation of the dispute (typical of traditional relativism), an advocate of the theory of reflection can see no obstacles in rejecting a relativism thus conceived, which is clearly a subjectivistic trend, and in admitting the correctness of their opponents, the absolutists.[14] What do the latter counterpose to the arguments of the relativists, who maintain that a given statement is true or false depending on when and where it is pronounced and who pronounced it? They maintain correctly that the arguments of the relativists are derived from a misunderstanding connected with a manipulation of ambiguous words (such as: "I", "now", "here") and elliptical expressions, that is, those in which there is no closer definition of the person, place and time of action (for example, "olives are tasty", "it is raining today", "it is hot here"). The appearance that the truthfulness of an expression alters with the subject, time and place, rests on a misunderstanding, since words have been employed here which render the given expression indeterminate (elliptical). It suffices to remove this indetermination (ellipsis) by introducing an additional precision in the expressions employed, for this misunderstanding to disappear. If instead of the statement "olives are tasty", one would say "for me (defining the person) olives are tasty"; if instead "it is raining"—"today, that is, on such and such a day, at such an hour, here (defining exactly the place of the event) rain is falling"; if we say instead of "it is hot here", "here (with a precise definition of place and time) I (giving a precise definition of the person) feel hot", then such sentences are either true or false, regardless of where and when they have been pronounced and by whom.

From the point of view of an advocate of the classical definition of truth and of the theory of reflection, the second manifestation of the dispute between the adherents of the positions of absolute and relative truth appears quite differently. In decidedly rejecting the position of relativism in its basic form, he will no less decidedly oppose the position of the defenders of absolute truth, where the second form of the dispute is concerned.

Let us cast aside the ambiguous and hence misleading verbal cloak. In effect, the dispute is waged between the advocates of the view that only a complete, dull, all-sided external and immutable cognition can be true, and the advocates of the view that truth may be, and apart from a few exceptions, must be partial, incomplete and thus mutable, in line with the development of our cognition of a given object.

Two questions draw one's attention here.

Firstly, the employment of the terms "absolute truth" and "relative truth". While the use of the words "absolute" and "relative" is understandable, when this characterization of the truth pertains to the attribution or non-attribution of the trait of truthfulness in references to the subject and to the circumstances of place and time, in the given case the employment of these words is justified rather by tradition, and not the best tradition at that. What does this reference to circumstances indicate in the given case? Only that total truth is immutable, and thus eternal, while partial truth is mutable and thus linked with a definite period. Nevertheless, this is a weak point of support, since "relativity" does not signify reference to circumstances of time and place (in some circumstances the proposition is true, in others it is false) but only that human cognition is cumulative, that it develops in time and that in line with this development the shape of the truths formulated on its basic changes. Thus, in order to avoid verbal misunderstandings and logical slips derived therefrom, it would be better also to distinguish terminologically these two pairs of opposites: absolute and relative truth and total and partial truth.

Secondly, the word "truth" itself has in both cases a different connotation. In the first case it means, in accord with our initial definition, a "true judgement" or a "true proposition"; in the second, the word "truth" is employed in an abbreviation of the expression "true cognition". Both meanings are closely bound up together, but they do not coincide. The cognition of a given object does not, after all, have to give rise to a single judgement; on the contrary, in furnishing a reflection of the various sides, aspects and developmental phases of the object, it is composed of many judgements; it is a process. Of course, judgement can also change, become fuller, more complete. It is always a function of the development of cognition and, in its own way, influences the shape of this cognition. Thus, judgement is also a process, but it does not have to be so (this pertains to partial truths which, due to this, are immutable, for example "2×2 is 4" or the statement of historical facts of the kind: "Casimir the Great was born on such and such a date"). On the other hand, cognition is always a process which is bound up with the infinity of the reality being examined (both in the sense of infinite number of links of every object with others, as well as the infinite development of reality).

Thus, we speak here not only of total and partial truth, but we can also qualify it further, from the point of view of its reference to time, as absolute (immutable) and relative (mutable). However, we must take into consideration the fact that, in simplifying the aim of cognition, one may obtain in certain cases an exhaustive and thus, as a result, an immutable cognition of some aspect of reality. This is an additional argument in favour of maintaining the terminological differentiation proposed above.

From what we have stated, and this is perhaps the most important argument, the conclusion follows that cognition and, therefore, in its wake, truth is a process.

This is an unusually significant conclusion for the elaboration of our concept of the theory of reflection. We have anyhow, to a large degree, built on it our concept that the Marxist theory of reflection can be constructed only on the basis of the objective-activistic model of the cognitive relationship.

The object of cognition is infinite; this assertion pertains to the object, both in the sense of total reality and of its fragments. For total reality, just like its fragments, are infinite when it comes to the quantity of their correlations and also their mutations in time. Therefore, the cognition of such an infinite object must also be infinite, must be an infinite process, a process of accumulating partial truths. In gathering them we enrich our cognition constantly, nearing to the "limes" of full, exhaustive, total cognition which, however, just as the mathematical "limes", is unattainable in one act of cognition and always remains an infinite process of striving towards. . . .

Engels had once stated aptly, in developing one of the fundamental concepts of Marx's gnoseology that: "If mankind ever reached the stage in which it can only work with its eternal truths, with conclusion of thought which possess sovereign validity and an unconditional claim to truth, it would then have reached the point where the infinity of the intellectual world, both in its actuality and its potentiality had been exhausted, and this would mean that the famous miracle of the infinite series which has been counted would have been performed." [15]

Thus, cognition is an infinite process, but a process accumulating partial truths which humanity has achieved at particular stages of its historical development; expanding, narrowing, overcoming these partial truths, but always basing ideas on them and accepting them as the starting-point for further development.

What we have stated above on the subject of cognition pertains to truth as well. "Truth" is only a "true judgement" or a "true proposition". But "truth" also means "true cognition". In this sense, truth is a process-like phenomenon: in gathering partial truths, cognition accumulates knowledge, striving in an infinite process towards a full, exhaustive and, in this sense, absolute truth.

The concept of cognition as a process, and truth as a process, is a general one and, therefore, to make it more concrete it would be necessary to apply this general concept specifically to the analysis of particular fields of science. Thus, the necessity arises of examining what partial truths a given branch of science employs, and how the process of coming closer to full and, in this sense, absolute truth takes place in connection therewith. An illustration of two extreme solutions in this respect is mathematics, on the one hand, and history on the other. Our further considerations shall be devoted, *inter alia,* to the investigation of this problem in the domain of history.

Notes

1. E. H. Carr, *What is History?*, p. 14, London, 1962.
2. H. J. Marrou, *De la connaissance historique,* pp. 10-11, Paris, éd. du Seuil, 1959.
3. Ch. A. Beard, "Written history as an act of faith", *The American Historical Review,* vol. XXXIX, p. 227 (1934).
4. E. Nagel, "Relativism and some problems of working historians", in Sidney Hook (ed.), *Philosophy and History,* p. 76. New York, 1963.
5. R. Aron, *Introduction à la philosophie de l'histoire,* p. 93, Paris, Gallimard, 1948.
6. K. R. Popper, *Die offene Gesellschaft und ihre Feinde,* vol. II, p. 262, Bern, 1958.
7. K. Mannheim, *Ideology and Utopia,* pp. 12 ff., London, 1968.
8. *Ibid.,* pp. 26 ff.
9. "The fiction of the isolated and self-sufficient individual underlies in various forms the individualistic epistemology and genetic psychology. . . . Both of these theories grew out of the soil of an exaggerated theoretical individualism (such as was to be found in the period of the Renaissance and of individualistic liberalism) which could have been produced only in a social situation in which the original connection between individual and group had been lost sight of. Frequently in such social situations the observer loses sight of the role of society in the moulding of the individual to the extent that he derives most of the traits, which are evidently only possible as the result of a common life and the interaction between individuals, from the original nature of the individual or from the germ plasm. . . . In this case, too, it is obviously no accident that the sociological standpoint was added to the others only at a relatively advanced date. Nor is it by chance that the outlook which brings together the social and cognitive spheres emerges in a time in which the greatest exertion of

mankind once more consists in the attempt to counteract the tendency of an individualistic undirected society, which is verging toward anarchy, with a more organic type of social order.'' (K. Mannheim, *Ideology and Utopia, ed. cit.,* pp. 25-26, 30.)

10. I expanded on these problems in my *Marksizm a jednostka ludzka* ("Marxism and the Human Individual") in the chapter "Marksistowska koncepcja jednostki ludzkiej" ("Marxist conception of the human individual"), pp. 70-146, Warsaw, 1965.

11. A. Schaff, *Niektóre zagadnienia marksistowskiej teorii prawdy* ("Some Problems of the Marxist Theory of Truth"), 2nd ed., pp. 47-65, Warsaw, 1959. *Język a poznanie* ("Language and Cognition"), chapter on "Language and reality", Warsaw, 1964.*Szkice z filozofii języka* ("Essays on the Philosophy of Language"); the essay, "Objectivity of cognition in the light of the sociology of knowledge and the philosophy of language", Warsaw, 1967.

12. *Ibid.*

13. See A. Schaff, *Z zagadnień marksistowskiej teorii prawdy* ("On Problems of the Marxist Theory of Truth"), 2nd ed., Warsaw, 1959.

14. Kazimierz Twardowski was one of the most eminent representatives of these views. See "O tak zwanych prawdach względnych" ("On so-called relative truths"), in *Rozprawy i artykuły filozoficzne* ("Philosophical Essays and Articles"), Lwow, 1927.

15. F. Engels, *Anti-Dühring,* p. 100, New York, 1934.

PART TWO

The Social Conditioning of Historical Cognition

CHAPTER 2

Two Concepts of History: Positivism and Presentism

"Mein Freund, die Zeiten der Vergangenheit sind aus ein Buch mit sieben Siegeln. Was ihr den Geist der Zeiten heisst, das ist im Grund der Herren eigner Geist, in dem ide Zeiten sich bespiegeln."

(Goethe, *Faust*, V. 575-579)

In beginning our excursion proper into the domain of reflections on historical cognition, let us commence with a confrontation of two great schools of thought in this respect. While it is true that they are rooted in the nineteenth century, they are, nonetheless, an important part of the contemporary scene. These schools are, on the one hand, positivism which voices the possibility of historical cognition as a faithful reflection of the facts of the past, free of the subjective factor; on the other hand, presentism, the most influential current variant of subjectivist relativism which negates the possibility of such cognition and regards history as the projecting of present thought and present interests into the past.

Leopold van Ranke was undoubtedly the most representative figure of the positivist trend. His words that the historian's task was not to appraise the past, or to instruct his contemporaries, but solely to show what really was "wie es eigentlich gewesen"[1] became something of a battle cry of the school and, regardless of all changes, continues to be such a cry for many historians up to the present day.

Ranke formulated his programmatic concept in the 30s of the last century. He had an excellent predecessor in Humboldt and excellent successors, such as Fustel de Coulanges, Acton and others. Thus, he was not an original, but an extreme exponent of the positivist position. Here are the premises on which this position is based.

Firstly, a total separation and mutual independence of the cognizing subject, the historian, and the cognized object, that is, history, in the sense of "res gestae", is assumed. This assumption is possible only when it is taken for granted that history, that is, "res gestae", exists not only objectively (in the ontological sense), but also in a ready and finite shape, as a definite structure of facts accessible to cognition.

Secondly, a cognitive relationship in accord with a mechanistic model, is assumed; that is, a passive, contemplative interpretation of the theory of reflection is adopted.

Thirdly, it is assumed that the historian as the cognizing subject can achieve not only impartiality in the current meaning; that is, overcome various emotions, phobias or predilections in his appraisals of historical events, but can also reject and overcome all the social conditioning of his perception of these events.

With such an interpretation of its tasks and on the basis of such a repertoire of premises, the concept of history is constructed in the spirit of classical positivism. What is important and sufficient is the collection of adequate quantity of well-documented facts, from which history will arise by itself. Theoretical and, in particular, philosophical reflection is superfluous and even harmful here, since it introduces an element of speculation into a positive science.

It should be recalled that the period in which Ranke formulated the programme of positivist historiography was one of universal revolt against speculative philosophy (the slogan "an end to philosophy" was shared—in spite of their opposition to positivism as a school—by such thinkers as L. Feuerbach, as well as by Marx and Engels) and, in particular, against "philosophical" (speculative) and moralizing historical writing. From this point of view, positivist historiography, which was completely dominant throughout at least the next three generations of historians succeeding Ranke, constituted an immense scientific progress and led to a veritable revolution in this field of science in respect to research techniques, the gathering and utilization of sources. The one-sidedness and limitation of this historiography rested, however, in the tacitly or consciously assumed theoretical premises which composed the specific philosophy of its representatives —the sworn enemies of philosophy. Here also rested the potential sources of an opposition and critique and ultimately of an open revolt against positivism in history.

In a later period, Ranke's opponents demonstrated that his writings were a negation of what he voiced. In spite of the postulated programme of history written impartially and unemotionally, "sine ira et studio", his programme was an expression of class and political involvement.[2] Nonetheless, this was not the most important, since it would have been, after all, a typical "argumentum ad hominem". The defeat of Ranke's school lay in its own assumptions. These could simply not be defended in the light of the progress of knowledge, both in the domain of the theory of cognition and the methodology of history.

One of the extreme opponents of the positivist school and an advocate of presentism, the American historian Conyers Read, presented the situation and the object of the dispute in the following fashion:

> . . . Historians and their critics have long been conducting a running fight between those who contemplate the past as an objective reality, which by diligence and dispassionate judgment can be described as it actually happened, and those who see the past simply as a projection of the ideas and interests of the present upon the accumulative data of remembered experience. The former group envisages the past as something finished and complete and unchanged; the latter group sees it as through a glass darkly, a coloured glass at once translucent and reflective, in which the light which comes through is not clearly distinguishable from the light which is thrown back.[3]

Another representative of presentism, Charles A. Beard, in an article devoted to the struggle of contemporary trends in historical writings, characterized the situation similarly, calling the criticized school "historicism":

> What then becomes of the historicism of the type under which the historian imagines himself able to know history as it had actually been? That philosophy, for such it was while denying philosophy, has been wrecked beyond repair. It can no more be recovered than the posture of ideas and interests of the year 1900 can be restored. The idea of history as an actuality fully structured over against the observing historian has been correctly characterized as cryptometaphysics. Fundamentally, this idea made out of history as actuality a sort of idol whose form and aspects could be discovered by assiduous research and notetaking. The idol has been scattered, and its devotees are powerless to put it together again at the same time the unlimited relativity which imagines that there are or can be as many schemes of reference or historical conceptions as there are human beings has been

destroyed as incompatible with knowledge, and in its place has come a limited relativity containing comparatively few schemes of reference. . . .[4]

The anti-positivist "rebellion" involved all the basic concepts and premises of the traditional school and put forth its own counter-propositions:

firstly, that the subject and the object constitute in historical cognition an organic whole, influencing each other mutually;

secondly, that the cognitive relationship is never passive-contemplative but activistic, due to the role of the subject in it;

thirdly and lastly, that a historian's cognition and involvement is always socially conditioned; that he is always "partisan".

As mentioned above, this "rebellion" assumed its sharpest form in the school of presentism. We shall seek now to outline the views of this school and its road of development, beginning with the spiritual father of this trend, Benedetto Croce, including John Dewey's pragmatism and Collingwood's view, up to the American presentism of the 1930s and 1940s. Nevertheless, before we do so—and this is important from the point of view of our further consideration of the problem—we shall devote a moment to the views of an unexpected precursor of these ideas, Hegel.

We have not the slightest intention here of turning Hegel into a relativist and an advocate of the view that history is contemporaneous thought projected on the screen of the past, as has been well said by one American presentist, Carl Becker. The views of Hegel, an absolute idealist, were rather the opposite of presentism. Nevertheless, we find in his writings thoughts which were forerunners of presentism and which are worthy of attention, for the reason that, although they demonstrate a lack of consistency even of such a thinker as Hegel, they constitute an additional proof of his brilliance. I should like, therefore, to present only a few of Hegel's ideas on the subject of historical cognition which, although very "unorthodox" from the point of view of his own system, lead superbly to the core of the problems concerning us.

In his *Lectures on the Philosophy of History* Hegel decidedly rejected the dogmas so dear to the positivist historians, regarding the passive-receptive character of historical cognition "which faithfully" reflects facts.

We could put forth as the primary condition the principle of a faithful interpretation of historical data; but already in such general expressions as "faithfully" and "interpret" there rests an ambiguity. Even the usual, average historian who believes and maintains that his position is purely receptive and that he only follows the facts is not passive in his thinking but introduces his own categories through which he contemplates that which exists. In particular, in relation to everything which is supposed to have a scientific character, reason cannot fall into slumber; there is no way of doing without thinking here. Whoever regards the world rationally is also looked at rationally by the world; the two things condition each other. But diverse ways of thinking, diverse viewpoints, diverse opinions even if pertaining only to the considering of certain facts as important or unimportant—which constitutes the closest categories here—all this does not pertain to our subject.[5]

These thoughts are truly brilliant and pioneering although they sound odd in the expositions of an author who recommends to his reader the few paragraphs above—in complete accord with his system—that they should maintain an inflexible belief in the manifestation of reason in history and that the world of intelligence is not a victim of accident or fate, but must manifest itself in the light of an idea conscious of itself.[6]

Hegel's ideas expounded above find an emphatic commentary in other fragments of his "Lectures".

The historian takes on its elaboration [of historical material—A. S.] in accord with the spirit which animates him and which is something different from the spirit of the events described. The principles which the author himself deduces partially from the content and purpose of the actions and events described and partially from the method according to which he intends to elaborate history will be of particular significance here.[7]

But from our point of view undoubtedly the most interesting are Hegel's reflections on the subject of pragmatic history which, according to him, is the present projected backwards into the past. Strictly speaking, two aspects of the problem emerge here: how the past becomes the present for the historian, and how the present projects backwards on the vision of the past. Here is how Hegel solved the first aspect of the problem:

The second, in turn, variety of reflective historical writing is *pragmatic* historiography. When we are dealing with the past and with some remote world then a certain type of present which is the fruit of its work and a reward for the effort exerted opens up before the spirit . . . pragmatic reflections, even so abstract are thus, in fact, the present and narratives from the past begin to live with a present-day life.[8]

In the context of these reflections, Hegel's remarks on the subject of history, as the present projected into the past, and on the necessity derived from this of continuously writing history anew, are for us of greater importance:

> Every reflective conception of history cedes place to the *subsequent one;* every writer has access to sources, everyone can consider himself able to elaborate and set them into order and to impose his spirit upon them as the spirit of the epoch described.[9]
>
> A saturation with such reflective historical writing has often caused a reversion to a description of events in a fashion which would throw light on them from all viewpoints. Such descriptions undeniably possess certain value but most often they have only the value of the material. We, Germans, stop at this; on the other hand, the French create in an unusually ingenious fashion a conception of the present and relate the past to the present state.[10]

Here are contained in an embryonic form the significant ideas of the contemporary anti-positivist "rebellion" regarding the subjective factor in history ("der Herren eigner Geist"), on the subject of history as the present projected backwards, and finally on the subject of the reasons why history is being continuously written anew. This is an authentic precursory phenomenon, although—let us repeat this once more—quite an unexpected one.

Benedetto Croce possessed an excellent knowledge of Hegel. We are not acquainted with the history of Italian philosophy, and in particular with Croce's philosophy, to a sufficient degree to be able to state whether a conscious affiliation of ideas is involved here, but this cannot be excluded with certainty. In any case, that which in Hegel appears in the form of certain embryonic thoughts, incoherent in respect to his system, has been developed by Croce into a coherent system of idealist reflection on history. Presentism, of which the prime concept is the view that history is contemporary thought projected into the past, is precisely derived from him. All the other ideas of presentism are but the consequence of this primary concept.

The dominant feature of Croce's world outlook is radical spiritualism and the negation of materialism closely bound up with it. According to Croce's philosophy of the spirit, the spiritual sphere embraces not only theoretical but also practical activity. He divided theoretical activity, in turn, into two domains: conceptual and intuitive. Science belongs to the conceptual domain; as a result, Croce denied history the character of a science. According to him, only a person who subsumes the individual into the general, deals with science; a person who presents the individual, as such, deals with art. Since the task of historical writing is to present that which is individual, it is therefore rather closer to art than to science. The difference was supposed to rest in the fact that history limits itself to what had taken place in reality, while art is free from such a constraint and deals also with what is possible. Croce, later on, modified his early views on the kinship of history and art. Nonetheless, he continued to maintain his fundamental concept that an historian's activity does not enter into the scope of the conceptual domain and stressed, on the other hand, so-called pure intuition.[11]

Croce's intuitionism is the second important element to which attention should be paid before engaging in an analysis of his presentism.

According to Croce, pure intuition is the fundamental form of the spirit's activity: fundamental, because it is independent of practical activity; on the contrary, practical activity is dependent on intuition. Intuition is the foundation of being, since it creates its object. This object is the "states of the soul", apart from which nothing exists. Croce's intuitionism, in fact, led his "philosophy of the spirit" to an extreme, since it eliminates everything which goes beyond the content of individual psychical make-up and creates a philosophy of "absolute immanentism". Croce criticized Vico and Hegel in that, by introducing into philosophy a metaphysical "transcensus" they obscured the fact that man possesses only immanent experience, that only one reality exists—the "Spirit", which is activity, liberty and the "eternal creator of life".

Croce closely connected intuitionism with the theory of historical judgement; according to him, the object of such a judgement is intuitively experienced by the historian. Nevertheless, inner contradictions of the doctrine arose from this, which even the most complex metaphysical elucidations could not overcome. If intuition is the expression of the state of the historian's soul and creates its object, the historian cannot, of course, experience anew the facts of the past or enter into direct contact with them. Even assuming, as Croce did, that the individual is a particle of the "Absolute", that it is the "manifestation and the instrument" of the "Universal Spirit", one should then assume that this "Spirit" manifests itself identically in various "instruments". Even Croce does not maintain this. The theory of pure intuition thus contradicts the concept that history is knowledge about what had happened in the past. Therefore, Croce, as a result of drawing the conclusion from this inner conflict of his doctrine, passed to the defence of the concept that all history is contemporary, that is, to the defence of the concept of so-called presentism.

Presentism, just like intuitionism, is a development of the "philosophy of the spirit" and is understandable only against its setting. The concept that all history is contemporary rests on another thesis of the "philosophy of the spirit", that is, that everything which enters into the make-up of history is the product of the spirit. Let us commence our reflections precisely with this concept. In order to illustrate it we shall quote a number of Croce's statements, taken from the works written by him in his later period.

Croce spoke out against the division of facts into historical and unhistorical, arguing as follows: "Since a fact is historical only to the degree to which it had been thought of, and since nothing exists apart from thought, the question which facts are historical and which are not, has no sense."[12]

He considered this whole question to be a pseudo-problem, since the selection of facts and documents by researchers is completely arbitrary. In spite of this arbitrariness of choice, one cannot err in history, just as in art, since it itself "creates the image, the unity of the image".[13]

This stand causes Croce to treat quite contemptuously all activity of collecting historical data, calling it, debasingly, "chronicle writing"; after all, history proper draws truth from inner experiences.

> The compilation of facts we call chronicles, notes, memoirs, annals, but not historical works; even if they have been critically examined, even if the sources of all the data have been given, and the testimonies exactly checked, then, in spite of all efforts, it is impossible to overcome the external nature of the source or testimony, since they always retain the essence of some "they say" or "they write" and they can never become our truth. On the other hand, history demands from us truth drawn from our most inner experience.[14]

This is a radically subjectivistic interpretation of history and the conception of presentism derives precisely from it. If everything which exists is the creation of the spirit, then historical facts are also its creation. Thus, there is no objectively given past; it is only facts which exist, created by the spirit in an eternally changing present. All history must, therefore, be contemporary as the product of the spirit acting always in the present, creating this historical image (apart from which no other history exists) under the influence of *present* interests and motives. Croce wrote: "Practical need, on which historical judgement is based, imparts to history the property of 'contemporary history' since it always refers to—regardless of to what remote past the facts might chronologically pertain—the contemporary need, the contemporary situation in which these facts enter into."[15]

According to Croce, the entire past is contained in every one of our spiritual acts (and, in his opinion, history is precisely such an act) and, vice versa, the past is revived only when the given documents evoke and render permanent the remembrance of definite spiritual states (which can, of course, appear only "now", that is, contemporaneously). Without such a spiritual activity, documents (for example, monuments, chronicles, archeological sites, etc.) are only inanimate objects. It follows that we can speak of history only when we ourselves experience certain states and feelings (for example, Christian charity, knightly chivalry, the radicalism of the Jacobins, etc.) and thus it is a particular projection of our "ego", brought forth by contemporary needs and possible because "man is a micro-cosmos . . . in the historical sense, a synthesis of the world's history".[16]

Elsewhere Croce wrote that contemporaneity is the proper feature of every history.[17]

However, Croce attacked not only the concept of positivism that the historical process is objective, and that the past in a "ready" state awaits the historian who, having collected a sufficient quantity of facts, presents its faithful image, but also a second concept—the pillar of the positivist doctrine—that the historian may and should be completely impartial, uninvolved and objective, in the sense of neutrality towards all types of social conditioning.

Croce maintained something quite to the contrary. According to him, historical cognition is always an answer to some need and in this sense is *always* "engagé". If it were different, if it were not connected with practice and with contemporaneity it would lose all sense and value. Nonetheless, it follows from this that the historian is and should be partial, "engagé" and "partisan".

Croce closely linked the problem of "partisanship" of history and the historian with the issue of evaluation in historical writing. If we write history without evaluations, the outcome is not a history but a chronicle. If we do evaluate, history must be partial, partisan. In view of the importance of this problem for our further consideration, we shall quote the relevant passage from Croce's work in its entirety.

> The idea of non-partisan history, completely devoted to truth, has been constantly counterposed to partisan historiography, regardless of which party was involved. The postulate of the non-partisanship of history . . . becomes muddled, dissolves and disintegrates into nothingness, as often as we reach the point where it is necessary to define more closely how history, which does not have a partisan nature, is to be understood. The unfortunate reasoning which leads to this confusion and ullity is derived from the premise that partisan history betrays the truth when, instead of being satisfied with the facts as they actually occurred, it evaluates them; this reasoning also leads to the conclusion that, if one wishes to attain unadulterated and unfalsified truth, one should refrain from all evaluations. . . . An examination of this issue would show that, by eliminating evaluation from historiography, one eliminates historiography itself, while partisan history, opposed to it and differing from it . . . remains unshaken.[18]

Such are the fundamental ideas of Croce's presentism. It is an extreme variant of relativism, since it relegates historical cognition to the subject which is its creator. In the light of this doctrine every history, as we have already mentioned—is contemporary history, while the truthfulness of historical cognition corresponds to the need which has evoked it. This linking of cognition and its truthfulness with an interest to which the cognition corresponds brings the doctrine of presentism close to the positions of pragmatism.

Croce's radical interpretation of presentism has, however, other far-reaching consequences. It makes it imperative to recognize that one cannot speak of a single history (in a sense of a historical process) since a mutliplicity of histories exist, equal to the number of minds who "create" this history. As a result, one should assume that not only every epoch, every nation and every social class, but, in fact, every historian and even every thinking individual possesses his own specific image of history. One should also assume that the sole criterion possible for evaluating these various and, of necessity, variable histories is reference to the degree to which they correspond to needs, concerns and demands. Whose? One can answer this question consistently only if, and when, one recognizes the individual as the "measure of all things".

These consequences, which follow ineluctably from an acceptance of Croce's doctrine, are catastrophic for historiography. An historian would have, for example, to acknowledge simultaneously as true two contrary reports and interpretations of one and the same historical event since they corresponded to some interests. As a matter of fact, if he were consistent, he would even have to protest against the concept that it is the same historical event which appears in different works, since, according to Croce, there are no objective events, there are only the products of the mind which are, of course, as different as the minds. Thus, history would be deprived of the criterion enabling it to distinguish truth from falsehood, and should even protest against the search for such a criterion. The radical subjectivism and relativism of Croce's presentism deprives historical writing of its scientific character. This was precisely what Croce wanted to attain. While he sought refuge from the annihilating results of the relativism, represented by himself, in the doctrine of the "Absolute Spirit", here, as well, he could find nothing more, but an eclectic admixture to his subjectivism. For, if one even assumes that the mystical "Absolute Spirit" were to be the judge resolving the dispute between contrary historical judgements, each of which is, after all, true in definite conditions, then this, from the viewpoint of the perspectives of historical writing, is actually of no avail. Apart from the sphere of thinking in terms of "Absolute Spirit", only the following conclusion is obvious: the last one to speak is correct. This is a verdict which deprives history of the name of science.

In the course of the further development of this doctrine, the advocates of presentism had to take this conclusion into consideration: some accepted it, while others strove to modify its extremeness.

R. G. Collingwood, who contributed greatly to popularizing Croce's works in the English-speaking world, belonged to the first group. As an idealist philosopher, Collingwood did not feel perturbed by the extreme nature of Croce's views. On the contrary, he even exacerbated this radicalism.

According to Collingwood, all history is a history of thought. An historian, in recreating anew the thought of the past, does so in the context of his own knowledge and, therefore, critically.[19] The activities which an historian studies are not for him an observation of a spectacle, but an experience which he must relive anew in his own mind. These experiences are objective, in relation to the knowledge regarding them, only because they are subjective as his own action.[20] The historical image is an image of the historian's imagination, and the imperative nature of this image is linked with the *a priori* existence of imagination. Hence, the historian's work differs from that of the novelist only in that the image created by the historian is considered to be a true one.[21]

When one accepts such premises, then nothing at all can be daunting. Thus, Collingwood discovered a direct transition from his metaphysics to presentism: only the present may serve as a justification for the choice of a given picture of the past.

> Historical thinking is that activity of the imagination by which we endeavour to provide this innate idea with detailed content. And this we do by using the present as evidence for its own past. Every present has a past of its own, and any imaginative reconstruction of the past aims at the reconstructing of the past of this present, the present in which the act of imagination is going on, as here and now perceived. . . .
>
> It is for the same reason that in history, as in all serious matters, no achievement is final. The evidence available for resolving any given problem changes with every change of historical method and with every variation in the competence of historians. . . . Because of these changes, which never cease, however slow they may appear to observers who take a short view, every new generation must rewrite history in its own way; every new historian, not content with giving new answers to old questions, must revise the questions themselves. . . .
>
> This is not an argument for historical scepticism. It is only the discovery of a second dimension of historical thought, the history of history; the discovery that the historian himself, together with the here-and-now which forms the total body of evidence available to him, is a part of the process he is studying, has his own place in that process, and can see it only from the point of view which at this present moment he occupies within it.[22]

Thus Collingwood's views are radical although, with regard to the presentism which they contain, they are not original. Nonetheless, it is worthwhile paying attention to them, even if only for the last sentences of the paragraph quoted above.

Presentism experienced its true growth in the United States during the 1930s and 1940s, although some foretaste of this "new history" appeared already at the beginning of the century in Robinson's work.

The significance of American presentism rests, above all, in the fact that it was developed primarily by eminent historians such as Charles A. Beard. Thus, it was not anymore a speculation of philosophers, such as Croce or Collingwood, but a stand taken by historians closely linked with their work.

Chester McArthur Destler published in 1950 an article entitled "Some observations on contemporary historical theory", in which he took up the history of relativism in historical writing, mainly after the Second World War. Destler was an opponent of relativism, and thus also of presentism; this renders his remarks, particularly those pertaining to the social function of this school, more interesting and caustic. In characterizing the contemporary condition of the theory of history in the United States Destler wrote:

> . . . there has developed among some historians in this country a conviction that in the light of present-day knowledge the scientific pretensions and other assumptions of the Ranke "Naïve Realist" school in Britain and America provide an insufficient basis for the conduct of historical research. Furthermore, recent struggles over domestic reform measures and the continuing international crisis have engendered among some of our fellows a desire for "functional" history that can contribute more largely to the solution of contemporary problems.[23]

Destler is an advocate of bourgeois liberalism, as evinced by his entire article. Nevertheless, he was able to grasp the essence of the political problem: the social aim of "functional historiography" which offers relativism for the purpose of the class struggle waged by the bourgeoisie. Historical relativism is by no means an invention of American historical writing. What is new, however, is the more extreme and open posing of this problem in conditions of the sharpened class struggle of the bourgeoisie in general, and the American bourgeoisie in particular. When the social content of presentism has been grasped, it is easier to understand the function of the historical predecessors of these views.

Relativist tendencies are of long-standing in American historical writing. Destler mentions its foreign sources, in particular the works of Benedetto Croce and R. G. Collingwood referred to above;[24] he refers also to American works and, in particular, to J. H. Robinson's *The New History* (New York, 1912) in which the principle of functional historical writing was advanced (subordinated, at that time, to aspirations towards liberal reforms), to H. E. Barnes' *History of*

Historical Writing (Oklahoma, 1937) which further developed this idea, and to C. Becker's works, to which we shall refer later. However, Destler considers the period after the Second World War to be a turning-point, in which the relativist "revolt" came completely to the fore. This is not fortuitous. This was a period of intensified class struggles in which the subservient role of ideology became especially prominent.

As we have already mentioned, American presentism is directly derived from Croce's presentism. His ideas were implanted in the American milieu by such an influential philosopher as John Dewey. Ideological kinship with pragmatism was one of the causes for this.

The starting-point of Dewey's reflections was the problem of the selection of research material by an historian. Dewey posed the question: on what basis is more belief ascribed to certain judgements regarding the past, as against others? Dewey maintained that one concludes about the past solely on the basis of judgements pertaining to things which can be observed contemporaneously (documents, relics, etc.). Such judgements, however, are the result of selection undertaken from the point of view of specific needs. In connection with this, they are relative to the problem and, simultaneously, they are always the product of a definite present.[25]

> *All historical construction is necessarily selective.* Since the past cannot be reproduced *in toto* and lived over again, this principle might seem too obvious to be worthy of being called important. But it is of importance because its acknowledgement compels attention to the fact that everything in the writing of history depends upon the principle used to control selection. This principle decides the weight which shall be assigned to past events, what shall be admitted and what omitted; it also decides how the facts selected shall be arranged and ordered. Furthermore, if the fact of selection is acknowledged to be primary and basic, we are committed to the conclusion that all history is necessarily written from the standpoint of the present, and is, in an inescapable sense, the history not only of the present, but that of what is contemporaneously judged to be important in the present.[26]

History is thus always linked with a definite contemporaneity which not only furnishes the principle of selection but is also thereby responsible for the "facts" of the past (or rather for what *we* recognize as such facts). Hence the conclusion that every present has its past and, therefore, it is understandable that history must be continuously written anew (an important conclusion to which we shall return in our further considerations).

The slightest reflection shows that the conceptual material employed in writing history is that of the period in which a history is written. There is no material available for leading principles and hypotheses save that of the historic present. As culture changes, the conceptions that are dominant in a culture also change. Of necessity, new standpoints arise for viewing, appraising and ordering data. History is then rewritten. Material that had formerly been passed by, offers itself as data because the new conceptions propose new problems for solution, requiring new factual material for statement and test. At a given time, certain conceptions are so uppermost in the culture of a particular period that their application in constructing the events of the past seems to be justified by "facts" found in a ready-made past. This view puts the cart before the horse.[27]

Destler correctly called this stand "subjectivist, relativist presentism". As mentioned previously, however, what is primarily of interest to us is the position of professional historians. Among the numerous representatives of this group of presentists we have chosen as the subject of critical analysis the views of Charles Beard and Carl Becker, authoritative representatives of the so-called Columbia school and Conyers Read, a representative of the younger generation.

Charles Beard, the noted historian of the American Constitution, was one of the principle leaders of the "revolt". He was particularly interesting as a historian, since in his writings he linked relativism with so-called economic interpretation of history. He not only attacked the theory of objective historical truth, but also openly praised class and partisan history. Beard's philippics against Ranke and his school were very characteristic in this respect. We shall begin our analysis with this instructive historical interpolation which throws a sharp light on the whole problem of relativism in modern American historical writing.

In 1909 when the attack began against the domination of Ranke's thesis, regarded up to that time as a dogma, the American historian George Burton Adams came forth in support of Ranke's school as being *par excellence* scientific.[28] While ascertaining that after fifty years of indisputable dominance of this school it had begun to be attacked, Adams consoled its advocates by stating thus: "Any science which is a true science must be based on proven and correlated facts."[29]

After several decades the old school found itself on the defensive and Beard attacked it, denying the scientific nature of historical writing. In doing so he sought to hit the opponents' most sensitive spot, the myth of "non-partisanship". ". . . Contemporary thought about history, therefore, repudiates the conception dominant among the schoolmen during the latter part of the nineteenth century and the opening years of the twentieth century—the conception that it is possible to describe the past as it actually was, somewhat as the engineer describes a single machine."[30]

In order to butttress this concept, Beard undertook a sharp critique of Leopold von Ranke, the principal representative of the school he fought against. This brought about a reaction of the followers of the old school. In the subsequent issue of the *American Historical Review* (no. 3, pp. 439-449) T. C. Smith's polemical response was published, which was answered immediately by Beard in an article entitled "That Noble Dream",[31] in which he developed the criticism of Ranke and his school.

Beard demonstrated that while Ranke voiced the ideal of an objective, "positive", "non-partisan" history, based exclusively on the study of documents, he in fact embraced a peculiar pantheism, interpreting history as "the manifestation of God", as the "den Gang Gottes in der Welt". While proclaiming "non-partisanship" of history he was in reality completely partisan. To support his statements Beard quoted a number of proofs: the partisan nature of the editorial policy which Ranke followed in the periodical *Historisch-Politische-Zeitschrift*; his negative attitude towards freedom of the press after the July Revolution; the assistance rendered in 1848 to William IV in the struggle against the democratic constitution; the positive appraisal of the results of the Franco-Prussian War of 1870-1871 as a victory of conservative Europe over the revolution. Beard summed up his appraisal in this way: "Ranke who, in disregarding stubbornly social and economic interests in history, avoided successfully any historical works infringing the conservative interests of the Europe of his times, may be correctly characterized as one of the most 'partisan' historians which the 19th century produced."[32]

Ranke's formula ("Wie es eigentlich gewesen"), Beard maintained, was implanted in the conception of historical writing, interpreted as an analogy to the natural sciences. It also was derived from class sources.

Beard rejected this conception just as he did determinism, the regularity of historical processes and the possibility of historical forecasting. By presenting in a vulgarized fashion the application of the method of natural sciences to historical research, Beard gained an easy victory over his foe and proclaimed the triumph of extreme subjectivism which radically negated the scientific character of historical writing.

In rejecting the similarity of the method of history to methods of the natural sciences Beard employed a social argument. According to him, this similarity implies a social neutralism (a Marxist would call this "objectivism"). Such a stand was derived from the specific needs of the ruling classes and would be rejected once conditions had changed.[33] According to Beard, a change of conditions had brought about a crisis as a result of which the dogma of neutralism and objectivism had been rejected and historians had acknowledged the fact that a historical work constituted the reflection of the author's thought in given conditions.

Beard built his own conception of history on the basis of this criticism of Ranke and positivist historical writing. He differentiated history as the "past reality" and history understood, following Croce, as "contemporary thought about the past".[34] The latter, i.e. historical writing, was the subject of his consideration. According to him, it follows from the fact that history is the thought about the past, that it is always the result of selection and thus facts are chosen and set into order by the historian "as he thinks".[35]

What conclusions did Beard draw from this regarding the character of history?

Formally he came out against relativism, while in fact he was inclined towards an extreme variant of relativism. According to Beard, history is "an act of faith" and hence the subjective creation of the historian, dependent on him and changing along with its creator.

> The historian who writes history, therefore, consciously or unconsciously performs an act of faith, as to order and movement, for certainty as to order and movement is denied to him by knowledge of the actuality with which he is concerned . . . his faith is at bottom a conviction that something true can be known about the movement of history and his conviction is a subjective decision, not a purely objective discovery.[36]

The subjectivism of this creed and its consequence of relativism are indubitable. While criticizing historicism (in the sense of Ranke's positivist doctrine) and accusing it of objectivism (in the sense of class neutralism) Beard simultaneously proclaimed a programme of partisanship of historical writing. In relation to Ranke's doctrine he speaks of its class roots, although he did not undertake a similar genetic analysis of his own views. But what Beard had not done himself was done for him by his colleagues and followers.

Among Beard's followers were such methodologists as J. H. Randall Jr. who repeated his idea that the acceptance of a given principle of selection is an act of faith.[37] Such a stand can, of course, lead only to *presentism*. Randall spoke of this thus: "It is the present and the future operating in the present that creates the past and makes history. It recreates the past which is the material for the present to work upon."[38] The selection of the material of the past is always relative and dependent on the present. Every past is *our* past, "*our* past is not in *the* past, but in the present, in *our* present".[39] Randall develops his conception of "objective relativism", that is, historical relativism which he calls "objective", since according to him what has been ascribed to specific conditions is objective, on the above basis.[40]

Carl Becker was also one of Beard's followers. He was likewise one of the main proponents of the relativist "revolt". We shall analyse Becker's views as presented in his "Presidential Address", delivered in 1931 at a meeting of the American Historical Association where, in accordance with the tradition, speeches of the president of the Association on this occasion are of a fundamental nature and present the author's credo in reference to certain basic problems in the realm of history.

Just as Beard did, Becker identified history with thought about history and with history as a science. He did maintain that one should accept the existence of two series; a series of the events themselves and a series of their mental images. ". . . But the actual series of events exists for us only in terms of the ideal series which we affirm and hold in memory. This is why I am forced to identify history with the knowledge of history." [41] Thus, history becomes a subjective image, while everything else is simply an empty phrase. However, if History is simply "the memory of things said and done" then every man is an historian in his everyday life. What is more: every man is the creator of a different history. Every man also creates history by referring it to the present since "he cannot recall past events without, in some subtle fashion, relating them to what he needs or desires to do. . . . In this sense all *living* history, as Croce says, is contemporaneous: insofar as we think the past . . . it becomes an integral and living part of our present world of semblance.''[42]

The conclusion which Becker drew from these views was tantamount to extreme subjectivism and relativism of the historical conception:

> It must then be obvious that living history, the ideal series of events that we affirm and hold in memory, since it is so intimately associated with what we are doing and with what we hope to do, cannot be precisely the same for all at any given time, or the same for one generation as for another. History in this sense cannot be reduced to a verifiable set of statistics or formulated in terms of universally valid mathematical formulas. It is rather an imaginative creation, a personal possession which each one of us . . . fashions out of his individual experience, adapts to his aesthetic or emotional needs, and adorns as well as may be to suit his aesthetic tastes. [43]

While Becker maintained further on that this "product of the imagination" is not completely haphazard, since it is limited by the existence of other people and that everyone could "create a world of semblance in accord with his own desire" only if there were no other people, it is impossible to see what could be the real effects of this statement. At most, the criterion of universal approval has been added to Becker's subjectivism, which does not in the least negate this subjectivism, while Becker expresses this apparent limitation only half-heartedly. His principal idea rests in the conviction that an historian should be alloted the "freedom of a creative artist";[44] that in writing history he, of necessity, presents a mixture of facts and fantasies; in a word, that history is, in one way or another, a subjective product conditioned by the specific present of the historian.[45]

Carl Becker was the author of the most drastic and, at the same time, most "picturesque" statement regarding presentism. For this reason it is worth quoting, although its content is not original. Becker links his statement with the problem of the constant re-interpretation of history.

> . . . each age re-interprets the past to suit its own purposes. Leaving aside the vagaries that distinguish individuals, historians cannot wholly free themselves, however detached they may strive to be, from the most general preconceptions of the age in which they live. In quiescent times . . . they are likely to be satisfied with the past . . . and at such times historians would easily fall into the habit of just recording what happened. . . . But in periods of stress, when the times are thought to be out of joint, those who are dissatisfied with the present are likely to be

dissatisfied with the past also. At such times historians . . . will be disposed to cross-examine the past . . . to sit in judgement on what was formerly done, approving or disapproving in the light of present discontents. *The past is a kind of screen upon which each generation projects its vision of the future, and so long as hope springs in the human heart the "new history" will be a recurring phenomenon.*[46]

Let us now take up another "Presidential Address" proclaimed eighteen years later, in 1949, by Conyers Read at the meeting of the American Historical Association. It carried the brave title "The Social Responsibilities of the Historian".

Marx had once said, as a metaphor, that the human anatomy provides us with the key to the understanding of the anatomy of a monkey; he sought in this manner to express the thought that a higher stage of historical development, by revealing the effects of certain events of the past, opens perspectives for an understanding of its tendencies and driving forces. The presentists were also aware of this. In the article quoted above Randall wrote that the understanding of results, and thus of the "significance" of the events of the past, changes along with later history, along with what appears in the world of events as the result of the possibilities inherent in events which had already occurred. This assertion, from which follows the necessity of changing the historical image, was utilized by him as an argument for the justification of relativism.

We shall be in accord with the relativists' own conception if we ascertain that the further development of their doctrine sheds a light on the nature of the earlier studies, on their role and tendencies. From this point of view an analysis of Read's speech is undoubtedly interesting. The 1940s brought in much that was new in comparison with the 1930s, as reflected by new accents in historical writing. This makes it possible for us to grasp better the content and social function of the relativist doctrine in its development.

Conyers Read did not add anything new to the contents of this doctrine. Just as Beard and Becker, he regarded history as the recollection of past human experiences, and thus purely subjectively, and similarly to his predecessors, he attacked the conception of objective truth as the principle enemy.[47] According to him, the main line of struggle divides the defenders of historical objective truth and those who "see the past simply as a projection of the ideas and interests of the present upon the accumulated data of remembered experience"[48] Read, of course, came out in favour of the latter employing the old, well-known argument of the selection by the historian of historical material. This selection is conditioned by the interests of the present and transforms history into a creation of the historian which constitutes an emanation of the requirements of the present. The models applied by us undergo change as do the questions referring to the past and this explains why every generation must write history anew.[49]

Thus far these are nothing more than the ideas of subjectivist-relativist presentism already known to us. In this respect Read is not original. His accusation of the defenders of objective truth, charging them with objectivism and social neutralism which facilitates his identifying their position with that of Ranke, is also not original. What is new, however, is Read's attempt to substantiate the social basis of his own position.

Read impressed historians regarding their social responsibility and stressed the need of taking an active stand in the task of "education for democracy". According to him, it was precisely this active stand which makes imperative the adoption of a relativist-presentist position. How did Read justify his demands? By the alleged defence of democracy against fascism and communism.

> The age we are leaving, the liberal age if you like, was characterized by a plurality of aims and values and by a neutral attitude towards the main issues of life. In that age neutrality went so far that we cease to believe . . . in our own objectives. Confronted by such alternatives as Mussolini and Hitler and last of all Stalin have imposed, we must clearly assume a militant attitude if we are to survive. The antidote to bad doctrine is better doctrine, not neutralized intelligence. We must assert our own objectives, define our own ideals, establish our own standards and organize all the forces of our society in support of them. Discipline is the essential pre-requisite of every effective army whether it march under the Stars and Stripes or under the Hammer and Sickle. We have to fight an enemy whose values system is deliberately simplified in order to achieve quick decisions and atomic bombs make quick decisions imperative. The liberal neutral attitude, the approach to social evolution in terms of dispassionate behaviourism will no longer suffice. Dusty answer will not satisfy our demands for positive assurances. *Total war, whether it be hot or cold, enlists everyone and calls upon everyone to assume his part. The historian is no freer from this obligation than the physicist.*[50]

The political meaning of Read's statement is exceptionally clear and, taking into consideration the American setting, there is no doubt that he was primarily concerned with the struggle against communism. Read stated that the historian must find support for his present position in the past. If he does not do so, then people will "seek for assurance in a more positive alternative, whether it be offered from Rome or from Moscow".[51] Hence the necessity for the historian to accept the principle of social control. In connection with this, Read maintained: "The important thing is that we shall accept and endorse such controls as one essential for the preservation of our way of life." Read considered that such a stand did not threaten the freedom of the individual nor deform science. An historian can continue to examine all phenomena, "but we must realize that not everything which takes place in a laboratory is appropriate for broadcasting at the street corners."[52]

It is quite clear that these postulates aim at turning history over to the service of the ruling classes and the social order represented by them. The past, history, should be shaped from the point of view of the present-day interests of these classes. This is precisely why, or at least one of the reasons why, Read, just as other presentists, fought against positivist historical writing and Ranke's ideals which in new conditions had ceased to serve the interests of the ruling class. Today historical writing must cast away the semblance of objectivity and neutralism, must reject the appearance of indifference in respect of problems of theory and world outlook. Why? The social-political groundwork of the problem furnishes an explanation of this phenomenon.[53]

In the statement quoted above Destler had emphasized this aspect of the problem by characterizing the social function of presentism in historiography. The object of his criticism was primarily Conyers Read, but his blows were aimed at the entire trend. Destler's criticism contained bold and correct moments; he pointed out the definite class character of the partisanship proclaimed by the advocates of presentism, the anti-communist tendency of this trend. This is particularly important, since presentism is most often proclaimed by individuals taking the position of bourgeois liberalism, which may render difficult a comprehension of the proper character of their ideology.

Presentism remains an influential trend in American, and only American, historical writing. This does not signify, however, that it does not meet with opposition from so-called liberal historical writing as well. On the contrary, one could name such representatives of the opposition as C. Destler, quoted above, or M. Mandelbaum, Arthur O. Lovejoy, C. H. McIlwain and others.[54]

After this relatively expanded exposition of the views of the presentists, it is time for a theoretical summing up which will simultaneously be a confrontation of presentism and positivism and a demonstration of the problems which arose as a result of the confrontation of these positions.

We began the present chapter with an enumeration of the theoretical premises of positivism of the Ranke school. How did the representatives of *presentism* regard these premises? In a most general fashion it can be stated that their attitude was completely negative. This is precisely why a consideration of the conflict of the ideas of positivism and presentism may be interesting from the viewpoint of the essential problems of historical writing which are concealed by this conflict.

Among the theoretical premises of Ranke and his school we had put forth in the first place the idea regarding the total separation and mutual independence of the historian and the object of his cognition, "res gestae". History, in the meaning of "res gestae", exists objectively, not only in the ontological sense, but also in the cognitive, as an extant and given once and for all (in its ideal shape) structure of historical facts accessible to cognition, facts which it is only necessary to collect and present.

The presentists counterposed a subjective-relativist position to this conception. We may leave aside the ontological aspects of the problem, which were important for Croce or Collingwood, while other presentists either did not attach significance to it or were even ready to accept the idea regarding the objective existence of historical processes ("res gestae") without altering their subjectivism in respect to history ("historia rerum gestarum"). As far as the last question is concerned all the presentists take a uniform position counterposed to that of positivists.

All presentists negate, above all, the conception regarding the separation and mutual independence of the subject and object in the process of historical cognition, that is, they decidedly reject the first of the models of cognitive relationship enumerated by us with its passive-contemplative conception of the cognizing subject, a model which rests at the foundation of the doctrine of positivism.

According to their conception, the cognizing subject is active and contributes to the process of cognition the entire intellectual and emotional charge of his personality. This is emphasized not only by the presentists but also by Hegel. As many presentists maintain explicitly, the subject and object create a single indissoluble whole in the process of cognition.

As a result, they also reject the conception of Ranke and his school that history is a ready (extant) structure of facts which it is only necessary to discover with the aid of documents, to collect and present in a raw form and from this history, "wie es eigentlich gewessen", will arise by itself.

The presentists maintain, on the contrary, that history is *never* complete, that one can *never* maintain that one has finished working on it. It is always an answer to the problem and questions contemporaneous with the historian and thus it is eternally changing and being rewritten; this is so not only because new facts are uncovered but also because our views regarding what is an historical fact change (that is, what is significant from the point of view of the historical process); that with the increase of our knowledge about man and society we understand these processes differently, that the historical process, which shows the effects of past events, makes it possible to comprehend better man and society, their character and tendencies, etc.

Thus, presentism rejects the mechanistic model of cognition and the passive-contemplative interpretation of the theory of reflection. The second and third model, that is, the subjective-idealist or the objective-activist remain, therefore, as an alternative. The choice of one of these depends on the world outlook premises accepted and takes a different shape among the various presentists: Croce and Collingwood indubitably adopted the subjective-idealist model, while Dewey and Beard (with different reservations) rather took up the objective-activist.

An essential battle is waged around the third premise of Ranke's school, that an historian can and should be an impartial and "non-engagé" observer of facts, restricting himself to their description and refraining from evaluation. All the presentists reject this postulate as impractical, contrary to experience, and impossible to fulfil; on the contrary, they put forth the postulate of partisan and "engagé" history.

History is contemporaneity projected into the past which should be understood in the sense that the interests and needs of the present-day condition both the historian's field of vision and his point of view: starting with what he considers to be an historical fact, including the interpretation and evaluation of these facts, up to the comprehension of the entire historical process. Thus, the historian starts, consciously or subconsciously, from contemporaneity, from the conflicts and struggles proper to it and simultaneously—regardless of whether he is aware of this or not—he participates in these conflicts and struggles and is their exponent. Hence, there is no history other than "engagé", "partisan" and, in one meaning of this word, partial history. It cannot and should not be different; if for no other reason than that history is not a chronicle and cannot be reduced to a simple enumeration of facts; history must evaluate and interpret which *eo ipso* assumes taking a stand, being "engagé", "partisanship". Thus, if someone, for example Ranke, proclaims the postulate of history "wie es eigentlich gewesen", then he either does not know what he is talking about, or simply engages in camouflage for an easier attainment of certain social aims (this is precisely what the presentists accuse Ranke of).

In my opinion, the presentists in their conflict with positivism were correct in all the principal points which have been somewhat schematically listed above. This correctness, however, is of a negative nature: they attacked pertinently the weak points of the positivist position and showed where and why positivism is at fault. It does not follow, however, that the stand of presentism is correct and acceptable. Not by any means. These are two different matters: a critique of positivism may be correct, precisely in its critical part, but the exposition of one's own stand, which serves as the starting-point for this critique, does not in the least have to be correct in its positive aspect. In order to take up the basic issue, that is, the comprehension of the real theoretical problems which rest at the foundation of the conflict of positivism and presentism in historical writing, it is necessary to throw light, if even briefly, on our evaluation of presentism.

This evaluation is decidely negative. Any evaluation requires a given system of reference and is undertaken from some given chosen positions. In rejecting presentism, although we agreed with the trend of its critique of positivism, we do so from specific philosophical positions, because it is precisely the philosophical background of this doctrine which is at stake. As has been mentioned previously, it is impossible, in spite of the opposition of positivistically inclined historians, to do without philosophy in the realm of meta-theoretical reflections. The principal problems in the conflict between positivism and presentism are, in reality, *par excellence* philosophical problems. It is thus best to treat them consciously as philosophical problems, and to do so with a knowledge of philosophy. In the contrary case, this will be done in an unconscious fashion, as Engels warned, thus falling into the embraces of the worst philosophy—electic philosophy.

The philosophical position from which we undertake an evaluation of presentism and reject its positive proposition pertaining to the problems of interest to us, is that of Marxist philosophy. It is tantamount, *inter alia,* to the acceptance of materialism in ontological problems and realism in the theory of cognition. This stand determines our negation of the philosophical premises of presentism which comes down to two fundamental issues, although it would certainly be easy to enumerate many more particular problems determining our negative appraisal.

Firstly, the negation pertains to idealism; strictly speaking, to the subjectivism of presentism.

The differentiation of two meanings of the word "history"—as the objective historical process and the description of this process, i.e. historical writing or, to put it differently, as "res gestae" and "Historia rerum gestarum", is commonly employed. A philosophical conception, according to which objective reality existing outside of any cognizing mind and independent of it differs from the thought about such a reality, rests in a conscious or unconscious fashion at the foundations of this differentiation. It is only on the basis of such a conception and such a differentiation that various problems of the theory of cognition arise which, as we have noted, are of value also in the field of the theory of history.

A characteristic trait of presentism, and this is true of all its variants, is the negation of this differentiation: according to presentism, history is no more than *thought about history*. Thus, the objective historical process in fact disappears, while only thought remains. This is not thought about the process, but thought which *creates* history. At least this is the way that Croce and Collingwood saw the issue. Others, especially the American presentist historians, limit the field of vision to the historical *image* and thus reduce the issue to thought about the historical process. Here thought becomes as if sovereign, while the problem of its conformity with the objective process, and thus the problem of the *objectivity* of historical cognition, if of no concern to them. They are unilaterally interested only in the subjective factor which, while being, according to their conception, social conditioned, nevertheless remains exclusively a realm of thought. In the given context it does not matter whether they start from any metaphysical, philosophical premises or not. The effect is the same: presentism takes the stand of philosophical subjectivism. This is the strangest theoretical position that an historian could take, since it is hard to know why a man, representing similar views, should trouble himself with the discovering of historical documents, their criticism, etc., that is, why he should be a historian. This amazement refers, of course, not to speculative philosophers, like Croce, but to historians who clearly show a concern for their profession. Nonetheless, this constitutes at most one more example of the fact that the principle of contradiction does not meet with general confirmation from a psychological point of view.

Secondly, the negation pertains to the relativism which is inseparable from presentism.

If one assumes that the interests and needs of the present determine in some fashion our vision of history, that it is nothing more than the projection on the screen of the past, as Carl Becker picturesquely stated, then, as a result, it is quite understandable that history must be constantly written anew and that there will be different and perhaps even mutually contradictory histories although all of them are true at a given moment. Along with losing the objective historical process, to which our historical cognition should relate, we lose also in the wastelands of subjectivism the objectivity of cognition and objective truth; the classical definition of truth also loses its place and meaning. What remains, at most, is a utilitarian definition such as we meet with in James' pragmatism: what is true, is that which is useful, in the meaning that it corresponds to specific needs and interests. This is precisely relativism, understood as a conception which makes the truthfulness of a judgement dependent on the system of reference: within a given form of reference (in respect to a given present, the presentists would say) it is true; with another system, it is false. It is not difficult to note that the acceptance of such a view is tantamount to a death verdict on science, at least on science of an intersubjective character, of general value, a science in the meaning of objective cognition, perhaps partial, incomplete but obligatory for all. Thus, relativism, as a result, negates history as a science, the very *possibility* of such a science, which is tantamount to catastrophe, to the self-destruction of the theory which leads to such conclusions. This is so in the case of presentism and this threatens also all theories which, by introducing a subjective element of cognition, interpret it as a function of variable social conditioning, eliminate the objective historical process and the objective cognition of this process.

Presentism, while effectively attacking the errors of positivist historical writing, itself suffers from an incurable disease of subjectivism and relativism which leads it to scientific disaster. This is utilized in polemics by its opponents from the positivist camp, although the demonstration of a critic's failings does not thereby minimize the value of his criticism. This is a typical "argumentum ad hominem".

The Marxist, while rejecting positivism for a given set of reasons, no less decidedly rejects presentism for other reasons. For a Marxist, the question which of these two stands is more erroneous or which is closer to his position is meaningless. He considers both of them to be erroneous, although for different reasons and in a different fashion; both are alien to him, although he may agree with the critical arguments which one of the schools puts forth against the other. What is essential for him, in this case, is not the measuring of distances and differences separating him from one school or the other, but the noting of the real theoretical problems which lie at the foundation of the conflict being waged between these schools. He must conduct these reflections by himself, on his own responsibility, in the field of theory as well.

What then are the problems which can be brought to light by analysing the conflict in historiography between positivism and presentism?

The first and fundamental problem which we encounter in analysing this conflict, a problem to which we shall have to revert in the determining of our own stand, is the issue of the character of historical cognition. Two conceptions have clashed here: the positivist, which recognizes that the historical process exists objectively and that human cognition, if it can manage to accumulate a sufficient quantity of facts, provides a faithful reflection of it without any subjective admixture; the presentist which, in principle, is not interested in the existence of the objective historical process, while it negates that cognition is its reflection and treats the historical process as the function of current interests and needs. Thus, presentism takes a subjectivist stand, while correctly emphasizing simultaneously the social conditioning of the cognizing subject. It is clear what, as Marxists, we accept in these two stands and what we reject.

What remains to be solved is the theoretical problem of how to combine into one uncontradictory theory the conception that history is an objective process which had taken place in the past and is examined by us and the conception that cognition is not passive contemplation but has an objective-activist nature. To put it differently, what is at stake is to transpose the third model of cognitive relation (according to our scheme) from the language of philosophical abstraction to the language of specific historical research. A number of detailed questions of immense theoretical significance are bound up with this general problem, such as: what are historical facts and what are the criteria for their selection? Can historical cognition be limited to description, or must it also elucidate? Why do we continuously write history anew? How does the matter of the progress of historical cognition present itself in this light?

The second fundamental problem which comes forth in connection with our analysis of this conflict is that of relativism. It pertains to the domain of the theory of truth and is bound up with the former problem as closely as possible. Do your judgements possess the value of truthfulness only within the framework of a given system of reference (subject, place and time) and are relative in this sense, or is their truthfulness independent of this system of reference and, in this sense, absolute? We have sought to answer this question in the previous chapter on the basis of abstract philosophical reflection, separating the problem of the relative and absolute nature of truth, in a sense of reference to given circumstances, from the problem of partial and complete cognition. The problem returns here in the shape of concrete historical cognition.

Presentism is linked not only with subjectivism, but also with relativism. To put it more precisely it is a specific exemplification of relativism. While relativism recognizes the relativity of truth, in the meaning of the necessity of referring cognition to given circumstances in order for it to be regarded as true, presentism raises this position to the rank of a principle. History is, after all, always the projection of present interests, needs and politics onto the past. It is always a function of the variable present and, because of this, the truthfulness of historical cognition is also referred to these circumstances of time and place.

The position of the Marxist, as of every other opponent of relativism, is clear in this case; he rejects both the relativism of presentism and its subjectivism. The negation of premises, or of philosophical conclusions which are bound up with real questions and problems of a given domain of science, should not, however, screen from us the problem itself. The erroneous solution to the problem does not liquidate the problem as such. What then is the real problem which remains after the rejection of relativism?

Presentism emphasizes, and correctly so, that the historian's viewpoint, his way of grasping the historical process, which facts of the past he recognizes as important and significant, i.e. which of them he elevates to the rank of historical facts, etc., is dependent on present social needs and interests, which condition the mentality and stand of the people examining the past—the historians. This is not only an accurate observation, but it is also significant for the scientific self-awareness of the historian, as well as of the representatives of other branches of the social sciences. This self-awareness makes a better understanding of the issue of historical knowledge's progress possible, makes it easier to comprehend why history is continuously written anew and why progress does not rest, as the positivists imagine, on a simple accumulation of fact which at a certain moment should result in perfect, absolute and unchanging knowledge. On the other hand, the theoretical difficulties already known to us spring forth. Our cognition and its product (knowledge) depend not only on the objective factor in the cognitive relationship, but also on the subjective factor connected with the variable conditioning of the cognizing subject. This is a subjective factor of particular significance since it always constitutes the function of social conditioning. Nonetheless, this question can be easily elucidated by transferring the analysis of the human individual from a purely individual to a social basis. On the other hand, a problem of the interpretation of the objectivity of cognition and truth remains open in this new interpretation; especially since what is at issue is not a general formula and scheme of cognitive relationship, but its concrete application in the domain of historical cognition.

Finally, the third great problem which we can note in connection with an analysis of this conflict: the problem of being "engagé", of partisanship—in the meaning of taking up a definite "engagé" stand on one side of the conflicts and social struggles of the past, as dealt with by history—that is, of the "partisanship" of history and the historian. This problem can also rest, as a partial one, within the framework of the large issue of the objectivity of historical cognition, but it opens new perspectives which make it possible to take up the specific aspects of this problem.

In proclaiming the postulate of descriptive history, which limited itself exclusively to the ascertainment of facts, "wie es eigentlich gewesen", Ranke simultaneously raised to an ideal the image of an historian noted for his impartiality, "non-engagé", standing above the disputes and conflicts which he examines, refraining even from evaluations and judgements on this subject; in a word, an historian treating the object of his research "sine ira et studio". Such an approach to the matter and such a postulate addressed to the historian was closely linked with a definite interpretation of the process of cognition and the cognitive relationship; according to Ranke, cognition has a passive-contemplative character and, therefore, the cognizing subject plays the role of a passive registrator of events. Thus, he assumed that a subject not only should not, but also could not play an active role and, as a result, be "engagé".

The position of presentism is exactly the opposite: both in respect to the interpretation of the cognitive process, as well as to the position and character of the cognizing subject. Proclaiming the postulate of an "engagé". partisan history (in the meaning referred to above of this term) presentism not only defines what history and the historian should be like but also ascertains certain consequences which result from the totality of this doctrine. If one voices the view that history is a function of the variable present and its interests, then one must recognize, as a result, that an historian's stand is also a function of contemporary needs, interests and struggles. Thus, the historian is "engagé" in terms of class, and this in the meaning of contemporary involvement of partisanship of the present day, although projected upon the screen of the past.

Of what does the issue raised by us consist? Of the linking into one harmonious whole of the postulate of "engagé", partisan, class history with the postulate of its scientific nature, that is, the striving towards objective truth and the attainment of this truth, even in the meaning of an infinite process of striving towards the absolute truth. This is an unusually significant and fascinating problem, especially for Marxism, in the light of its own philosophical premises and difficulties.

The consideration of the conflict of presentism and positivism was important for us primarily from the point of view of extrapolation of essential research problems. As we have seen, they concentrate themselves around the conflict between the postulate of the scientific nature of history on the variability of the historical perspective. The debate of presentism and positivism throws a specific light on this problem. This is nevertheless a field for research and investigation of other scientific disciplines as well, which also influence our meta-historical considerations in a very essential, although indirect fashion. We have in mind here, above all, the so-called sociology of knowledge, with which we shall deal in the next chapter.

Notes

1. In his introduction to *Geschichten der romanischen und germanischen Völker von 1494 bis 1514,* Sämtliche Werke (Leipzig, 1885, Verlang von Duncker, dritte Auflage, t.XXIII, p. vii) Leopold von Ranke wrote: "History has been ascribed the office of judging the past, of instructing contemporaries for the good of the future; the present work does not undertake to fulfil such high offices: it desires only to show what really was."
2. For example, Charles Beard in a discussion article entitled "The noble dream", the *American Historical Review,* vol. XLI, no. 1, pp. 74-87 (1935).
3. C. Read, "The social responsibilities of the historian", the *American Historical Review,* vol. LV, no. 2, p. 289 (1950).
4. C. A. Beard and A. Vagst, "Currents of thought in historiography", the *American Historical Review,* vol. XLII, p. 481 (1937).
5. G. W. F. Hegel, *Lectures on the Philosophy of History* (Polish ed.), vol. I, pp. 17-18, Warsaw, 1958.
6. *Ibid.,* p. 16.
7. *Ibid.,* pp. 7-8.
8. *Ibid.,* p. 10.
9. Hegel repeats here the words of Goethe's Faust: "Was ihr den Geist der Zeiten heisst, das ist im Grund der Herren eigner Geist, in dem die Zeiten sich bespiegeln."
10. *Ibid.,* pp. 11-12.
11. This point of view is by no means original. Among Croce's many predecessors in this respect let us mention Arthur Schopenhauer who voiced similar views in *Die Welt als Wille und Verstellung* (Band II, Kapitel 38, "Uber Geschichte").
12. B. Croce, *Zur Theorie und Geschichte der Historiographie* p. 96, Tübingen, 1915.
13. *Ibid.,* p. 98.
14. B. Croce, *Die Geschichte als Gedanke und als Tat,* p. 37, Bern, 1944.
15. B. Croce, *Zur Theorie . . . , ed. cit.,* p. 100.
16. B. Croce, *Die Geschichte : . . , ed. cit.,* p. 42.
17. B. Croce, *Zur Theorie . . . , ed. cit.,* p. 4.
18. B. Croce, *Die Geschichte . . . , ed. cit.,* pp. 275-276.
19. R. G. Collingwood, *The Idea of History,* pp. 215, 217, 305, etc., Oxford, 1946.
20. *Ibid.,* p. 218.
21. *Ibid.,* pp. 245, 246.
22. *Ibid.,* pp. 247-248.
23. C. A. Destler, "Some observations on contemporary historical theory", the *American Historical Review,* no. 3, p. 503, (1950).
24. Let us cite, as an example, other English works which also exerted their influence. Already in 1874 F. H. Bradley in his *The Presuppositions of Critical History* voiced ideas similar to presentism: "The past changes together with the present and this can never be different, since it is always based on the present" (vol I, *Collected Essays,* Oxford, 1935, p. 20, as quoted by M. G. White in "The attack on the historical method", the *Journal of Philosophy,* no. 12, p. 318, fn. 7 (1954)). R. B. Haldane in his *The Meaning of Truth in History* (London, 1914) maintained that history is akin to art thus, in fact, denying the scientific character of historical writing. "History based exclusively on scientific methods would be an irony", wrote Haldane, who saw in the artist's activity the prototype of the historian's work which allegedly had, of necessity, to deform the picture of relativity. (As quoted by P. J. Teggart, *Theory and Process of History,* U.S.A., 1941, p. 55.) Charles Oman in his *On the Writing*

of History (London, 1939, pp. 7-8) wrote: ". . . History is not purely a subjective matter; it is the way in which an historian interprets and co-relates a given series of events. As the French say: 'Il n'y a pas d'histoire—mais seulement des histoires'."

25. J. Dewey, *Logic. The Theory of Inquiry,* p. 233, New York, 1949.
26. *Ibid.,* p. 235.
27. *Ibid.,* p. 233.
28. G. B. Adams, "History and the philosophy of history", the *American Historical Review,* no. 14, pp. 221-236 (1909).
29. *Ibid.,* p. 236.
30. Charles A. Beard, "Written history as an act of faith", the *American Historical Review,* no. 2, pp. 220-221 (1934).
31. The *American Historical Review,* no. 1, pp. 74-87 (1935).
32. *Ibid.,* p. 78. (Emphasis—A. S.)
33. Charles A. Beard, "Written history . . .", *ed. cit.,* p. 221.
34. *Ibid.,* p. 219.
35. *Ibid.,* p. 220.
36. *Ibid.,* p. 226. The theses of relativism appear in a less radical form in: Beard and Vagst, "Currents of thought in historiography", the *American Historical Review,* no. 3, pp. 480-483 (1937).
37. J. H. Randall, Jr. and G. Haines, "Controlling assumptions in the practice of American historians", in *Theory and Practice in Historical Study,* Social Science Research Council Bulletin, vol. 54, p. 21 (1946).
38. J. H. Randall, Jr., "On understanding the history of philosophy", the *Journal of Philosophy,* no. 17, p. 462 (1939).
39. *Ibid.,* p. 467.
40. *Ibid.,* p. 472.
41. C. Becker, "Everyman his own historian", the *American Historical Review,* no. 2, p. 222 (1932).
42. *Ibid.,* p. 227.
43. *Ibid.,* pp. 227-228.
44. *Ibid.,* p. 229.
45. *Ibid.,* p. 234.
46. C. Becker, "Mr. Wells and the New History, everyman his own historian", *Essays on History and Politics,* pp. 168-170, New York, 1935. (Emphasis—A. S.) It is worthwhile to mention an older, but very interesting from the viewpoint of the general characterization of presentism, essay of Becker's "Der Wandel im geschichtlichen Bewusstein", *Die Neue Rundschau,* 28, zweites Heft, pp. 113-121 (1927).
47. C. Read, "The social responsibilities of the historian", the *American Historical Review,* no. 2, p. 275 (1950).
48. *Ibid.,* p. 280.
49. *Ibid.*
50. *Ibid.,* p. 283, (Emphasis—A. S.)
51. *Ibid.,* p. 284.
52. *Ibid.*
53. *Ibid.*
54. See M. Mandelbaum, *The Problem of Historical Knowledge,* New York, 1938; A. O. Lovejoy, "Present standpoints and past history", the *Journal of Philosophy,* no. 18 (1939); C. H. McIlwain, "The historian's part in a changing world", the *American Historical Review,* no. 2 (1937).

CHAPTER 3

The Class Character of
Historical Cognition

"De plus, il s'en faut bien que les faits décrits dans l'histoire ne soient la peinture exacte des mêmes faits tels qu'ils sont arrivés: ils changent de forme dans la tête de l'historien, ils se moulent sur ses interêts, ils prennent la teinte de ses préjugés."

J. J. Rousseau, *Emile*

Presentism proclaims in general that history is always a function of a given present: social interests and needs emerging at the present moment condition the way of seeing the past, the selection of facts and thus the image of this past. In addition to the charge of subjectivism and relativism which can be put forth against presentism, another one, that of generality in reference to its conception regarding the social conditioning of an historian's stand, can also be made. What does this really mean? How does this take place? What are these needed interests and what is the mechanism of their reaction? Here are but a few questions selected from many to which presentism does not give an answer. The natural supplementation of presentism in this respect, although the supplementary nature was neither intended nor perceived by the representatives of the given trends, is the sociology of knowledge in the form represented by Karl Mannheim and his school.

The Sociology of Knowledge on the Social Conditioning of Cognition

The sociology of knowledge which has a "career" for itself during the past decades is derived from Marxism and, in particular, from its theory on the basis and superstructure as well as from its theory of ideology, Karl Mannheim spoke of this loyally, but most often the origin of the sociology of knowledge is passed over in silence which is incorrect not only due to the issue of scientific priority but also due to the possibility of correcting certain conceptions of the sociology of knowledge which are open to considerable criticism. They change their interpretation, in particular in respect to the charge of relativism, within the framework of the doctrine from which they were originally derived, within the framework of Marxism.

The fundamental operation of the sociology of knowledge is immensely simple, although heuristically significant and fertile. It is not satisfied with the assertion, which many other trends consider to be a sufficient starting-point, that given views emerge in respect to certain social problems, but also possess the question of *why* do they emerge precisely in a given shape which differs from others, both past and present. The raising of this seemingly banal question relating to origin is linked with the statement that a dependence, not in the least banal, appears between the views of people on social problems and social conditions. It is the latter which cause people to maintain precisely a given set of views, which elucidate why people who lived or live in differing conditions also tend to hold different views.

The comprehension of this connection is closely bound up with the acceptance of the Marxist thesis on the mutual dependence of the social basis and the social superstructure.If one accepts the thesis that a movement of the basis, that is, changes in the field of the material conditions of social existence, gives rise to changes in the views of people on social matters, that is, changes in the superstructure, then it is understandable why we pose the question regarding the origin of these views and, in particular, regarding the social relations and the material conditions of social existence resting at their foundations which bring them forth.

This question which constitutes the core of the sociology of knowledge and its specific trait is clearly borrowed from Marxism, just as is the interest shown in a particular part of the superstructure— ideology.

Let us consider further how Mannheim applied and interpreted the Marxist theory of the basis and the superstructure as well as the theory of ideology. Before we undertake this, however, I should like to emphasize that the genetic links of the sociology of knowledge with Marxism and its intellectual debt to Marxism are much more profound since they embrace the fundamental elements of Mannheim's doctrine which has not been always sufficiently stressed and brought to light. I have in mind specifically Mannheim's conception of man and his conception of cognition as a process. Without comprehending the connection of these elements of the sociology of knowledge with Marxism, we cannot understand to what degree and to what a great extent Mannheim based himself consciously on Marx.

In discussing the gnoseological premises of our considerations we remarked about Mannheim's conception regarding the origin and role of individualist fiction in the theory of cognition. He linked it with a definite type of social relations in which the original connection of the individual and the group becomes lost. Similarly, he bound up the justification of this view with the disintegration of the foundations of an individualist society, bordering on anarchy. The starting-point for the analysis of the process of cognition should thus be not an autonomous individual, separated and counterposed to society, but the social group in the framework of which the individual, by acting and co-operating with it, takes on a proper shape.[1]

The shifting of the accent from the individual interpreted autonomously to the social group and thus to the socially interpreted individual has a decisive meaning for the sociology of knowledge. It is only on this basis, clearly taken from Marxism, that Mannheim was able to put forth the conception which lay at the foundation of his further considerations on the subject of the social conditioning of human knowledge.

> . . . knowledge is from the very beginning a cooperative process of group life, in which everyone unfolds his knowledge within the framework of a common fate, a common activity, and the overcoming of common difficulties (in which, however, each has a different share). Accordingly the products of the cognitive process are already, at least in part, differentiated because not every possible aspect of the world comes within the purview of the members of a group, but only those out of which difficulties and problems for the group arise. And even this common world (not shared by any outside groups in the same way) appears differently to the subordinate groups and strata in a functionally differentiated society have a different experiencial approach to the common contents of the object of their world.[2]

Another element which links the sociology of knowledge with

Marxism, and to which I wish to draw special attention, is Mannheim's method of interpretation of the process of cognition.

Firstly, Mannheim—clearly following Marx—emphasized that cognition is not abstract-theoretical action, but is based on collective action.[3]

Secondly, and this once more shows the close ties with Marxism, Mannheim sought to interpret cognition both dynamically as a process and statically. This is an extremely important conception for the solution of problems derived from the sociology of knowledge.

> Hence it has become extremely questionable whether, in the flux of life, it is a genuinely worthwhile intellectual problem to seek to discover fixed and immutable ideas or absolutes. It is a more worthy intellectual task perhaps to learn to think dynamically and relationally rather than statically. In our contemporary social and intellectual plight, it is nothing less than shocking to discover that those persons who claim to have discovered an absolute are usually the same people who also pretend to be superior to the rest. To find people in our day attempting to pass off the world and recommending to others some nostrum of the absolute which they claim to have discovered is merely a sign of the loss of and a need for intellectual and moral certainty, felt by broad sections of the population who are unable to look life in the face.[4]

After this initial noting of the genetic links between the sociology of knowledge and Marxism we shall take up a proper presentation of Mannheim's views on the problems of interest to us. We shall begin with his interpretation of the problem of ideology in view of the role which it plays in his entire conception. Mannheim's views on this are to be found primarily in his *Ideology and Utopia*, already quoted by us, and in his *Sociology of Knowledge*.[5]

A fundamental idea of historical materialism is the conception regarding the social conditioning of human consciousness. The theory of the basis and the superstructure is devoted precisely to this problem. In interpreting ideology as a specifically qualified part of the super-structure and in indicating the connection of every ideology with the situation, aspirations and interests of given social groups, Marxism provided Mannheim with the impulse for the development of the theory of ideology. This genetical connection (referred to by Mannheim himself) is indubitable, although by radicalizing Marxist conception Mannheim has in fact departed from it.

Starting from the premise that ideology is always socially conditioned, that it reflects the aspirations and interests of a given social group, Mannheim took the stand that any ideology is *ex definitione* a "false consciousness"; that is, it gives a one-sided, partial and thus distorted image of reality. Since he placed all ideology on the same platform he could not defend himself against relativism. However, this did not prevent him from carrying out what was, from a certain point of view, a penetrating analysis of the concept "ideology".

He differentiated, above all, the partial and total concept of ideology ("partikularer und totaler Ideologiebegriff"). Mannheim called the ideas and suppositions noted for their more or less conscious concealment of the state, whose true cognition does not lie in the interest of the groups or individuals entertaining these ideas and suppositions, a partial concept of ideology. An entire gamut of possibilities enters into the picture here: from conscious lying to semiconscious, instinctive concealment of the true state of affairs, from deceiving others to deceiving oneself. This concept of ideology which, according to Mannheim, only gradually became distinct from the concept of ordinary lies, is partial in many meanings of this word. Its partiality, Mannheim stated, becomes immediately apparent when the total concept of ideology is counterposed to it; ideology in this second meaning implies the character ("die Beschaffenheit") of the entire structure of consciousness of a given period or of a given group; for example, a class.[6]

According to Mannheim, what both concepts of ideology have in common is the fact that in order to understand them it is insufficient to comprehend the ideological statement in itself; it is also necessary to take into consideration the social position of the subject and to interpret the given statement as the function of this position. According to Mannheim, "These conceptions of ideology, accordingly, make these so-called 'ideas' a function of the individual who holds them and of his position in his social milieu."[7]

In Mannheim's interpretation the two concepts of ideology differ primarily in that the partial concept of ideology embraces only a part of the view of the partner in the cognitive conflict as "false consciousness" and functionalizes only the psychological side, maintaining for both partners of the conflict a common cognitive (noological) stand while the total concept of ideology embraces the entire world outlook of the partner, including his conceptual apparatus, as a "false consciousness", and functionalizes his entire cognitive platform. In addition to this counterposing of the partial and total concepts of ideology a new pair of contradictions is proposed: the particular and general ("speziell und allgemein") comprehension of the concept of ideology. The first takes place when we functionalize the entire structure of the opponent's consciousness; the second "when he has the courage to subject not just the adversary's point of view but all points of view, including his own, to the ideological analysis".[8]

Mannheim was concerned not with the partial but precisely with the total concept of ideology; he was interested in the variable noological platform, the determining platform of cognition. This was supposed to be the subject matter for the sociology of knowledge. It is to concern itself with situations "in which the entire social structure together with all its manifestations appears of necessity differently to observers placed in various points of this structure. It is not the intention to conceal which brings forth in all these cases a 'one-sidedness' and 'falseness' of statements, but the inevitable variety of structure of consciousness among the subjects which are placed differently in the historical-social space."[9]

For Mannheim this possibility of "false consciousness" in general, a consciousness which is false in view of its fundamental functionalizing, constitutes the principle problem of the sociology of knowledge. In particular, the concept of a general shape of a total concept of ideology (that is, the functionalizing of the entire noological platform of all the partners of a cognitive conflict) led him to the thesis that all stands are only variants of a "false consciousness". Mannheim criticized Marxism only for failing to apply its own theory of ideology to itself. In such an interpretation all the cats become grey in the dark. The difference between scientific ideology (in fact in this light this term itself is by definition a "contradictio in adiecto") and non-scientific ideology and Marxist and, for example, fascist ideology disappears. Marxism becomes, in fact, only one of the many "points of view", endowed with equal rights to be spoken of by the history of thought. Thereby, it loses, of course, its exceptional position and its scientific value. Mannheim wrote:

At the present stage of our understanding it is hardly possible to avoid this general formulation of the total conception of ideology, according to which the thought of all parties in all epochs is of an ideological character. There is scarcely a single ideological position, and Marxism furnishes no exception to this rule, which has not changed through history and which even in the present does not appear in many forms. Marxism, too, has taken on many diverse appearances. It should not be difficult for a Marxist to recognize their social basis.

With the emergence of the general formulation of the total conception of ideology, the simple theory of ideology develops into the sociology of knowledge. What was once the intellectual armament of a party is transformed into a method of research in social and intellectual history generally. To begin with, a given social group discovered the "situational determination" (*Seinsge bundenheit*) of its opponents' ideas. Subsequently the recognition of this fact is elaborated into an all-inclusive principle according to which the thought of every group is seen as arising out of its life conditions. Thus, it becomes the task of the sociological history of thought to analyze without regard for party bases all the factors on the actually existing social situation which may influence thought. This sociologically oriented history of ideas is destined to provide modern men with a revised view of the whole historical process.[10]

In our further considerations we shall revert once more to an analysis of this "general conception of the total concept of ideology", in particular to the problem of the ideological character of Marxism. Here we shall concentrate on the general gnoseological consequences of this doctrine and primarily on the relativism which follows from it.

All views on social problems are, according to Mannheim, ideological; every ideology is a cognitive deformation, a "false consciousness". Since according to him, every ideology is simultaneously the function of a definite social situation (Seinslage) it is, as a given truth, relativized to *given* conditions. Hence, there are as many truths as there are "social situations", that is, complexes of conditions of social existence.

Such a stand is relativism and a consistent application of this doctrine to social sciences in general, and to history in particular, must give rise to results destructive to this science. Since scientific truth depends on the system of reference, then the possibility of obtaining an intersubjectively obligatory objective truth is eliminated and thereby the foundation of scientific cognition is extinguished. Mannheim defended himself against this consequence, which was tantamount to scientific catastrophe, and his weapon of defence is supposed to be the *sociology of knowledge* and, in particular, the differentiation between *relativism* and *relationism* within the framework of this theory.

We should like to add, at this point, a remark of a historical and self-critical nature.

A number of years ago, while engaged in a project on historical cognition, then put aside for a longer period of time, I published as a by-product an article devoted to Mannheim's sociology of knowledge.[11] At present, while upholding the principle ideas of this article, I believe that I was unjust in treating the idea of relationism as presented by Mannheim. Not in the sense that I consider that it saves him from relativism, which is the Achilles' heel of Mannheim's theory, but in that it contains a number of correct ideas which I unnecessarily and unfairly lost sight of in the general criticism. I shall now seek to apply here a more subtle method of analysis and criticism.

In the problem which we are concerned with, Mannheim puts forth two fundamental concepts. He maintained that:

1. One can speak of relativism in connection with his theory only when one does not expand the category of the sociology of knowledge to include the theory of cognition, modernizing it thereby;

2. that his own views are not relativist but relationist, which constitutes an essential difference.[12]

In his *Ideology and Utopia* Mannheim pointed out how the concrete development of the total concept of ideology leads to the sociology of knowledge. He emphasized here that extending the concept of ideology to entire human thought, that is, interpreting the entire structure of the consciousness of subjects as the function of definite conditions, we are faced with the fact of the conditioning of the "viewpoint"; not only of a given act of cognition, but of the cognitive process as a whole. Thus, such concepts as "ideology", "false consciousness", "reality", and so on, change their meaning as a result. Mannheim wrote: "This point of view ultimately forces us to recognize that our axioms, our ontology, and our epistomology have been profoundly transformed."

The aim here also is to change the outdated theory of cognition and the concept of truth bound up with it by introducing into them the interpretation that the subject and the process of cognition are socially conditioned. It is only in the case when one does not take this moment into consideration that relativism arises. Mannheim wrote:

Relativism is a product of the modern historical-sociological procedure which is based on the recognition that all historical thinking is bound up with the concrete position in life of the thinker (Standortsgebundenheit des Denkers). But relativism combines this historical-sociological insight with an older theory of knowledge which was as yet unaware of the interplay between conditions of existence and modes of thought . . . was necessarily led to the rejection of all those forms of knowledge which were dependent upon the subjective standpoint and the social situation of the knower, and which were, hence, merely "relative". Relativism, then, owes its existence to the discrepancy between this newly-won insight into the actual processes of thought and a theory of knowledge which had not yet taken account of this new insight.[13]

According to Mannheim it is necessary, in order to overcome such a state of affairs, to undertake a revision of the outmoded theory of cognition, taking into consideration its historically changeable nature. In another place (cf. *The Sociology of Knowledge, cit. ed.,* pp. 82-83) Mannheim put forth this same postulate in relation to the concept of truth which, according to him, is also variable and dependent on the conditions of the epoch.

Relationism is supposed to rest in the fact that what is "essential for certain statements is that they cannot be formulated in an absolute fashion but only by taking into consideration the 'viewpoint' dependent on the social position in which the expressing individual finds himself".[14]

According to Mannheim the taking into consideration of the social conditions of human knowledge must lead to the conclusion regarding the "relational" structure of human cognition. But this, Mannheim maintained, is not relativism:

> Thus a relativism in the sense of an arbitrariness of every statement does not follow from this; relationism in our understanding ascertains, on the other hand, that every statement can be formulated, from its essence, only in a relational fashion; *relationism transforms itself into relativism only when it is linked with the old static ideal of eternal truths, deprived of any subjectivity and lacking in perspective and when the ideal of absolute truth is used as a measure.*[15]

In his *Die Zerstörung der Vernunft* (Berlin, 1954) Georg Lukacs discussed, *inter alia*, Mannheim's sociology of knowledge. He rejected Mannheim's attempts at discarding the change of relativism by using the argument of relationism and considering this to be exclusively a terminological trick. The difference between relationism and relativism Lukacs considered to be analogous to the one which Lenin character-ized polemically and picturesquely in a letter to Gorky as the difference between a yellow and a green devil. Apart from Mannheim's assurances, how, in fact, does relationism differ from relativism, Lukacs asked, if it is based on the rejection of objective truth and the subjectivization of the cognitive process?

My criticism of Mannheim's relationism in the article mentioned above was basically similar. As I have already said this criticism was incorrect since it lost sight of certain valuable ideas presented by Mannheim.

Relationism does not rescue Mannheim's conception from the charge of relativism, but this is so not because relationism is identical with relativism but because Mannheim did not see clearly the difference between them and, in addition, was unable to put forth consistently his own relationist stand.

Thus, firstly, the assertion that all cognition is relative in the meaning that truth is dependent on the position of the cognizing subject (on his individual traits, on circumstances of time and place) is not identical with another assertion that *certain* statements cannot be formulated without taking into consideration the social conditioning of the subject. The first assertion is represented by *relativism* the second by Mannheim's *relationism*. Here are the differences which exist between them:

(a) Relativism employs a larger quantifier (*all* cognition is relative), while relationism employs a small one (*certain* statements cannot be formulated . . .), leaving a large part of cognition (cognition which has no direct social implications) outside of its field of vision.

(b) Relativism is indissolubly linked with subjectivism and the negation of non-relative truth in respect to the circumstances of time, place and the individual traits of the subject, and it is thus absolute, in the specific meaning of the word, according to one terminology, and objective according to another. On the other hand, relationism proclaims only the negation of the passive-contemplative model of cognitive relation and, as a result, the negation of absolute truth understood as a static, complete and thereby unchangeable truth. Thus, relationism, as distinct from relativism, does not imply either subjectivism or the negation of objective truth; on the contrary, it lends itself exceedingly well, within the framework of the objective-activist model of cognitive relation, to being linked with the doctrine of objective truth, although not static-absolute but dynamic-changeable.

The differences between relationism and relativism are thus sufficiently significant to be noted and to recognize the stand of relationism as theoretically independent. This is the more important in that relationism is based on accurate observations in relation to human cognition (the social conditioning of the subject and the process of cognition, the active role of the subject in cognition, the process-like nature of cognition and truth, etc.). On the other hand, the differentiation between relativism and relationism, as carried out by Mannheim (relativism in the meaning of the *arbitrariness* of every statement), is erroneous and this is why, *inter alia*, he was unable to grasp this problem which remained the Achilles' heel of his doctrine.[16]

Secondly, Mannheim was unable to present consistently the position of relationism and to separate it from relativism.

Mannheim stated that relationism transforms itself into relativism when it is interpreted in the context in a theory of cognition which, failing to understand the role of the subjective factor in the process of cognition, employs the ideal of eternal and absolute truths understood statically. Thus, according to him, the charge of relativism in relation to relationism is based on a misunderstanding or error. In one sense this is also true when one approaches the appraisal of relationism from the stand of a mechanistic, passive, contemplative model of the cognitive relation. It is impossible then to understand the role of the subjective factor in cognition and, as a result, to understand the sense of the idea of relationism. However, in the case of the sociology of knowledge the issue cannot be reduced only to error or to an incorrect charge of relativism, derived from a misunderstanding. The matter rests more deeply and is bound up, above all, with the fact that Mannheim was unable to carry out consistently the stand of relationism thus going over, as a result, to a position of relativism.[17]

Here are the charges which can be made in this respect against Mannheim without in the least eliminating the reasons speaking in favour of relationism.

Firstly, Mannheim betrayed his own theory by proclaiming simultaneously with the concepts of relationism the theory that all ideology is a "false consciousness". The line of reasoning in his theory of ideology is, as we recall, the following: *every* ideology is socially conditioned, bound up with a definite "point of view", and thus limited in its perspective and deforming reality. Hence, *all* ideologies are deformations and thus a false picture of reality, a "false consciousness". It follows clearly from this that he evaluated the role of the subjective factor in cognition negatively, so negatively in fact that the gradiations and even the differences in the functioning of this factor, as for example, in the case of scientific and religious ideology, ceased to interest him. At the same time, however, we know that relationism calls for the "calculating" of the subjective factor as a necessary component of the process of cognition and accuses even the so-called traditional theory of cognition of being unable to take it into consideration in its construction. Hence, the role of the subjective factor to the degree to which it is an expression of the social conditionings of the subject should not, according to relationism, be evaluated negatively but one should solely ascertain its appearance and undertake, in connection with this, specified intellectual actions to be referred to later. In developing relationism consistently one cannot simultaneously proclaim the theory of ideology as a "false consciousness". This is a contradiction within the framework of the doctrine which substantiates our thesis that Mannheim was unable to apply his own ideas consistently, thus, arriving, as a result, not at relationism but at authentic relativism.

Secondly, the charge against Mannheim's theory of truth follows the same path of reasoning. It is a partial problem, as compared with the above, but it throws light on it additionally and from a special viewpoint.

Mannheim treated the theory of cognition for which, *inter alia*, "The ideal of absolute truth is the measure" is outmoded; not only because it did not take into consideration "the point of view", but also due to the "static idea of eternal truths". Relationism is supposed to take into consideration the partial character of truth attainable in fact in cognition and, as a result, the process-like dynamic nature of human cognition and the truths acquired in this way. Here once again, however, the contradiction appears clearly between this postulate of relationism and the theory of ideology, as well as the sociology of knowledge in the shape given it by Mannheim. While protesting against the recognition of absolute truth as a measure in one case, he postulated it in another. After all, if ideology does not present total truth and thus an eternal, absolute truth, he disqualifies it as a "false consciousness". Thus, he did not make allowance for a category of partial truth, subject to change and a specific evolution. Thereby, he accepted the premise against his own postulates, that "the ideal of absolute truth is the measure". In this manner, he committed a fundamental error of confusing objective truth with absolute truth. This opened the path for relativism, although the sociology of knowledge simultaneously postulated relationism.

Mannheim clearly felt this effect since, in spite of assurances that the change of the postulates of the theory of cognition had supposedly solved the question of relativism, he undertook further attempts to overcome it. Why would he have done so, had he believed in the efficacy of his relationism?

Even on the basis of relationism the concept still persists that no statement interprets a historical subject "in itself" ("Ansichsein") but as a result of its ideological character; it is a function of the historian's social position and volitional processes. Thus, in spite of the new terminology the question reappears of referring cognition to the subject and the social conditions in a way which makes the possibility of objective knowledge questionable. Mannheim sought a way out of this difficulty by means of the "theory of perspective". If we interpret reality from different "points of view" then objectivity is obtained by an indirect road, a road of "recalculating" or "transforming" these different "perspectivistic views":

> Just as we resolve a conflict pertaining to visual objects which by their essence . . . can be seen only in a perspectivistic fashion and not by constructing a non-perspectivist image (since this would be impossible) but by seeking to understand on the basis of an image independent on a certain viewpoint why, for a man standing on a different position, things appear thusly and not otherwise, here too we can achieve objectivity in the same fashion by proper "transposing" and "recalculating". Of course, the problem appears immediately as to which of the existing points of view has an optimum character, but here a certain criterion also exists; just as in visual perspective, when certain given points of view are best suited to bring out the most important objective links, here too a certain test exists, i.e. the greatest adaptability and the greatest effectiveness in respect to empirical material.[18]

As is usual in such cases an accumulation of arguments only

complicates the situation. With the "theory of perspectives" new serious difficulties emerge for the sociology of knowledge.

It was Mannheim's concern to show that his conception is not relativist, that it recognizes the objectivity of cognition, only understood differently from within the framework of the traditional theory of cognition. Similarly, in a relational solution, Mannheim stated that, "the aim is not to resign from the postulate of objectivity and the ability to resolve factual discussions or to proclaim illusionism according to which everything is an illusion and nothing can be resolved; what is maintained here is merely that this objectivity and ability to resolve can be attained only in a roundabout fashion".[19]

According to Mannheim this objectivity appears in two variants.

Firstly, when we have a common noological platform. As follows from Mannheim's theory of ideology the "mental structure" ("Aspekstrucktur, Denkstill") is derived from definite social conditions and volitional processes. In this way a definite conceptual and categorical apparatus arises which defines the contours of our image of the world while a change of the conceptual apparatus brings about a change of this image.[20] Thus, as long as we remain within the framework of one and the same system (have the same "mental style", as, for example, the members of a single class in the same historical period) we may attain the same results and reject views contrary to them as erroneous.

Secondly, when we find ourselves within the framework of different systems and the conflict of different perspectives ensues. Then "objectivity" would have to be attained in a roundabout way, by "recalculating" these perspectives. But how is this to be done?

Mannheim proposed to arrive at a synthesis by soaring above the conflicting perspectives which would make possible the comprehension of the conditions giving rise to them. But, after all, in accord with the theory of ideology the synthesizer would also have his own "mental style", and would not be an impartial judge but would introduce his own deforming "point of view" into the issue. Thus, as in the case of other relativist systems we would be forced to reach the conclusion, so destructive to science, that the last one to proclaim a judgement is correct.

Mannheim proposed still another solution: the resolving of a conflict between different "perspectives" by means of a criterion of the greatest effectiveness of a given "point of view" in respect to empirical material.

Here also difficulties of the type mentioned above arise immediately. After all, the conflict pertains, *inter alia*, to the "point of view" regarding this effectiveness and the judge also possesses his "point of view" which eliminates objectivity. Here, once more, the last one to speak is correct.

In this critical situation Mannheim decided to perform a theoretical "salto mortalis"; he simply *assumed* the objectivity of knowledge of a given social group in reference to its "mental structure", and thus in reference to the social position conditioning it. As a consequence he *assumed* the possibility that it could attain objective historical truth. This is not possible for all; only for the intelligentsia which is above the classes and whose call is "always to discover that point from which general orientation in events is possible".

This final "salto mortalis" signified a twofold bankruptcy of Mannheim's conception.

Firstly, because Mannheim came into conflict with his own theory by voicing the special position of the intelligentsia which breaks with the general concept on the social conditioning of all knowledge.

Secondly, because in assuming the possibility of objective knowledge regarding "mental structure", and thereby the possibility of objective historical truth, Mannheim contradicted the fundamental thesis of the theory of ideology (ideology is "false consciousness") and thereby negated the foundations of his own system.

Thus, it appears that the price which Mannheim had to pay for seeking to avoid relativism was the negation of the foundations of his own conception. This seems to justify Maurice Mandelbaum's criticism who, coming out against all forms of relativism, spoke of Mannheim and, in particular, of his conception of "recalculating perspectives" in this way:

> . . . His (Mannheim's) attempt to put relationism in the place of relativism by means of the sociology of knowledge leads him to the acceptance of that which he previously negated: the possibility of objective historical knowledge. Along with Croce and Dilthey, Mannheim provides in this way a proof of the ultimate futility of any attempt to avoid the consequences of historical relativism after accepting the philosophical basis of this relativism.[21]

Regardless of the criticism of the inner contradictions of Mannheim's doctrine it should be remarked here—this will be an assistance for our further considerations—that the theory of "recalculating perspectives" and the concept of the intelligentsia as a social stratum which has special qualities for this, undoubtedly offers some fertile ideas to which it will be necessary to revert.

Firstly, this pertains to the idea of "recalculating perspectives" itself. If we disrobe it from its metaphorical shape it can be expressed simply: the awareness of the fact that cognition, due to various types of conditions (level of knowledge, social interests, etc.), is not full, all-sided and finite, but, on the contrary, is partial and limited, even deforms the image of reality and opens the road to an overcoming of these limitations. Taking even into consideration that such an overcoming is also not final and absolute and that this new higher level of cognition will be limited in its perspective and partial in scope, it is, after all, significant—taking the matter realistically, only this is really significant—that given limitations and deformation can be overcome. This, and only this, can be the road for the progress of knowledge. Similarly, in learning to overcome a given disease, tuberculosis for example, one does not guarantee a patient that he may not succumb to a different one; it is, however, considered an achievement that this disease has been mastered and the patient cured, thus seeing in this correctly both progress of knowledge and progress from the point of view of human life.

In drawing attention to the fact that a self-awareness of the limitations of human cognition and an understanding of their nature is the best road for overcoming them, Mannheim expressed a significant thought, although he was not the sole discoverer of this truth nor an original one, apart from the form in which he expressed it. Nonetheless, the thought itself, as we have already stated, is valuable and noteworthy for further considerations regarding the mutual relations and connections of the subjective factor in cognition with the problem of the objectivity of cognition. The more so in that Mannheim did not proclaim an abstract judgement, but sought to link it with an indication of the potential social bearer of his ideas.

Secondly, this pertains to Mannheim's suggestion that the

intelligentsia is that group or social strata which is best suited to the function of social auto-reflection on cognition.

Within the framework of Mannheim's system this conception leads, as we have seen, to immense difficulties and becomes an additional, although important element in his theoretical débâcle. This follows, however, from the postulates of coherence of a system which cannot stand for internal contradictions. On the other hand, it does not by any means negate the value of the idea as such.

This idea shows that in order to carry out this "recalculating of perspectives", i.e. in order to become aware of the limitations and deformations of cognition, a corresponding level of knowledge and professional training which would enable the undertaking of this auto-reflective operation is necessary. If we understand the word "intelligentsia" as the name of a group or social stratum marked, above all, by a higher level of education than that which is generally accepted in society, then it becomes understandable that it is precisely this stratum which is predestined to undertake the function of auto-reflection, since it is better prepared for this than others and, last but not least, a part of it engages in this reflection *professionally*.

It cannot be denied that these are convincing, commonsensical thoughts. Two consequences follow from them, pertaining both to the theoretical as well as the practical aspects of the problem.

The first rests in the fact that the general concept regarding the self-awareness of the limitations and deformations of cognition as a path leading to their overcoming and, thereby, to raising human knowledge to a higher level, is placed on a concrete social basis in respect to the realization of this auto-reflection. This does not signify, of course, that *everyone* who belongs to the stratum of the intelligentsia, that is, who possesses, among others, the required formal education and training, can engage in such auto-reflection and will, in fact, undertake it. This would be a utopia since education and proper professional training constitute a necessary, but by no means sufficient, condition for this possibility to transform itself into reality. The concept is much more modest, although no less important because of this: it is most likely that the people undertaking this auto-reflection will come from the intelligentsia, or even exclusively from it. The understanding of this state of affairs makes it possible to ascertain that the postulate of undertaking proper reflection is a realistic one and makes it also possible to comprehend better the social role of the intelligentsia.

Here, then, is the second consequence which can be drawn from Mannheim's conception. To the various other characteristics and appraisals of the intelligentsia as a stratum and of its social role the above can now be added, which certainly should not be made light of when discussing the role of the intelligentsia and its social prestige, even if the assertion itself sounds banal: the intelligentsia constitutes that part of society which, due to its education, is best prepared to undertake reflections on the limitations and deformations of human cognition, thus overcoming them and, in this fashion, perfecting human knowledge. The function of the intelligentsia in creating knowledge is, in fact, undertaken (or at least, above all) by that part of it which we call the creative intelligentsia or the intellectuals. This group, however, is a constant emanation of the intelligentsia as a stratum and without the existence of the entire stratum as a basis from which the selection of the individuals best suited to fulfilling this function takes place, the group of the intellectuals could not exist. Thus, Mannheim spoke of the intelligentsia as a stratum, of its social role and prestige. It may be ascertained, with sadness, that these are matters which are seldom understood socially and still more rarely put into practice, when it comes to the fitting of the appearances of the intelligentsia's social prestige to the functions actually fulfilled by it, and the merits, in the social sense connected with this.

Summing up our critical review of Mannheim's doctrine we may put into order the results of this review in the following fashion.

Firstly, an undoubted merit of Mannheim's sociology of knowledge rests in the fact that in developing and, to a certain degree, concretizing the corresponding ideas of Marx, it confirmed the conviction in the modern period, at least among competent scientific circles, that the process of cognition is socially conditioned, that both the shaping of a scholar's personality (in particular of his stands and inclinations), as well as the shaping of value systems and their selection in the process of cognition are subject to the overwhelming influence of social, primarily class, needs and interests. These are essentially Marxist ideas as Mannheim clearly notes. Already the fact itself of introducing these ideas to the so-called official academic milieu and their dissemination in this milieu in such a fashion that today they are already, in principle, regarded in the broadest circles of the world of science as a truism, is something quite significant and constitutes a right to scientific praise (even those who charge Mannheim—and correctly so—with relativism, do not by any means, deny a moderate version of his concept relating to the influence of social factors on the stand and views of scholars, which earlier would have been regarded as a heresy). These same people (this is undoubtedly an interesting psychological observation) who vehemently reject Marxist conceptions of the class character of cognition and, in particular, of ideology, today enthusiastically defend Mannheim's theory regarding ideology as a false consciousness, his concepts of the social "point of view", of the links of cognition with the social situation, in particular, in its class aspect and so on.

Secondly, it can be stated about Mannheim's conception that it is—in contrast to the definition of the devil in Goethe's *Faust*—a force which desires that which is good and does that what is evil. This pertains both to the conception of relationism which Mannheim violates and thus descends to relativism, as well as to the conception of "recalculating perspectives", as a path towards the overcoming of the subjective factor, and the role of the intelligentsia in this field. In the context of Mannheim's system these conceptions lead to inner contradictions and explode this system. Mannheim's sociology of knowledge is full of thoughts, suggestions and new ideas while those who in the heat of criticizing Mannheim's relativism throw out the proverbial baby with the bathwater do not perceive the strong aspects of his conceptions or disregard them, in order to facilitate their criticism (I myself belonged to this category) commit the cardinal error of so-called nihilistic criticism.

In bringing out the mental stimuli derived from Mannheim's sociology of knowledge one should not dull the edge in the criticism of relativism. As we have already pointed out, Mannheim's relativism is connected, above all, with his conception of ideology as a false consciousness and with the utilization of absolute truth as a measure, in contradiction to his own postulates, for judging the truth and falseness of views regarding social problems. This relativism gives rise to the danger of negating the possibility of the social sciences in general, and of history in particular, as well as to all the further troubles of Mannheim's doctrine connected, above all, with operations aimed at avoiding this danger.

From our point of view, however, the most important problem connected with the sociology of knowledge, and lying in the sphere of our interests, is the problem of the possibility of objective cognition and objective truth in the social sciences and especially in history.

As we have already stated the sociology of knowledge may be regarded as supplementary in this respect to presentism: in undertaking a certain segment of the problem matter raised by presentism it concretizes the issues, points out their particular aspects and states anew the problem of the objectivity of cognition. The central problem in this respect may be put into the form of a question: is objective cognition in the social sciences possible, if it has a class character?

We shall have to return to this problem once more and seek to provide our own answer to it. This is precisely why it is important not to lose sight of it and not to forget those thoughts, suggestions and partial solutions which the sociology of knowledge presents. As has been stated, they may not fit Mannheim's system, they may cause its incoherence, but this does not deprive them automatically of all heuristic value.

In connection with the central problem regarding the possibility of objective cognition, two other questions arise which, while forming, in fact, a part of the principle question, call, however, for a separate examination and distinct answers. These are:

Does every social conditioning of cognition with which a given "point of view" is linked lead inevitably to cognitive deformation?

Does every social conditioning of cognition with which its partial character is connected lead inevitably to falsehood (false consciousness)?

One more operation should be undertaken, *inter alia,* for the purpose of a more precise elucidation of the problems mentioned above. As is known, the sociology of knowledge avails itself of Marxist inspiration and propounds Marxist ideas of its own fashion. Much of that which is of value in the suggestions of the sociology of knowledge is derived from Marxism. Thus, it is logical to return to these sources, especially since our intention is to base our own conclusion consciously on Marxism. Therefore, the need to examine the concepts of the sociology of knowledge from the positions of Marxism is apparent.

Marxism and the Sociology of Knowledge

Contemporary sociology of knowledge links up consciously with Marx and Marxism. Are its troubles with relativism also inherited from Marxism? A negative answer to this question calls for proof based on pointing out the differences between the corresponding concepts of Marxism and of the sociology of knowledge. This is the more interesting and necessary since, if the substantiation were to prove convincing, we can obtain an advantageous perspective for a way out from the theoretical troubles of the sociology of knowledge while preserving its achievements in the realm of the interpretation of the process of cognition.

When we mentioned above that Mannheim based his ideas on Marxism, this pertains to historical materialism. We do not intend, of course, to present here the totality, or to give a full interpretation of the theory of historical materialism. We are interested, in particular, in certain concepts of this theory and shall focus our attention on them.

The sociology of knowledge is based directly on two elements of historical materialism—its theory of the basis and the superstructure, and its theory of ideology. Of what do the differences and similarities of the two doctrines in this respect consist?

The theory of historical materialism was expounded in a number of works by Marx and Engels, beginning with the early ones up to those of the final period of their creativeness. These are works of a theoretical character as well as attempts to apply the doctrine, especially in historical works. In our opinion, the works which are particularly important for our considerations here are the joint works of Marx and Engels, *The German Ideology* and the *Communist Manifesto;* Marx's *Theses on Feuerbach,* his preface to *A Contribution to the Critique of Political Economy, The Eighteenth Brumaire of Louis Bonaparte,* Engels' *Anti-Dühring, Ludwig*

Feuerbach and the End of Classical German Philosophy, as well as a number of letters (to Bloch, Mehring, Starkenburg and others) devoted to the problem matter of historical materialism. It is on these sources, above all, that we shall base our review and analysis of Marx's and Engels' views.

The theory of the basis and the superstructure takes up the question, which is central from the point of view of the sociology of knowledge, pertaining to the origin and development of human ideas and views, in particular in relation to social problems. Noting the existence and significance of such ideas and views and their diversity and variability in time, the creators of historical materialism posed a fundamental question: is this an autonomous phenomenon, a simple filiation of ideas spontaneously arisen, or is it a heteronomous phenomenon in the meaning that the consciousness of people (understood as an ensemble of their ideas and views) is derivative in relation to something else, which cognition in a given meaning of this word reflects? Marx and Engels answered this fundamental question with a statement equally fundamental from a theoretical viewpoint: human consciousness, being the reflection of the social existence of people, is heteronomous. This answer which sounds seemingly banal today (it has become trite for many due to its obviousness) had become from the time of its formulation a platform for much thought and many acute theoretical conflicts.

Marx and Engels maintained that it is not consciousness which determines social existence but, on the contrary, social existence which determines consciousness. Taking advantage of the possibility which the German language offers in this respect they expressed this thought in *The German Ideology* in a disputatious fashion, resembling a pun: "Das bewusstsein kann nie etwas anderes sein als das bewusste Sein" (Consciousness never can be anything else than realized existence).

The relation of social consciousness to social existence, although it did not by any means take on the nature of a unidirectional cause-effect dependence, as we know especially from Engels' correspondence on this subject dating from the latter part of his life, was presented by the creators of the theory in the image of a relationship between the basis and the superstructure. This is, of course, only an image but one which so appealed to the imagination that theoretical misunderstandings have arisen due to the overly literal comprehension of this formula. This impelled Engels in a later period to engage in a number of polemical interventions.

Social existence is called the "basis" upon which and depending on which (as Engels stated in the later period "in the final analysis", taking into consideration the mutual dependencies and influences between the basis and the superstructure) there arises "a superstructure", a complicated edifice of human ideas and views on reality, and of corresponding institutions.

The "basis" or, to put it differently, "social existence", was understood by the creators of the theory of historical materialism as a complicated structure of things and inter-human relations. Thus, they included *productive* forces, a category which includes both technological (instruments and machines) resources and people possessing the abilities to utilize a given technology. For the existence of a given mode of production it is necessary that the socially corresponding *relations of production* be present, together with the productive forces. The creators of the theory took this category to mean all the relations between people which, with the existence of given productive forces, are necessary for a real process of production to occur. Thus, these are diverse relations, from the organization of people in the direct process of labour to property relations regulating the rights of people, to instruments of labour and to raw materials. The productive forces together with the relations of production of a given period, whose mutual relations and adjustment play a large role in all of social movement and development, create that which we call the "social basis", "social existence", or "mode of production".

Changes in the "basis" give rise (in "final analysis" and hence in the process of mutual interaction) to changes in the "superstructure". The category of the "superstructure" is a name embracing social consciousness (ideas, views, theories) and corresponding institutions (legal views and institutions serving to implement them as, for example, courts). The theory proclaiming the dependence of social consciousness (the superstructure) on the mode of production (the basis) concentrates on the genetic conditioning of consciousness, as the reflection of objective reality in the mind of people, by means of this reality and its changes. Consciousness is neither completely self-generated (in the meaning of exclusive dependence on the will of the subject) nor autonomous (in the meaning of a pure filiation of ideas). It is a reflection, but a reflection of a special philosophical sense of the word and does not negate either a relative autonomy of its development or its mutual interaction on the development of the basis. It is impossible to predetermine how this reflection takes place and a number of Marxist theoreticians voiced the need for taking into consideration social psychology as a link which is intermediate between the motion of the basis and the superstructure (in the past, Labriola and Plekhanov, in the present, Eric Fromm, influenced by Marxism, in his theory of "Filters").

Anyone who accepts the theory proclaiming the influence of the basis on the motion of the superstructure recognizes, thereby, the social conditioning of consciousness and its changes. This general thesis finds its concrete application, in reference to social groups and individuals belonging to them, in the theory of the class nature of consciousness and cognition. If one accepts the social conditioning of consciousness due to its dependence on the basis, on social existence, then one recognizes, thereby, the influence on consciousness of the relations of production which are, after all, an indispensable component part of the basis. The relations of production and, in particular, property relations determine the division of society into classes which represent definite interests effecting also the cognitive attitudes of people. Since the interests of these social classes differ, or are even completely counterposed, then there is nothing strange in the fact that their influence on the cognitive attitude of people gives rise to divergent results in the products of their cognition.

Such is the theoretical foundation of the concept of the sociology of knowledge regarding the social conditioning of human cognition and the various "angles of views", as created by classical Marxist theory. However, for its fuller comprehension and, even more, for a proper appraisal of its relation to the sociology of knowledge, a presentation of the Marxist theory of ideology is called for.

In order to avoid a fundamental misunderstanding, which has been the cause of more than one inconsistency in the analysis of ideology, in general, and of Marxist ideology, in particular, it is necessary to elucidate initially what we intend to analyse, what questions we wish to pose in respect to the concept "ideology". One may question the definition of ideology and reply to this from a genetic, structural or functional concept of ideology,[22] but one can also pose a question regarding the character and value of ideological cognition and its relation to objective truth. It is true that these are connected problems but they are not identical. Therefore, one should distinguish a definition of ideology from answers to the question pertaining to the character and value of ideological cognition, even if it may assume outwardly the shape of a definition. The statement, for example, that "ideology is false consciousness" is exactly an answer to this question and not a definition, although it gives the appearance of a definition.

The concept of "false consciousness" in Marxist theory has been interestingly and, as far as I am aware from the corresponding literature on the subject, most profoundly presented and analysed in a sketch by Jerzy Szacki entitled "The Marxian Concept of 'False Consciousness'".[23] I do not agree with the author's main thesis that the concept of "false consciousness" is not gnoseological but solely sociological. This implies an interpretation of Marx in the categories of the sociology of knowledge, an interpretation which takes "false consciousness" to be a partial truth and not a deformation. Simultaneously, however, the author did not succeed in bringing out certain traits of the concept of "false consciousness" which, heretofore, have not been subjected to analysis, while the literature on the subject avoided them, failing to show any particular interest in them.

These problems include Szacki's differentiation of three types of "illusions" which Marx covered with the joint name of "false consciousness", that is:

(a) those which, according to Marxist terminology, created the "tone" of the epoch (Mannheim's "Denkstil") and thus pertain to the noological platform the society of a given epoch;[24]

(b) those which, still in Marx's terminology, create the "false consciousness" of a class and, thus, have a particularist significance;[25]

(c) finally, those which create the "false consciousness" of the ideologists.[26]

This differentiation of three types of "illusions" is based on considerable factual material drawn from Marx's and Engels' works.

Herein lies the significance of this typology; it sets the subject-matter in order and simultaneously renders its analysis more profound. It appears that modern sociology of knowledge is to a much more considerable and serious extent derived from Marx than it might seem at first glance.

Let us return, however, to the issue which interests us directly; to the definition of ideology in connection with its characterization as a "false consciousness".

We shall take up, in the first place, the *origin* of "false consciousness". The founders of Marxism linked this clearly with the division of labour and the separation of consciousness from historical data, that is, also from the division of society into classes and from the influence of class interest on the attitudes of the members of a given class.[27] This also explains why the ideology of a ruling class in a class society (Marx noted that the ideas of ruling classes are the ruling ideas in a given society) is always a "false consciousness" is distorted. This is why a social situation makes it possible to absolutize specific judgements and a specific viewing of the world from the position of the ruling class. A remedy can hence be found in the separation of general judgements and hypostasis concepts from their abstract shape. The defalsification of "false consciousness" can be achieved by its historical concretization, by placing a given ideology on the concrete basis of a *class* society. By extracting the class content of ideology we overcome its condition as a "false consciousness".

Hence, the postulate calling for the reducing of ideology to a determined class interest. This is a moderate postulate, for the aim is not (as was sometimes unfortunately done, giving rise to the opposition of the founders of Marxism themselves) to find for every idea an interest which gave rise to it but to interpret certain ideologies as a whole and refer them as a whole to the social interests and relations which constitute their genetic basis.

Marx, in employing the concept "ideology", referred to that meaning of the word which had become historically established from Destutt de Tracy through the Napoleonic tradition, bound up with Napoleon's distaste for "ideologies" which he identified with abstract reasoners, also inconvenient for those in power. Hence, the meaning was pejorative. Ideology is tantamount to "false consciousness", to a distorted vision of reality. The founders of Marxism even employed a corresponding image: the vision of social reality, as in a "camera obscura", upsidedown. But ideology was for them always class, *bourgeois* ideology.

One should note that for Marx and Engels their own theory, which constitutes the reflection of the interests of the proletariat, was not an ideology. It is precisely on the basis of this fact that Mannheim accused Marx of failing to apply the theory of ideology to his own views and, thus, not attaining what in the sociology of knowledge is referred to as the general and total concept of ideology.

Contrary to Mannheim, we believe that this was not an inconsistency, but a difference of conceptions, in Marx's favour. It made it possible for Marx to avoid those difficulties in which the sociology of knowledge is enmeshed.

Marx and Engels spoke of ideology to the end of their days as a "false consciousness". They did not employ such expressions which, since Lenin's times, have become current among Marxists as, for example, "proletarian ideology" or "scientific ideology" (from the Marxian understanding of the word "ideology" this last expression even contains a "contradictio in adiecto").

Marx and Engels did not set themselves the task of defining the concept of "ideology" in some broader meaning of this word, as utilized at present, but characterized solely the cognitive value of "ideology" in the narrower meaning then accepted, when the word "ideology" was by definition tantamount to class deformation of cognition. Hence, we are dealing with two cardinal differences in the employment of the word "ideology" by Marx and Engels and by modern theorists, Marxists included. Firstly, the present-day usage of this word is broader in its meaning than in the times of Marx and Engels: secondly, at present we pose distinct questions regarding the definition of "ideology" and its cognitive value, which was not done in Marx's era.

When Marx spoke of "ideology" this was tantamount to the expression "the bourgeoisie's class ideology" and its class conditioning explained the fact that ideology is, and has to be, a deformation, a distorted vision of the world. There are no reasons or need to defend the Marxian concept of "false consciousness" against identification with cognitive deformation. On the contrary, for Marx *it is* always a deformation and cannot be otherwise since, by definition, ideology is compared to an image in a "camera obscura". However, for Marx his own theory *is not*, as we have noted, an ideology, and he would have rejected such a suggestion with indignation. This brings into light the difference in the employment of the word "ideology" by the founders of Marxism and by modern theorists: no one today, including the Marxists (perhaps they, above all), will entertain any doubt as to the fact that Marxism is an ideology; Marx, on the other hand, considered that it was not, but then Marx understood the word "ideology" differently.

Mannheim charged Marx and Marxism with failing to apply the theory of ideology as a "false consciousness" to their own doctrine. In this respect Mannheim substituted for Marx and, acting on the assumption that he was in accord with the spirit of Marxism since he proclaimed that every ideology is a "false consciousness", formulated the idea of a general and total concept of ideology. It is precisely here that he departed from Marxism; he did not draw, in spite of what they seemed to him, consistent conclusions. Mannheim's error rested in the fact that he erroneously construed the formulation "ideology is a false consciousness" to be a definition of ideology and identified the word "ideology", as employed by Marx in respect to its content, with the meaning of the term "ideology" in contemporary language.

If Marx, as Mannheim had done later, really identified ideology in the present-day meaning of the word with "false consciousness", then he would not have escaped, similarly as the sociology of knowledge later on, the accusation of relativism. Marx, however, did not do so; on the contrary, he decidedly rejected such a generalization, endowing the word "ideology" with a narrower meaning.

Lenin and other Marxists in a later period did not identify ideology with false consciousness. They did, however, counterpose to bourgeois ideology proletarian ideology which is considered to be scientific, as distinct from non-scientific, for example, from religion or fascist ideology. None of the contemporary Marxists who struggle, after all, for the victory of proletarian ideology and battle in the name of scientific ideology, which they consider to be identical with Marxism, do not in the least consider that what is at stake is a "false consciousness''; on the contrary, they are convinced that Marxist proletarian ideology overcomes the "false consciousness" of bourgeois ideology. Simultaneously, they consider it undoubted that Marxist ideology is also *class* and even that it is *par excellence* class by nature, as a proletarian ideology. Is there no inner contradiction here? Do they not negate in this way Marx's doctrine, while officially defending it? Not in the least. While their starting-point is a different understanding of the word ideology they remain, simultaneously, faithful to the line of reasoning of their masters.

Marx ascertained the class conditioning of human views on social problems and endowed this observation with the form of theory. What is more, he understood also the functional role of ideas in social struggle, maintaining already in a work written in his youth that ideas as well can become a material force when they attract the masses. These are two fundamental elements of a functional definition of ideology. But, as we know, Marx did not employ the word "ideology" in a broad sense. In restricting it to a specific social phenomenon he did not negate, in the least, that such fundamental traits of "ideology" as the connection with the interest of a given class, and this both in the genetic as well as in the functional meaning (in the sense of the defence of this interest), are common to "ideology" in his own meaning, as well as in the meaning of other systems of views and convictions in relation to which he did not employ this name. What is important is not whether, as employed by Marx, the word "ideology" has a broader or narrower meaning, but how he saw and characterized phenomena which, at least partially, were regarded by him as covered by this name.

How then does the question of the definition of ideology present itself? The assertion that ideology is a false consciousness is not a definition. It is simply a statement determining the cognitive value of ideology (with a corresponding detonation of this concept) and only as a result of the ambiguity of the word "is" and the structure of the sentence does it resemble a definition. There is no obstacle in the way of constructing such a definition, while remaining in complete accord with the spirit and discoveries of Marxism: either a genetic one (views on social problems which are shaped under the influence of interests of a given social class) or a functional one (views on social problems which serve the defence of given class interests) or finally, a mixed, genetic-functional one. On the other hand, whether we consider ideology *always* to be a "false consciousness" (cognitive deformation) or not, depends on the scope of this term as accepted by us. In certain cases ideology is a deformation, and in others it is not, unless we were to determine, "ex definitione", that the term "ideology" is to be employed only for cognitive deformations.

Let us commence with a definition of ideology. In another work[28] we proposed the following definition: "Ideology" is a term for views, based on some accepted system of values, regarding problems pertaining to a desired aim of social development, views which determine the attitudes of people, i.e. their readiness to behaviour in given situations and their real behaviour in social matters.

This definition can be given a genetic-functional form: "Ideology" is the term for views on problems of a desired purpose of social development which are shaped on the basis of definite class interests and serve their defence.

Finally, one may carry out various combinations on the basis of these same elements, thus endowing the formulation of the definition with differing forms. In all these variants it will remain, however, in accord with the ideas of historical materialism, and it will not *presume* in any of them that ideology must imply a cognitive deformation ("false consciousness"). If one has not assumed, by definition, that "ideology" is a term for such views which due to class interests deform the image of society, then there is no obstacle—although one fully recognizes the class conditioning of human views on social problems—for these ideologies to be adequate and not deforming, as well as for them to be scientific, "quod, est explicandum".

If we do not tie our hands with the premise that cognition has a nature of passive reflection, and truth an absolute character (in the meaning of complete and eternal truth), if, in other words, we accept the third model (in accord with our typology) of cognitive relation (the activist interpretation of the theory of reflection), and if we take truth to be a process of accumulation of partial truths, then there is no reason why we may not consider class-conditioned truth to be true, and in this sense adequate. It is, after all, a reflection of reality, although always relative in the sense of its partiality, in a sense of a cognition which is incomplete and thus changeable in time. If we understand the term ideology in accord with the above cited attempts at definition, that is, more broadly than the meaning given to this word by Marx and his contemporaries, then, of course, we may deal with true and adequate ideologies (always with the mental reservation that we are not dealing with absolute truthfulness), as well as with ideologies which do constitute a class deformation and which are a "false consciousness".

With such an interpretation of truth and with such an approach to the problem of ideology it is also understandable that one may speak (as Marxists have been doing since Lenin) about scientific, non-scientific and even anti-scientific ideology. Starting *from the assumption* that ideology is by definition "a false consciousness", then the expression "scientific ideology" suffers from a "contradictio in adiecto". However, nothing impels us to accept such an assumption. If we accept a functional or a genetic-functional definition of ideology, then we may, and even should, pose the question as to what type of assertion a given ideology is based on; in the genetic sense, from what statements, views and convictions it is derived. If we state generally that ideology means human views regarding the aims of social development, or human views regarding the aims of social development which have arisen from class interests and which serve its defence, then we have not remarked anything, thus far, on the relation of these views to scientific theories. It is clear, after all, that they may be derived from scientific statements from which corresponding conclusions relating to the roads of social development are drawn, that class interests and their defence may be linked with science and be based on scientific foundations. It is also clear and well known in the history of thought that corresponding views may accept as a premise religious beliefs or pseudo-scientific ideas such as racism, that class interests and their defence may be linked with positions clearly contrary to science, with some type of mysticism or anti-scientific speculations seeking to pass themselves off as science. We know of ideologies of this sort, not from speculation but from experience and practice. What is more, we are able to determine, by analysing such examples, which classes are connected with which ideologies or, to put it differently, to which choices a specific situation and set of interests social classes are impelled.

In contrast to Mannheim, Marxism differentiates the class conditioning of cognition and, as a result, also the effects of this conditioning in the realm of the adequacy of the reflection of social reality by cognition, depending on the nature of the class and the relation of its interests to the tendency of social development. In particular, it distinguishes between "rising", revolutionary classes and "falling", conservative classes. This terminology is obviously metaphoric and image-like, but the meaning of the corresponding concept is clear. There are classes which struggle in accord with their interests for the abolishment of the existing social order which has become a brake on development; these are revolutionary classes as, for example, the working class under capitalism. There are also classes struggling, in accord with their interests, for the maintenance of the existing social order which is the foundation of their rule and the privileges derived therefrom; these are conservative classes and, in a situation of sharpened conflict, counter-revolutionary, as the bourgeoisie under capitalism. Since crises of a system and the conflicts and class struggles connected with them are bound up closely, according to the Marxist theory, with a dissonance and with growing contradictions between the developing productive forces and the relations of production, which tend to stagnation (due to the hampering influence of the ruling classes) within the framework of a given mode of production, the revolutionary classes represent the developmental tendency with which they identify themselves, in accord with their interests, while the conservative classes represent the departing system and their interests are clearly contrary to the developmental trend in society.

It is clear what influence such a situation can have on the attitudes (in the sense of a readiness to corresponding conduct) and the conduct of people belonging to one or the other class.

In a fashion which is most often unconscious but, at times, also fully conscious, the members and supporters of a class which finds itself objectively in a revolutionary situation, since their group and individual interest coincides with the developmental trend in society, are not subject to the mechanism of psychic restraints when it comes to reflecting in cognition that which is actually taking place in society; on the contrary, their interest leads to a more acute observation of the phenomenon of changes, of the disintegration of the old order and the manifestation of the birth of a new order whose victory they are expecting. Their cognition of social processes and their ideology, which is the groundwork of their social action, are a true, accurate reflection of reality since, in this respect, they do not encounter the restraints and obstacles derived for a corresponding social conditioning. It is clear, we repeat this only for the sake of safety, that this is a partial reflection, that this is a relative truth in the sense of being incomplete, since we are dealing with human cognition and the process-like character proper to it.

On the contrary, the members and supporters of a class, which objectively finds itself in an anti-revolutionary situation due to the conflict of its group and individual interests with the objective trend of social development, are subject to the mechanism of various restraints in the realm of the cognition of reality; their social situation drives them to a position of a conservative deformation of the image of reality. It removes, most often unconsciously, from their field of vision that which is contrary to the interests of the class; at times it consciously falsifies the image of reality and the regularities of its development. In any case, the cognition of social reality from the "angle of view" of the conservative class is conservative and in this sense deforming; the ideology resting at the groundwork of this class's social activity is earmarked by an antipathy towards the changes occurring and is thus directed against them. It is characterized by deformation, by "false consciousness".

Thus, we see that in the light of Marxist theory, maintaining consistently the position of a class character of cognition in the realm of social problems, we are not in the least impelled to identify *every* ideology with "false consciousness". In any case, this is not resolved by the indisputable fact that cognition is conditioned socially and on a class basis; cognition which would take place *outside* of a social, class *milieu* is simply a fiction. However, the character of cognition, *always* class based, differs, as we have seen, depending on the character, interest and place of a given class in the social structure. It may be adequate, scientific, in the sense of its truthfulness, when its bearer is a "rising" class and thus revolutionary, it may be deforming when its bearer is a "falling" class and thus conservative.

This position not only dissociates Marxism from Mannheim's sociology of knowledge but also, in one sense, counterposes Marxism to the sociology of knowledge. This was not understood not only by Mannheim, who charged Marxism with failing to apply to its own doctrine the theory of ideology as a "false consciousness", but also by authentic followers of Marxism. As a result they approached, as Mannheim does, the edge of a relativist scientific catastrophe. The position of the eminent Marxist historian M. N. Pokrovsky may serve as an example.

Pokrovsky considered all historiography to be ideology and on this basis rejected the possibility of utilizing even the factual material assembled by bourgeois authors. Pokrovsky answered the question pertaining to what is ideology thusly: "It is the reflection of reality in the minds of people through the prism of their interests, primarily their class interests. This is what ideology is. In this meaning every historical work is, above all, a sample of a distinct ideology."

So far, everything is in order, since he expressed the concept of the class character of ideology merely in a different fashion. However, Pokrovsky subsequently elaborated his understanding of ideology, and primarily of its cognitive value:

> All ideologies are composed of fragments of reality. There is no completely imaginary ideology; nonetheless, every ideology is a *distorting* mirror which in no way provides a *true reflection of reality* but rather something which cannot be compared even with the reflection in a distorting mirror. In a distorting mirror one can recognize one's face in accord with certain traits: there is a beard or there is no beard, there is a moustache or there is no moustache. Here, on the other hand, reality may be ideologically camouflaged to such a degree that a brunette may appear to be a blonde, while a bearded man may be as beardless as a cherub, etc. etc.[29]

The conclusion: every ideology is a "false consciousness". Marxist ideology is here in the same position as every other. Thus, there is no objective scientific truth in the social sciences; there are as many truths as there are classes, historical epochs and so on. Pokrovsky's conception, which he took from Bogdanov, is in accord with Mannheim's views (both positions were formulated more or less at the same time). It is characteristic that it is in accord also with the views of *presentism*, since it proclaims that history is contemporary politics projected into the past. In defending these positions Pokrovsky did not refrain from a total negation of the objective science of history and this not only in the sense of the class conditioning of an historian's views but also in voicing a more radical concept, that an historian selects his facts in an arbitrary fashion and interprets them subjectively on the basis of his class position. In characterizing the slogan of an objective science of history as a bourgeois invention, Pokrovsky wrote: "Bourgeois democracy, in its system of stupifying the masses, has elaborated the formula of 'objective history' which unfortunately, obscures the vision of many of our comrades even up to the present." [30]

The problem which we face rests precisely in the question whether, in the light of Marxist theory, objective cognition in the domain of social sciences in general, and in history, in particular, is possible. On the basis of the preceding arguments pertaining to the relation of Marxism to Mannheim's sociology of knowledge we have sought to show why, starting from certain common concepts of social conditioning of human cognition, Mannheim became enmeshed in relativism while Marxist's theory does not face this peril. These arguments also contained an implicit answer to the question whether objective cognition is possible, if one recognizes simultaneously its class, "partisan" nature. This issue deserves to be discussed separately.

In this connection it is necessary, however, to present a particular semantic explanation in order to avoid possible verbal misunderstanding. I have in mind here such expressions, often employed in Marxist vocabulary, pertaining to the characterization of cognition as, for example, "class based", "partisan". There are no particular troubles with respect to the first of these expressions; we have used it often and the implications connected with it are clear, if one understands the meaning of the sociological category, "social class". On the other hand, the word "partisan", which in everyday Marxist language is often employed as a determinant for the words "cognition", "attitude", "stand", and so on, does call for an explanation.

The word "partisan" appears in this context in at least three various, although linked, meanings. An understanding of their differences in content is imperative in order to avoid a logical error in reasoning.

Thus, firstly, we say that someone, for instance as an historian, takes a "partisan" stand (not only the Marxists use this now but also, for example, the presentists) when he assumes an "engagé" stand on the side of one of a number of competing and battling scientific schools. In this meaning one speaks of the "party" of idealists and materialists in philosophy, the "party" of advocates and opponents of historicism and so on. If I come out in favour of the concepts of one of these "parties" in science when I support its position and fight against the concepts of his opponents, then I take and "engagé", "partisan" stand.

Secondly, a "partisan" stand may signify representing the interests of a particular class within the framework of a given domain of science. In this meaning an economist who, for example, scientifically substantiates the superiority of socialism or, on the contrary, of capitalism, takes the stand of a particular social class and in defending its interests, by means of correspondingly formulated scientific theories, assumes a "partisan" position.

Thirdly, and finally, we speak of a "partisan" stand when someone in proclaiming particular scientific theories is in accord with the official line of a given political party.

It can be easily noted that the three situations dealt with above are linked together primarily by a common but ambiguous name. In addition, the differences are much more profound than the similarities, although in employing this word attention is seldom drawn to this fact which creates the possibility of very dangerous scientific confusion. After all, taking the side of a particular scientific theory (the first meaning) is something quite different from the defence of the position and interests of a given social class, derived from conviction (the second meaning), and even more different from disciplined subordination to party decisions (third meaning). What matters here is not so much, and not only, the difference in the meaning of the words, as the varying scientific values of these assorted problems concealed by an homonimous name.

"Partisanship", in the first instance of the meaning outlined above, is a significant matter from the point of view of analysing scientific cognition and its conditioning; what is more it determines a position which may be considered proper and desirable from the viewpoint of science and its representatives, a position of taking sides between conflicting positions in science. "Partisanship" in the second meaning of the word is interesting and significant, when it comes to analysing science from the aspect of the social conditioning of scientific cognition, that is, from the aspect of the sociology of knowledge. On the other hand, "partisanship" in the third meaning can be of interest as a sociological and psychological fact since, as we know from experience, such positions of scientists do, in fact, appear although from the viewpoint of science and the sake of its development they must be appraised negatively. No less than Marx himself wrote at one time that "The first duty of an inquirer of truth is to proceed towards it on a straight path, looking neither to the left nor to the right".[31]

In referring, further on, to partisanship pertaining to science and recalling all the three meanings of the word outlined above we shall be concerned with the first and second meanings. Thus, further on, we shall employ the word "partisanship" exclusively in these two meanings.

In accordance with Marxism, a student of society and, thus, an historian is subject to the influence of social conditionings connected with the epoch and common to all the people living in it ("the tone of the epoch"), as well as those specific to the class, social stratum and group to which the student belongs and which he represents in one way or another. His position as a student is tinged on a class basis and even if he is aware of this it is difficult to overcome. However, most often he is not aware of this fact and regards his own attitudes and actions as "purely" scientific, that is, not conditioned by any considerations outside science.

The class conditioning of a student's cognition implies his partisanship above all in the second meaning of this word, that is, in the sense of taking the side of the interests of a particular social class (partisanship in the first meaning or in the sense of taking the position in a conflict of scientific schools is indirectly bound up with class affiliation, but is autonomous to a considerable degree). Thus, let us take it as given that a student's cognition of social problems is conditioned on a class basis and is partisan in a given meaning of this word. In connection with this, two questions immediately arise: Does this not lead to relativism? Can cognition arrived at in this fashion be regarded as objective?

An analysis of the position of the sociology of knowledge and that of Marxism provides us with sufficient material for an answer. The recognition of the social conditioning of cognition does not lead in itself to relativism unless one were to accept simultaneously the premise that absolute truth is employed as a measure. If one does not accept such a premise, which leads necessarily to the absurd conclusion that the entire history of mankind consisted in the accumulation of falsehoods (that which we call partial or relative truths appear as falsehoods in the light of such a measure), then it is obvious that socially conditioned cognition (which in the case of *human* cognition is a necessity, while in accord with Dietzgen's formula, we shall not concern ourselves with angelic cognition) does, or at least can, furnish partial, but objective truth.

Such a presentation of the problem, which follows from our foregoing considerations, offers a solution to both the questions raised above.

Scientific cognition, although conditioned on a class basis, is objective cognition furnishing partial, objective truths.

This ascertainment abolishes the charge of relativism: *partial truth* is objective truth, while the concept of relativism that the truthfulness of a given view depends on a system of reference, that is, that it is a truth for some and not a truth for others, or that it is a truth in one period and not truth in another, is simply not so.

Notes

1. K. Mannheim, *Ideology and Utopia,* pp. 25-30, London, 1968.
2. *Ibid.,* p. 26.
3. *Ibid.,* pp. 27-28.
4. *Ibid.,* p. 77.
5. K. Mannheim, *Wissensoziologie Handwörterbuch der Soziologie,* pp. 659-680, Stuttgart, 1959. (Polish translation in *Przeglad Sociologiczny* ("Sociological Review"), vol. V, pp. 56-101 (1937).)
6. Cf. K. Mannheim, *Ideology and Utopia, ed. cit.,* p. 53, and *Sociology of Knowledge, ed. cit.,* pp. 57-58.
7. K. Mannheim, *Ideology and Utopia, ed. cit.,* p. 50.
8. *Ibid.,* p. 69.
9. K. Mannheim, *Sociology and Knowledge, ed. cit.,* p. 57.
10. K. Mannheim, *Ideology and Utopia, ed. cit.,* p. 69.
11. A. Schaff, "Mannheima socjologia wiedzy a zagadnienie obiektywności prawdy" ("Mannheim's sociology of knowledge and the objectivity of truth") in *Myśl Filozoficzna* ("Philosophical Thought"), no. 1, pp. 116-134 (1956).

12. K. Mannheim, *Ideology and Utopia, ed. cit.,* p. 68.
13. *Ibid.,* p. 70.
14. K. Mannheim, *The Sociology of Knowledge, ed. cit.,* p. 73.
15. *Ibid.,* pp. 90-91. (Emphasis—A. S.)
16. It is worthwhile at this moment to shed light on a certain unsuccessful attempt at criticizing the theory of the social conditioning of human cognition, a critique, which consistently pursued relationism overcomes. The meaning of this criticism, as employed by Ernst Grünwald (*Das Problem der Soziologie des Wissens,* Wien, 1934) and Maurice Mandelbaum (*The Problem of Historical Knowledge,* New York, 1938) rests in the charge lodged against the sociology of knowledge that it lapsed into a vicious circle in its reasoning. If one maintains that cognition is socially conditioned then this pertains as well to this very statement regarding the social conditioning, which undermines the entire reasoning. It is interesting to note that Mannheim himself had earlier drawn attention to this danger. ("Das Problem einer Soziologie des Wessens", in *Archiv für Sozialwissenschaft und Sozialpolitik,* Bd. 53, Tübingen, 1925) although his proposal to avoid this trap by recognizing thinking as the expression (*Ausdruck*) of reality of which thinking is a part, does not resolve the problem. However, by consistently differentiating relationism and relativism this problem can be successfully eliminated. The statement that cognition is socially conditioned signifies something other than the statement that the truthfulness of such cognition is a function of changeable circumstances and depends on who voices a given judgement as well as where and when. If the first stand is called relationism, and the second relativism, then it is clear that the second does not, by any means, follow from the first. Mannheim, anyhow, expressed this clearly (*ibid.,* pp. 580-581).

   Relationism, after all, proclaimed only the non-autonomous nature of cognition in the meaning of its social conditioning. It is clear that this refers also to the concept of the sociology of knowledge (as we know Mannheim also developed this aspect of the problem in an interesting fashion) as well as in the meaning of a definite "point of view" of this theory. But what follows from this? Only that we are not dealing here with absolute truth in the meaning of total exhaustive truths; but nobody maintains this. Hence, this is not relativism which attacks the concept of the objectivity of truth and thus the problem of the vicious circle, which seems so ominous, disappears.

   Werner Stark (*The Sociology of Knowledge,* London, 1958, pp. 194-196) attacks Grünwald's paradox somewhat differently. He summarizes Grünwald's position in the following way: If no statement pertaining to reality is an absolute truth, then neither is the concept of the sociology of knowledge which, after all, refers also to social reality; thus, it is false. Stark's criticism attacks the lesser premise of Grünwald's syllogism. The concept of sociology of knowledge, Stark stated, does not refer to social reality, but to the invariable traits of man as such and the way in which he constructs his spiritual world.

17. An interesting illustration of the concept that the failures of Mannheim's sociology of knowledge are bound up with an inconsistency in the carrying out of his own stand is his letter of April 15, 1946 to Kurt H. Wolff written in connection with the charges voiced against the sociology of knowledge during the seminar conducted by the latter. (Kurt H. Wolff published this letter in the essay "The sociology of knowledge and sociological theory" contained in *Symposium on Sociological Theory,* ed. by Llewellyn Gross, p. 571, Evanston, Ill., 1959. Mr. Rainko drew my

attention to this letter: ". . . if there are contradictions and inconsistencies in my work, then it seems to me that they are caused not so much by the fact that I do not perceive them, but rather by the fact that I seek to pursue every line of thought to its conclusion even if this contradicts other statements. . . .

"I hope that this is understandable or that it will at least convince you and your seminar that if contradictions appear they are not caused by my short-sightedness but by the fact that *I desire to break radically with the old epistemology although I have not been successful so far in doing this completely.* This does not rest, however, within the possibilities of one man. I believe that our whole generation will have to work on this since it is obvious that in every field we have already departed from the idea that the human mind is tantamount to absolute reason, rejecting this in favour of the theory that we think on the basis of variable systems of references, the elaboration of which is one of the most exciting tasks of the near future. . . ."

18. K. Mannheim, *Sociology of Knowledge, ed. cit.,* pp. 91-92.
19. *Ibid.,* p. 90.
20. It is worthwhile to draw attention to the similarity of Mannheim's conception to neo-positivism and especially to so-called radical conventionalism which maintained the dependence of the images of the world on the conceptual apparatus. Similarities also occur between this conception and the theories of linguistic relativism, in particular the so-called field theory (Jost Trier and others).
21. Maurice Mandelbaum, *The Problem of Historical Knowledge,* p. 82, New York, 1938.
22. Cf. J. J. Wiatr, *Czy zmierzch ery ideologii* ("The End of the Era of Ideology?"), pp. 67-74, Warsaw, 1966.
23. *Studia Socjologiczne* ("Sociological Studies"), no. 2, pp. 7–19 (1966).
24. "The 'idea' had always fallen into disgrace when it differed from 'interests'. On the other hand, it is easy to understand that any mass 'interest' clearing a path for itself in history, when it appears for the first time on the world's arena, surpasses in the 'idea' or 'imagination' its real boundaries and is considered as a *general,* human interest. This *illusion* gives rise to what Fourier calls the *tone* of each historical epoch." (Marx and Engels, *Collected Works,* vol. 2, p. 99, Warsaw, 1961.)
25. "Upon the different forms of property, upon the social condition of existence, rises an entire superstructure of distinct and peculiarly formed sentiments, illusions, modes of thought and views of life. The entire class creates and forms them out of its material foundations and out of the corresponding social relations. The single individual, who derives them through tradition and upbringing, may imagine that they form the real motives and the starting point of his activity." (K. Marx, "The Eighteenth Brumaire of Louis Bonaparte", *Selected Works,* vol. I, p. 247, Moscow, 1951.)
26. "But the democrat, because he represents the petty bourgeoisie, that is, a *transition class,* in which the interests of two classes are simultaneously mutually blunted, imagines himself elevated above class antagonisms generally. The democrats concede that a privileged class confronts them but they, along with all the rest of the nation, form the *people.* What they represent is the *people's rights*; what interests them is the *people's interests." (Ibid.,* p. 252.)
27. "Division of labour only becomes truly such from the moment when a division of material and mental labour appears. From this moment onwards consciousness *can* really flatter itself that it is something other than consciousness of existing practice, that it is *really* conceding something without conceding something *real*; from now

on consciousness is in a position to emancipate itself from the world and to proceed to the formation of 'pure' theory, theology, philosophy, ethics, etc." (Marx and Engels, *The German Ideology*, p. 20, New York, 1939.)

"Ideology is a process accomplished by the so-called thinker consciously, it is true, but with a false consciousness. The real motive forces impelling him remain unknown to him; otherwise it simply would not be an ideological process. . . . because it is a process of thought he derives its form as well as its content from pure thought, either his own or that of his predecessors. He works with mere thought material, which he accepts without examination as the product of thought, and does not investigate further for a more remote source independent of thought; indeed this is a matter of course to him, because, as all action is *mediated* by thought it appears to him to be ultimately *based* upon thought." ("Letter of Engels to F. Mehring", July 14, 1893, in *Selected Works*, vol. II, p. 451, Moscow, 1949.)

28. A. Schaff, *Język a działanie ludzkie, Szkice z filozofii języka* ("Language and Human Action, Sketches on the Philosophy of Language"), p. 122, Warsaw, 1967.
29. M. N. Pokrovski, *Istoricheskaya mauka i bor'ba klassov* ("Historical Science and the Class Struggle"), vol. I, pp. 10-11, Moscow, 1933.
30. *Ibid.*, vol. II, p. 394.
31. K. Marx, "Remarks pertaining to the new Prussian Regulation on Censorship", in Marx and Engels, *Collected Works*, vol. I, p. 6, Warsaw, 1960.

CHAPTER 4

Historicism and Relativism

"For to make relativism the basis of the theory of knowledge is inevitably to condemn oneself either to absolute scepticism, agnosticism and sophistry, or to subjectivism. Relativism as the basis of the theory of knowledge is not only the recognition of the relativity of our knowledge, but also a denial of any objective measure or model existing independently of humanity to which our relative knowledge approximates."

V. I. Lenin, *Materialism and Empirio-Criticism,* English ed., Moscow, 1947, p.135

On the threshhold of reflections on historicism we encounter a warning made by competent people: beware of the ambiguity of this expression.

Heussi, the author of a work on historicism, which was of considerable importance in the inter-war period, concluded his analysis of the meaning of the word "historicism" with the words: "What has been said so far shows how remote we are at present from a uniform application of this concept. Such confusion exists in its employment, *that no one should utilize it without defining, at the outset, what he understands by it.*" [1]

In a well-known French philosophical dictionary the item "historicism" concludes with the following warning: "One should avoid (this term) as most terms of this type since they lead easily to verbal discussions." [2]

It is sufficient to browse through a few selected works on historicism in order to become convinced that these warnings are correct. [3] The word "historicism" covers not only different but also quite contra- dictory meanings. It became, at one time, a true battle cry, in a positive sense for some and in a negative one for others.

It would be best, in such a situation, to refrain from using this word; however, it is very difficult and probably impossible to do without it.

"Historicism" has acquired such a permanent usage in the literature of the subject that it cannot be eliminated without the risk of employing an outlandish language. In addition, it has become "useful" and adapts itself well as a name for the collection of ideas with which we are concerned. Since some authors employ it to refer to various and sometimes very different collections of ideas then, in accord with Heussi's postulate, we should define, at the outset, the meaning in which we shall utilize the word "historicism".

We shall begin not with a definition but with an explanation of an historical nature. This will be an explanation by contrast, but such an approach is, at times, advantageous for obtaining a clear picture and a precision of meaning connected therewith.

As all authors of works on historicism emphasize, it is a trend which arose in opposition and even in struggle with the ideas of the Age of Enlightenment. We have in mind here, primarily, such consequences of Enlightenment rationalism as the concept of an unchanging human nature and of an unchanging law of nature. Thus, historicism is, above all, a tendency to interpret all of nature, society and man in constant motion and change.

This juxtaposition of the ideas of historicism and the Enlightenment offers us a proper prospective and the possibility of understanding the aim of those who fought under the banners of historicism regardless of other differences dividing them (we disregard totally odd usages of this word such as, for example, Popper's misleading terminology where "historicism" is defined as a method leading to historical prognostication).

Their aim concerned primarily a method of perceiving the world, its dynamics, its constant change in respect to things, animated nature, thought, etc. Troletsch's concept was not quite the same since he identified historicism with the historicizing of our knowledge and our cognition, that is, reduced it to a historicization of thoughts and ideas. Nonetheless, a common trend is apparent here: introduction of the factor of constant change into the image of the world.

However, the issue does not concern only how we see the world, but also how we comprehend and elucidate it. The result of interpreting the world as motion and change (as history) is an interpretation of everything that exists at present as the outcome of changes which have occurred in the past (hence of history in the meaning of an objective historical process) and as the starting-point of changes from which the future shall be born. A genetic explanation is the inevitable consequence of historicism. The problem of whether changes, to which reality is subject, always and continuously constitute a development (in the sense of a transition from "lower" forms) is already a question of conception and may be resolved variously on the basis of historicism in some general meaning of the word.

Anyone who recognizes these two principles is faced, nonetheless, as a result with a disturbing phenomenon which requires reflection and the taking of a stand. If it is really true that everything, all reality and its manifestations are in constant motion and change, then this pertains as well to human ideas, human principles, in particular, moral, etc. Historicism, by linking human ideas with historical cognition, thus leads to a negation of absolute principles. Does this not lead, however, to relativism, that is, to recognizing that a true idea in one set of conditions becomes false in others and vice versa? As we have previously stressed, relativism constitutes a danger to the very existence of science. Science is, in fact, impossible without the intersubjective objective cognition which is a negation of relativism. Is historicism actually identical, as some maintain, with relativism? Does it lead, as a result, to relativism? This is the problem with which we shall be primarily concerned.

We shall not enter into an analysis of the ambiguity of the term "historicism" on the basis of the particular meanings ascribed to it in the literature of the subject. This has already been done many times and, in addition, this is not the central problem for us. The relation of historicism to relativism can be extrapolated from the multitude of interpretations of the problem which actually exists, while we can satisfy ourselves with a projective definition. This will be a Marxist definition of historicism.

Marx stated once in *The German Ideology* that he recognizes only one science: the science of history which embraces both nature and society.[4] While this sentence was contained only in the manuscript and Marx himself struck it out, it nevertheless reflected certainly the position which corresponded to his views at the time. If the sentence were to be understood literally, then it would have to be regarded as erroneous; not only does history of nature and science, that is, a diachronic approach to reality exist, but a synchronic one as well. What is interesting and important for science is not only the discovery of the dynamic laws of reality but also of coexistential and structural laws. However, this sentence can—and in our opinion should—be understood not in a sense that negates the validity of any research, apart from the historical, but in the meaning that it emphasizes the particular significance of the latter and postulates a genetic interpretation of the subject of research. This does not, however, signify a negation of the value of research on the structure of the object or, still more, an *a priori* rejection. With such a moderate interpretation this sentence sounds like a declaration of faith in historicism. In what meaning of this word? In the meaning which is bound up into a coherent totality with all of Marxist philosophy, with all of the Marxist world outlook.

The dialectical view of the world, as developed by classical German idealist philosophy, and, in particular, by Hegel had a profound influence on Marx. It is true that Marx endowed it with an ontological interpretation completely counterposed to that of Hegel and consistently took the position of materialism, but the filiation of ideas here is distinct. These ideas were the philosophical reflection of the revolution in the realm of world outlook caused by the development of the natural sciences at the end of the eighteenth and beginning of the nineteenth centuries. Astronomy, geology, physics, biology and chemistry, as well as other strict sciences, continued, due to their discoveries, to furnish constant new proofs of the dynamic nature of reality. Darwin's theory of evolution was the supreme achievement in this domain. Marx's historicism was its equivalent in the domain of knowledge regarding social phenomena in respect to the strength of its cognitive influence.

At first glance, especially if one approaches the problem *ex post*, with hindsight, the statement that social phenomena are historically changeable may seem to be banal. The history of the problem shows, however, that it was not always banal. Proof of this may be found in the Enlightenment ideas referred to above pertaining to the unchanging law of nature and the unchanging nature of man. While divergent views had appeared earlier, mention may be made of Vico and of Helvetius' views on human nature during the Age of Enlightenment, it was nonetheless anti-historicism which was dominant. Classical German idealist philosophy and, above all, Hegelian idealism brought changes into this field as well, but it was idealism which endowed this conception with a metaphysical, if not a totally mystical character. The concepts which derive their stimuli from historiography itself developed on a different path, although closely linked with the dominant philosophical trends of the epoch. These were the positivist conceptions fought against by Hegel, whose supreme expression was to be found in the work of Ranke. Nevertheless, this is indubitably historicism in a particular meaning of the word. Marx's historicism was thus not an exceptional or distinct phenomenon, in the sense of a lack of analogous intellectual trends among his contemporaries. It was, however, a different historicism from that represented by his predecessors and his contemporaries, and it was original in this sense. What were the characteristic features of this historicism?

They embraced, above all, a radically historicizing interpretation of all of reality, both natural and social. However, this was not limited to an intellectual interpretation of this reality, to its *intellectual image* but pertained to *reality* itself; everything that exists is a becoming, is a process. All things and phenomena, as well as thought about them, are interpreted as processes, as becoming, in the meaning of a series which, from the arising of a thing through subsequent changes, leads to its disappearance in its former shape and to its transformation into a new shape. Marxism puts forth an additional concept according to which in the process of historical changes processes of development also appear, regarded as a transition from "lower" to "higher" forms. This dynamic, process-like vision of reality is the foundation of historicism in the meaning that everything that exists is interpreted from a historical viewpoint and *is*, in fact, history.

It may be stated that this most general principle of historicism is simply another expression of a dialectical vision of the world. This is undoubtedly so, but we find here, at the same time, a second characteristic feature of Marxist historicism. It is a historicism based on a consistently materialist ontology. Everything is a process, but "everything" is not only the thought about the world, not only our interpretation of reality but the world itself, reality itself, which is material and exists objectively, outside of any mind and independent of it.

Historicism, understood thusly, does not limit itself to an ascertaining of the dynamic, process-like nature of all of reality, but, as a result, recognizes that the cognition of every thing or phenomenon calls for reference to its history for a genetic explanation. This does not signify that the cognition of reality has an exclusively genetic character, that it rejects the examination of the structure of the object in the static sense, or that it neglects this aspect of the problem. On the contrary, historicism not only does not exclude examination of the structure, but recognizes it as an indispensable complementation of a genetic explanation. It is important, nevertheless, not to lose sight of the connection between these two methods of examination. From this point of view one can specifically understand the meaning of Marx's statement that he acknowledged only one science—history; this is simply a postulate for a genetic approach to the examination of reality.

Thus, by "historicism" we understand here the interpretation of all of reality, hence, both the objective world as well as its reflection in the minds of people, as a process of unceasing changes and development which leads, as a result, to the postulate for a genetic explanation of the phenomena of this reality.

Marxist historicism leads to two concepts which must draw our attention from the cognitive viewpoint: to the concept of the mutual connection of things and phenomena in the historical process which also effects the evaluation of the cognitive value of human ideas and to the concept regarding the concrete nature of truth.

In our previous considerations, especially those pertaining to the sociology of knowledge, we have already encountered the concept regarding the connection of human ideas and views with the conditions of the social environment, their "being tied" by these conditions ("Standortsgebundenheit" in Mannheim's terminology). This problem, when seen from the viewpoint of historicism, reveals, however, new aspects. Here this "Standortsgebundenheit" pertains to eternally changing historical conditions. This is the source of important warnings for every historian pertaining to the error of modernization or archaization in the interpretation of historical events, and also, of a conclusion regarding the concreteness of truth, which, methodologically, is extremely significant. What matters is not to create apparent generalizations by employing elliptical sentences, that is, sentences which contain partially defined and thus ambiguous expressions. On the contrary, when we enounce sentences pertaining to some historical processes, then we must concretize them from the point of view of their "Standortsgebundenheit", that is, in this case from the point of view of the historical conditions in which they took place. In opposite case, truth has an abstract character (by this we mean the failure to take into consideration the conditions of time and place) which transforms it either into a banality or into an utter falsehood.

The problem which now rests before us—similar, but not identical to that with which we were concerned in our previous reflections—consists of the question: does not the taking into consideration of the postulate of treating events in their concrete conditioning, and historical truth as a concrete truth, lead to relativism? Let us, in the first place, elucidate the source of this suspicion.

If all of reality is an infinite process of changes and development then, in accord with the above-cited attempt at a definition of historicism, man's cognition of the world is of the same nature. However, this signifies not only that the image changes together with the subject reflected by the human mind, not only that cognition is always *different,* but also that it is always *richer,* in a meaning similar to that which we employ when speaking about "richer" systems in mathematics. The historical process of the development of human cognition rests not only in the fact that our knowledge is constantly different, and not only in that it is ever richer, that we know always *more,* but primarily in that the changes do not have a purely additive, purely quantitative nature, but that they are *qualitative* changes. The difference between, for example, classical and quantum mechanics in the field of the cognition of the laws of nature is not purely quantitative; we not only know more, but we know in another way, and this in a qualified sense (not in the sense of a simple ascertaining of differences, but in a sense of such a "difference" which is the result of development, the result of a transition from lower to higher forms).

This may be expressed in another way. Cognition is an infinite process, not only because the subject reflected in cognition (in a special meaning of the word "reflected") is an infinite process of changes but also because the subject of cognition is infinite from the point of view of mutual relations and influences, of a specifically comprehended structure of things and phenomena which compose that what we call "objective reality". Starting, thus, not only from the category of change but also from the category of totality we attain, as a result, a comprehension of the process-like nature of cognition and, consequently, an understanding of the process-like character of truth and its concreteness.

It is here, however, that the trouble with relativism begins or, to put it more precisely, may begin, given a certain interpretation. If the subject of cognition is infinite (in both the dimensions specified above), then the cognition of this subject cannot be terminated and thus finalized. Simultaneously, being an infinite process, cognition is hence referred at each topical stage to the conditions of that stage. It is not absolute. Is it then relative?

The answer depends on how we understand here the word "relative".

Let us look at the problem from the point of view of the axiological aspect, which is classical in this respect. Historicism is opposed to all theories proclaiming absolute values (in particular moral ones), absolute appraisals (in particular aesthetic), absolute norms (in particular ethical). In all these cases of negation it employs the argument of empirically ascertainable historical variability. In the light of an historical analysis of the life of human societies, all absolutes—values, appraisals, norms—become dissolved and changeable and very different historical shapes appear in their place. They must be referred to specific conditions of time and place, to concrete historical conditions, since outside this context they cease to be comprehensible: why did the system of values (appraisals, norms) change? Why did it take on precisely such a shape and not another? and so on and so forth. If an absolute value (appraisal, norm) does not need a system of reference, since precisely due to its unchangeability it aspires to be a universal value, historicism does not admit an interpretation of them without the employment of a system of reference and thus interprets them relatively. In this sense, as well, historicism *is* relativist. However, philosophical relativism means something else and here again we face the ambiguity of the word which may lead to logical slips.

Philosophical relativism maintains not only that cognition is not endowed with an absolute nature and is historically conditioned (historicism maintains the same) but asserts, in addition, that the truthfulness of judgements is also historically conditioned (historicism does not maintain this in the least or, in any case, such a statement does not derive logically from the premises which it recognizes).[5] Thus, it is characterized by the conviction that the truthfulness of a given judgement depends on who proclaims the given judgement, and when and where; in other words, according to relativism, a true judgement in given circumstances becomes false in other circumstances and vice versa. On the other hand, historicism does not voice such a conviction, which is possible only in the case of elliptical judgements referred to above. On the contrary, historicism *ex professo* condemns elliptical judgements and replaces them by concretized historical statements. In consequence, historicism only maintains the historical changeability of cognition and hence its fundamental partiality on each actual stage of development, which does not mean that the same utterance is sometimes a truth and sometimes a falsehood, but that it is always a partial truth and that absolute truth is solely the boundary of an infinite process. If historicism thus rejects the possibility of attaining absolute truth, in the meaning of total truth in one act of cognition, then it also proclaims a type of relativism, taken as anti-absolutism. But here the words "relativism" and "absolutism" appear in a different meaning than previously. The crux of the issue rests precisely in this; the problem of the objectivity of truth is something quite different from the problem of its fullness and completeness. To put it differently, the issue of the objectivity and absoluteness (in the meaning of fullness and unchangeability) of truth should not be confused. Partial truth is not absolute but it is objective. The anti-relativist solution of the problem of historicism rests in this assertion.

In analysing historical relativism Raymond Aron started from an obvious ascertainment of the historical variability of moral, philosophical, religious and other views. According to him, the problem may be reduced to the question as to which arguments are employed in passing from this assertion to relativism. He distinguishes two basic arguments which bound up one way or another with the relativist systems. The first rests in the reduction of moral, philosophical, religious and other views to a changeable social reality, while the second, in the rejection of the cumulativeness of truths, i.e. on the rejection of progress. Aron speaks of this as the "Philosophy of becoming and not of evolution".[6]

The core of the argumentation of historical relativism has been grasped here and it is the second argument, the rejection of the cumulativeness of historical truths, which is particularly important for us. It is only under such a condition that relativist conclusions may be drawn from the ascertaining of the historical changeability of human views. It is *assumed* here, since it is bound up with a particular metaphysical background, that we are dealing with a series of views, unlinked with each other, that we are dealing not with evolution, not with development, but with mutually isolated phenomena which may be reduced to given historical conditions and the whole issue thus terminated. The unveiling of this peculiar mental mechanism is the best defence against the charge of relativism or against the voluntary dressing up of historicism in relativist apparel. In order to be able to do this, that is to accept a relativism thus comprehended, it is necessary, after all, to accept simultaneously a metaphysics which makes it possible to identify the absoluteness of truth with its objectivity, a metaphysics which permits a type of conduct contrary to the warnings which we have made time and again. Whoever assumes that truths which appeared historically are not cumulative and do not compose themselves into developmental series, assumes, thereby, that cognition which is not absolute in character is not objective. This is simply a falsehood which in this case serves a mythologization of historical cognition. Hence, not historicism, as such, should be identified with relativism, but only a certain interpretation of historicism which, with the aid of a definite metaphysics, assumes that which was supposed to have been proven.

In the literature of the subject one encounters very often the idea that the identification of the problem of the absoluteness of truth and of its objectivity is erroneous. This idea recurs precisely in the context of the struggle against the argument voicing the alleged necessary relativist conclusions derived from the acceptance of the concept of the historical or social conditioning of human cognition. We shall examine, as an example, one of such attempts, which is particularly striking, at least in its destructive part. We have in mind W. Stark's work on the sociology of knowledge; the arguments contained therein have, however, a broader significance, since they pertain also to the problem matter of historicism.

> The problem of truth—the properly epistemological problem—raised by the sociology of knowledge as we understand it, springs from the fact that every society sees, possesses and holds only one aspect of objective relativity, in other words, one part of the truth, but is inclined to regard it as the whole truth, beside which all other world-views must need appear erroneous. All human perception is limited; but all human beings are loathe to acknowledge their limitation. All concrete thought-structures have arisen through the realization of one limited possibility out of an unlimited potentiality . . . and yet the naïve assumption is almost always that this one possibility which has actually come to fruition is the only one that was antecedently possible. The fallacy with which the sociology of knowledge has to deal, so far as the search for truth is concerned, is thus the fallacy of *pars pro toto*—taking the part for the whole.[7]

According to Stark the sociology of knowledge, by rendering people aware of this state of affairs, that is by bringing out the partial nature of the truth which they attain, leads to a scientifically fertile modesty and humility. In this fashion the sociology of knowledge provides a valuable correction to the dangerous error which arises from the abuse of truth. Is this relativism? Stark answered this question in the negative. The problem of the partiality of truth is not a problem of its relativeness. All truth is absolute, Stark maintained, clearly interpreting the word "absolute" as "objective". The partial nature of truth gives rise, on the other hand, to the postulate of the co-ordination of partial truths, their synthesis.[8]

This line of reasoning is in accord with our final conclusion: historicism leads to relativism only when the problem of the absoluteness of truth (in the sense of its fullness) is erroneously identified with the problem of its objectiveness and when, as a result, the assertion that truth has a partial character is identified with the negation of its objectiveness. This, however, as has been already stated, is a fallacious premise which affects the appraisal of the value of historicism as a theory.

In the last three chapters we have undertaken an analysis of the objectivity of historical cognition as reflected in presentism, the sociology of knowledge and historicism. These are not, by any means, strictly delimited spheres of problems; on the contrary, they often intertwine and certain themes and arguments often repeat themselves. However, what we are concerned with here are different aspects of the same problem—the active role of the subject in the comprehension of social problems. Presentism accents the conditioning of the attitudes of the student of the past by his actual interests, while the sociology of knowledge broadens this subject-matter and is concerned with the influence of social conditioning on the "angle of view" of social problems in general; finally, historicism introduces the problem of historical variability of human views on social problems from the point of their cognitive value. Thus, the issue pertains clearly to one and the same problem—the problem of the objectivity of historical cognition, inasmuch as social problems are always of an historical nature. Nonetheless, the approach to this central problem (in the sense of a different perspective and different aspects) is varied. This is why it constituted a useful preparation for the considerations of the ultimate part of this work. They will be devoted to the problem of the objectivity of historical cognition from the meta-theoretical point of view. We shall take up a collection of problems with which we have already dealt in the second part of the work but we shall do so differently, not from the point of analysing particular theoretical trends pertaining to historical cognition but from the point of the problems connected with it. Thus, these will be considerations of an analytic nature but aimed clearly at an ultimate synthesis.

Notes

1. K. Heussi, *Die Krisis des Historismus,* p. 15, Tübingen, 1922.
2. A. Lalande, *Vocabulairie technique et critique de la philosophie,* p. 417, Paris, 1956.
3. See F. Meinecke, *Die Entstehung des Historismus,* Munich, 1936; E. Troeltsch, *Der Historismus und seine Probleme,* Tübingen, 1922; K. Heussi, *Die Krisis des Historismus, ed. cit.*; D. Lee and R. Beck, "The meaning of 'historicism'", the *American Historical Review,* no. 3 (1954); W. Hofer, *Geschichtesschreibung und Weltanschauung,* Munich, 1950.
4. Marx and Engels, *Collected Works, ed. cit.,* vol. III, p. 18.

5. Similar arguments are presented by Eduard May in his *Am Abgrund des Relativismus,* Berlin, 1942, for example, pp. 59, 63-65, etc.
6. R. Aron, *Introduction à la philosophie de l'histoiré. Essai sur les limites de l'objectivité historique,* pp. 369-370, Paris, éd. Gallimard, 1968.
7. W. Stark, *The Sociology of Knowledge,* pp. 155-156, London, 1958.
8. *Ibid.,* p. 60.

PART THREE

The Objectivity of Historical Truth

CHAPTER 5

Historical Facts and Their Selection

> The facts are really not all like fish on the fishmonger's slab. They are like fish swimming about in a vast and sometimes inaccessible ocean; and what the historian catches will depend, partly on chance, but mainly on what part of the ocean he chooses to fish in and what tackle he chooses to use—these two factors being, of course, determined by the kind of fish he wants to catch. By and large the historian will get the kind of facts he wants.
>
> E. H. Carr, *What is History?*, p. 18

We shall commence our reflections on the objectivity of historical truth quite naturally with the historical fact, if only for the reason that it is usually considered—and this is correct in one sense—that the differences in views among historians appear at the time when they commence to interpret facts, while the groundwork itself, assuming a certain level of knowledge and research techniques, is identical for all competent historians. Adhering to such a view it is possible to avoid the extremities of Ranke's school and to postulate the limiting of an historian's tasks to the exposition of "pure" facts, refraining from any interpretation or comments. It is sufficient, if one recognizes that in enouncing the word "fact", in reference to history, we express ourselves in an unambiguous fashion. Thus, if anyone has determined it for all the students of the problem and, therefore, historical facts as acts of research and the products of such determinations, are not subject to the influence of so-called subjective factors in the process of cognition, taken both in the individual as well as in the social meaning.

Anticipating our further reflections, we may state that in opposing the above position as a crude one we find ourselves in a situation analogous to that of a physicist who, taking the stand of quantum mechanics, must consider the present-day employment of the conceptual apparatus of Newtonian mechanics as the sole instrument in research and cognition to be crude and scientifically incompetent; or, and this example is even more convincing, in a situation analogous to that of a physicist who on the basis of contemporary knowledge regarding the structure of the atom would have to assume an attitude to the scientific claims of those who would wish in present-day research to apply the conceptual apparatus dating back to the beginning of the nineteenth century when, following ancient theories, the atom was regarded as the minutest, indivisable particle of matter in the shape of an elastic ball. Such a position is, of course, crude and shows a lack of competence and an ignorance of contemporary physics, but it is not simply only a falsehood. Under certain conditions Newtonian mechanics may and can be employed; Dalton's model of the atom does convey cognition which is true, in a certain respect, and its outdatedness in relation to contemporary knowledge is true also of other models, much more highly developed and more adequate such as, for example, Rutherford's. It follows from this well-known fact that the process of cognition is infinite, that every truth achieved at a given time within the framework of this process is only partial, and in this sense relative, and thus fated to become outmoded and overcome by more complete truth. It does not follow from this, however (we have discussed this more extensively in the first part of our work), that partial truth, the product, amongst others, of the present-day level of knowledge about the world, is not at all an objective truth, that it is simply a falsehood.

It is impossible at the present, without leaving oneself open to the charges of ignorance, to defend the concept that the atom is an indivisible, elastic material ball; similarly, it is impossible today to defend the concept that an historical fact is something like a brick which always and for everyone maintains this same shape and that different totalities may be built from these bricks depending solely on the fashion in which they are put together.[1] But it does not follow from this that it is a common falsehood. The task becomes the more difficult and the more complicated when, on the one hand, we wish to oppose the primitiveness of views which are unable to incorporate and take into consideration the role, obvious today, of the subjective factor in cognition and, on the other hand, without throwing out the proverbial baby with the bathwater, to preserve out of the theory of historical fact that which constitutes an objective truth within it.

In order to achieve this we must begin with an operation which is fundamental from the point of view of semantic analysis, to define precisely the expressions employed by us. Hence, let us begin with an attempt to analyse the expression "historical fact".

Carl L. Becker, the representative of American presentism referred to previously, was the author of one of the most interesting essays, in our opinion, on the subject of the historical fact. He commenced his elucidations in a way which brought out the subject exceedingly well and this is why we shall begin by quoting the corresponding passage:

> When anyone says "facts" we are all there. The word gives us a sense of stability. We know where we are when, as we say, we "get down to the facts"—as, for example, we know where we are when we get down to the facts of the structure of the atom, or the incredible movement of the electron as it jumps from one orbit to another. It is the same with history. Historians feel safe when dealing with facts. We talk much about the "hard facts" and the "cold facts", about "not being able to get around the facts", and about the necessity of basing our narrative on a "solid foundation of facts". By virtue of talking in this way, the facts of history come in the end to seem something solid, something substantial like physical matter . . . something possessing definite shape and clear persistent outline—like bricks and scantlings; so that we can easily picture the historian as he stumbles about in the past, stubbing his toe on the hard facts if he does not watch out.
>
> That is his affair, of course, a danger he runs; for his business is to dig out facts and pile them up for someone to use. Perhaps he may use them himself; but at all events he must arrange them conveniently so that someone—perhaps the sociologist or the economist—may easily carry them away for use in some structural enterprise.[2]

Ascertaining, further on, that things are only seemingly as simple and obvious as they appear, that the expression "historical fact" is just as ambiguous as the category "freedom", "cause" and so on, Carl Becker proposed, in order to elucidate the matter, a consideration of three questions: (1) what is an historical fact?, (2) where is it to be found? and (3) when does it appear?

Let us then, in line with Becker's proposal, start with the question: what is an historical fact?

In starting our reflections on the subject of the historical fact we employed an analogy from the domain of the nature sciences. Let us repeat here, as well, that the question what is a fact?, is by no means specific to history or the social sciences in general. It had appeared much earlier in the domain of the natural sciences along with the whole ballast of the role of the subjective factor. The conventionalists of the

French school led in this. The line of Boutroux-Poincaré-Duhem and Le Roy was of particular significance in this respect. Starting with the problem the role of language (conceptual apparatus), definition and theory in the development of science theyarrived (in particular Le Roy) at questioning the "independence" and "sovereignty" of the scientific fact, including in their conception also the "raw fact", that is, the fact which does not constitute a component part of some theory. Regardless of all the deformations of conventionalism, especially in the direction of subjectivism, its undoubted merit was to put forth the problem of the role of the conceptual apparatus in the building of science and, in particular, in the observation and formulation of so-called scientific facts.[3] Although this might seem odd in view of the special obviousness and importance of this problem in its field, history is retarded in its development in this respect and could, particularly as far as the active role of language in the study of historical fact is concerned, learn much, both in the positive sense and in the sense of warnings as to the dangers threatening on this road, from meta-theoretical reflection in the natural sciences.

Nonetheless, let us return to the question. In the first place it is necessary to define what we shall call an *historical fact* in the domain of history. Since this question is ambiguous and is, in fact, composed of a number of concrete questions, the answer to it assumes a different shape depending on the meaning which we ascribe to the question.

Let us begin with an elucidation as to what historical phenomena *may be* bearers of the term "historical fact". We state, after all, that Caesar's crossing of the Rubicon is an historical fact. Thus, a single event may be an historical fact (may be, but does not have to be; the overwhelming majority of everyday events, of which there are billions, is not placed by us into this category). Certain processes which point to specific regularities may also be historical facts: we say that the weakening of feudalism in rural areas by the growth of capitalist relations in the towns is an historical fact in the history of nineteenth-century Russia. Certain institutions and their role in social life (for example, the structure and functioning of the Diet in eighteenth-century Poland) may also be historical fact. The materialized products of certain events and processes, for example, constitutions, laws, etc., may also be a fact; material culture goods such as, for example, archaeological sites, ornaments discovered in old tombs, instruments of labour, pottery, scientific works, works of art and even preserved seeds of grains, etc., may be historical facts.[4]

Diverse elements and aspects of history in the sense of *res gestae* may also be an historical fact such as single events, long-term processes, processes earmarked by repetition, as well as various material and spiritual products of these events and processes. Thus, as can be seen, the scale of the possible designates of the term "historical facts" is very rich and varied. In principle, everything, every manifestation of man's social life *may be* an historical fact. *May be,* but does not have to be. Hence, let us distinguish clearly between an event which took place in the past (we may call it a "fact" in the sense of what had really occurred) and an historical fact, that is, such an event which, due to its significance for the historical process, has become (or may become) the subject of interest for history. It follows clearly from this that every historical fact is some event which had taken place in the past (a fact), but not the reverse, not every event of the past is automatically an historical fact.

This is an extremely important assertion since it follows therefrom that the "differentiam specificam" between what is and what is not an historical fact should be sought in the system of reference, in the specific context which transforms a usual thing or event into something qualified to such a degree that it is called an "historical fact". In our further considerations we shall deal precisely with this criterion which distinguishes historical facts from usual facts.

Let us now take up another aspect of the question: what is an historical fact? The issue now is to differentiate among the manifold manifestations of social life (facts) those which, in accord with the definition, are to be termed an "historical fact". Thus, the aim is not, as previously, to ascertain whether this term should be ascribed to some particular manifestations of life, to some special categories but, since it has been shown that potentially *all* manifestations of life enter into the picture, how a manifestation of life is to be qualified in order to have this term ascribed to it, which we do not ascribe to others belonging to the same typological group.

The definition of an historical fact usually begins with the assertion that it is a fact out of the past. This statement is true, but so banal as to be superfluous. Since we are dealing always with something which has already happened, even if in the given moment, then it is understandable that we are always speaking about facts out of the past since by definition nothing else can enter into the picture. Therefore, there is no need to dwell on this question. It is sufficient to state that all manifestations of the life of individuals and society may be an historical fact (understanding the dialectical connection between these apparent poles of contradiction, since an individual is always social and society exists always in the form of the action of individuals who compose it). They may be, but do not have to be. What is important here is to answer the question as to when this possibility becomes a reality.

Caesar crossed the Rubicon in 49 B.C. and this is undoubtedly an historical fact. But the Rubicon had been crossed before him and after him by thousands of people and we do not believe, in the slightest, that these were historical facts. To the question why, the answer in this case is easy: it is the context of this event which is essential, its connection with other events, both from the point of view of causes as well as results. Caesar's crossing of the Rubicon in 49 B.C. brought about the end of one societal form of ancient Rome and marked the beginning of a new one. The crossing of this river by thousands of other people did not have such implications. They were, as we say, historically insignificant; by this we mean that they did not bring about corresponding results.

A similar reasoning can be carried out in many varied fields of life, in respect to its different manifestations. There exist events and processes, as well as their different material and spiritual (for example, customs and usages) products which we do not hesitate to call "historical facts"; there are others, in this same category, to which we shall not ascribe this term; the former are significant due to their effects, the latter are not.

Thus, it is a certain context, a connection with a certain totality and a certain *system of reference* which determines the issue. The system of reference is extremely important for understanding the relative character of that which we term "historical fact". It is only when we become aware of this that it becomes clear why one and the same event, one and the same process or their material and spiritual products are insignificant historically in one interpretation and become important historical facts in another, and vice versa. The scholar searching for sources for the political history of a given country will pass by indifferently the testimonies of the culture and art of this country if they are not directly connected with political life; they will have no historical meaning for him. On the other hand, if he places them in the context of the history of a given country or a given epoch, they will become transformed (of course not always, but in any case they may become transformed in proper conditions) into important historical facts. This is a rather banal observation, but it is, nonetheless, important for an understanding of the concept "historical fact" which we are analysing.

Thus, it can be seen that historical facts are those manifestations of the life of individuals and society which have been selected from among many others, belonging to the same category, because of their cause and effect connections and interactions within the framework of larger totalities. It is the significance of a given event, process or of their products which constitutes the criterion of selection. A certain system of reference is therefore assumed, within which and due to which evaluation and subsequently selection takes place; the existence of the subject who undertakes this evaluation and selection is also assumed. Alongside the subject who is indispensable, an anthropological factor enters into the domain of historical facts, with all the complications caused by the active role of the subject and the influence of the subjective factor on the process of cognition.

The literature of the subject contains also a different view regarding this problem. It is worthwhile to become acquainted with this view, due both to the author and to the possibility of bringing out our own position more clearly.

Henry Levy-Brühl wrote in his article "Qu'est-ce que le fait historique?"

> Only a fact which has truly taken place may claim the status of a historical fact, i.e., a fact which has given rise to some effects in the past. However, if one takes into consideration that a fact cannot produce effects except in and through public opinion, then it follows rigorously that the historical fact is essentially a social fact. The statement that a certain fact caused effects means that it was reflected in a given milieu, either extensive or narrow. It is social opinion in respect to a given fact which endows it with an historical character. From this moment on the nature of a

given fact has little significance. Whether a fact is isolated or repeats itself, whether it is individual or general, is also of little significance. In the case where collective opinion has been formed regarding some fact, it belonged to history. In the case where no such collective opinion exists, we have no historical fact on hand.[5]

Three theses have been put forth here:

1. only a fact which has caused effect in the past is an historical fact;
2. an historical fact is a social fact since it can bring out effects only in public opinion;
3. an historical fact is shaped by public opinion.

It is clear, of course, that these three sentences should be taken together to form a certain whole. In the contrary case, treated separately, they are simply false. The statement that the criterion for qualifying certain manifestations of life as historical facts is to be found in the effect caused by them in the past, without an additional qualification of these effects, is tantamount to a recognition that every such manifestation is an historical fact since, after all, each one of them did produce some effect. Similarly, the statement that an historical fact is a social fact endows all the manifestations of life with the meaning of an historical fact, since all of them are social to one degree or another. It is equally easy to abolish the thesis that an historical fact is a fact constituted by public opinion since, apart from all other possible charges, this would signify an overwhelming narrowing of the concept "historical fact"; the eliminating from this category, for example, of all material products such as edifices, instruments and so on. On the other hand, the matter is different if one links these three sentences into a statement that, in addition, the expression "to cause effects" should be understood in the meaning "to cause effects in public opinion".

This position differs clearly from the one presented by us above due to its proclaimed idealism, interpreted in the spirit of Durkheim. Social facts are facts in the realm of collective consciousness: such an interpretation narrows the category of historical facts, eliminating from it everything which possesses a material character in the domain of products, as well as everything which is not consciously present in social life. The similarity of both positions rests, on the other hand, in the fact that in both cases the social significance of a given manifestation in the life of an individual or a society is taken as the distinctive criterion. However, here Levy-Brühl again limits the question to the effects brought about in public opinion and by this opinion, while we, on the other hand, extend the field of vision to all social effects.

The third version of the question—what is an historical fact?—pertains to its structure. What is at issue here is whether the fact is "simple" or "complex", as some would have it, or "partial" or "total", as others put it, or perhaps something else again.

Let us return to Becker's essay quoted above in which he commenced his discourse with this version of the question.

> First then, what is the historical fact? Let us take a simple fact, as simple as the historian often deals with, viz: 'In the year 49 B.C. Caesar crossed the Rubicon'. A familiar fact that is known to all and obviously of some importance since it is mentioned in every history of the Great Caesar. But is this fact as simple as it sounds? Has it the clear, persistent outline which we commonly attribute to simple historical fact? When we say that Caesar crossed the Rubicon we do not, of course, mean that Caesar crossed it alone but with his army. The Rubicon is a small river and I do not know how long it took Caesar's army to cross it; but the crossing must surely have been accompanied by many acts and many words and many thoughts of many men. That is to say, a thousand and one lesser "facts" went to make up the one simple fact that Caesar crossed the Rubicon; and if we had someone, say James Joyce, to know and relate all these facts, it would no doubt require a book of 794 pages to present this one fact that Caesar crossed the Rubicon. *Thus, this simple fact turns out to be not a simple fact at all. It is the statement that is simple—a simple generalization of a thousand and one facts.*[6]

In continuing this trend of thought the author emphasizes further on that Caesar's crossing of the Rubicon may be considered by us as an historical fact, as against the thousands of everyday facts of the crossing of this river, because we see and understand its connection with other events and circumstances, such as Caesar's relations with Pompey, the Senate, the Roman Republic; such as the Senate's order that Caesar should resign the command of the army in Gaul; such as Caesar's refusal to obey the Senate and the significance of his crossing the Rubicon in the march on Rome, etc. As a result of these reflections Becker concluded:

> The truth is, of course, that this simple fact *has* strings tied to it, and that is why it has been treasured for two thousand years. It is tied by these strings to innumerable other facts, so that it can't mean anything except by losing its clear outline. It can't mean anything except as it is absorbed into the complex web of circumstances which brought it into being. . . .
>
> Thus the simple historical fact turns out to be not a hard, cold something with clear outline, and measurable pressure, like a brick. It is, so far as we can know it,

only a *symbol*, a simple statement which is a generalization of a thousand and one simple facts which we do not for the moment care to use and this generalization itself we cannot use apart from the wider facts and generalizations which it symbolizes. And generally speaking, the more simple an historical fact is, the more clear and definite and proveable it is, the less use it is to us in and for itself. [7]

The thesis is clear: there are no simple facts, their simplicity is apparent and the illusion is caused by the simplicity of the statement which, in generalizing, disregards the richness of concrete reality. This reality in every case, even in the case of seemingly the simplest fact, the simplest assertions of single events, is composed of countless links of the given fact with other events, processes, their products in the context of which the given fact appears and is understandable. True reality is always a determinate totality and its elements possess countless ties and interactions. The so-called simple fact is precisely such an element taken out of the context of the totality. The shape of the statement referring to it is, in fact, simple, due to its abstractedness. However, if one were to transfer this simple form of the statement to the fact itself it would lose all meaning and would cease to be an historical fact.

Thus, there are no simple facts and all historical facts are immensely complex. Lenin had said once that an electron is equally infinite from the point of view of the possibilities of studying it and from its analysis as matter. "Mutatis mutandis", the same may be said of so-called simple facts in history.

Becker's analysis and his conclusion (his other conclusions to which we are opposed will be discussed later on) are correct and profoundly dialectical. It is well known that a badly posed question may confuse the entire process of research. If one takes some elements out of the context of a totality and if one assumes the abstractedness of a statement, as the "simplicity" of reality which is discussed in the given statement, then the blame for this does not rest with the "facts", but with the authors of these typologies and theories. This is precisely why we believe that a typology which separates facts into simple and complex or into partial and total, etc., leads to an error.[8] The boundaries between them are conventional and connected with the nature of the statement and not with the nature of the reality under discussion. It is not the fact which is simple but it is we (to facilitate narration, to simplify consciously a situation, by doing without details which are unimportant for us in a given context, etc.) who are interested in simplifying it; it is not the fact which is partial (and what is a "complete fact"), but it is we who are interested in bringing out only a certain aspect of the problem, etc.

Wanda Moszczeńska correctly protested against this typology and against the division of historical facts into "simple" and "complex". She maintained that historical facts are complex structures but warned against the temptation of reducing these complex structures to simple elements.[9]

Stefan Czarnowski took up this problem in an interesting fashion, approaching it not from the aspect of static typology but dynamically. In dealing with the analysis of the variability of social facts and their dynamics, Czarnowski wrote:

> Social facts differentiate and integrate themselves. This means that "complete" facts which show a many-faceted aspect decompose themselves in time into a series of facts of a particular nature; on the other hand, this means that facts possessing particular features, or different principle features and similar secondary features become a single whole. . . .
> This differentiation and integration are inevitable. Every fact, even the most primeval is complex. It contains within itself the possibility for an actualization of inner contradictions and identities. . . .[10]

This interpretation, although here, as well, "complete" facts are dealt with (the existence of "partial" facts is thus assumed), differs from the one mentioned above: here we meet with dynamics, a tendency towards . . . while the mutual dependence and the mutual transition of differentiation and integration is emphasized.

Therefore, the problem whether partiality or completeness, a simple or a complex character, may be ascribed to historical facts themselves (in the meaning of historical events) or to statements about them leads us directly to the fourth version of the question what is an historical fact? This time the question reveals the following problem: does an "historical fact" signify "an event from history", that is, some segment of the change *res gestae*, or does it signify a "statement about history", that is, some element of "historiae rerum gestarum", or, finally, does a third possibility exist?

Theoretically speaking, the expression "an historical fact" may mean both the first and the second. The advocates of idealism will maintain decidedly that it is a spiritual fact which is always involved, while the advocates of materialist views will emphasize the objective character of the historical fact (the element of *res gestae*). This dispute has important theoretical and methodological implications and deserves attention, if only for this reason.

Let us return, once again, to Becker's essay, which we have already quoted, who in this case comes forth decidedly as an idealist with the aim of buttressing presentism. He wrote:

> What then is the historical fact? Far be it from me to define so elusive and intangible a thing! But provisionally I will say this: the historian may be interested in anything that has to do with the life of man in the past—any act or event, any emotion which men have expressed, any idea, true or false, which they have entertained. Very well, the historian is interested in some event of this sort. Yet he cannot deal directly with this event itself, since the event itself has disappeared. What he can deal with directly is a *statement about the event*. He deals in short not with the event but with a statement which affirms *the fact that the events occurred*. When we really get down to the hard facts, what the historian is always dealing with is an *affirmation*—an affirmation of the fact that something is true. There is thus a distinction of capital importance to be made: the distinction between the ephemeral event which disappears and the affirmation about the event which persists. For all practical purposes it is this affirmation about the event that constitutes for us the historical fact. If so, the historical fact is not the past event, but a symbol which enables us to recreate it imaginatively. Of a symbol it is hardly worthwhile to say that it is cold or hard. It is dangerous to say even that it is true or false. The safest thing to say about a symbol is that it is more or less appropriate.[11]

We have quoted this entire long passage since it represents, in an exceptionally clear and expressive fashion, the idealist conception of an historical fact, furnishing thereby concrete material for discussion and controversy.

Becker's reasoning may be condensed in the following way:

(a) an historical fact is a statement about some event;

(b) the historian deals directly only with the statement, since the event itself has already passed;

(c) therefore, an historical fact is not the event itself, but a symbol which makes it possible to bring to mind the image of the event;

(d) in connection with this it is incorrect to qualify historical facts as "hard", or even to say that they are true or false; bearing in mind that we are speaking of symbols they should be qualified as more or less appropriate.

It is, of course, points (b) and (c) which are central in this reasoning and reflections should thus be started from them.

Is it correct to state that since we are unable to observe *directly* the events of the past, because they have already lapsed, then we deal *directly* only with statements regarding these events or with judgements about them? Let us draw attention to the circumstances that this apparently pertains solely to historical fact; in fact, this pertains to all of cognition which does not take place in a given temporal moment and, since the "moment" is an idealization for, in reality, we are always dealing with processes extended in time, this pertains to the *entirety* of our cognition. Hence, this is nothing more than an idealist credo and it is also clearly a case of *subjective idealism*. This is, however, only an observation and not an argument against Becker's thesis. What arguments do we have?

Let us commence with the word "directly" which appears so innocently in Becker's reasoning.

Is it true that when we say "Caesar crossed the Rubicon in 49 B.C." that we do not observe directly how Caesar crossed the Rubicon, but only imagine this? It is without doubt that Caesar does not cross the Rubicon in the moment when we speak of this. But then no one maintains this. If anyone were to expect such a "direct" experience, then he should be locked up in an insane asylum. This question, is in any case, completely meaningless for the issue of the objectivity of our cognition, that is, for the problem of whether that which we state corresponds to some event which had really taken place. Our problem pertains precisely to this objectivity of cognition and not to verbal juggling connected with the use of the word "directly".

In order to realize clearly what the dispute rests in, let us separate ourselves for a moment from the historical fact dealt with in the sentence about Caesar crossing the Rubicon and let us draw our attention to any indicative sentence, such as the thousands of which we make use of in everyday life. I utter the sentence: "I met Henry on the street yesterday"; the truthfulness of this statement can be verified not only by Henry and myself, but also by some friends who were present and the photograph which one of them took during the meeting. But Carl Becker comes forth and says: "You are not dealing directly with the fact of this meeting since the event has already passed but you are dealing directly only with a statement asserting that this meeting had taken place and hence it is not your real meeting which is a fact but only the statement—the symbol of that meeting.'' In everyday life we would simply wag our head and look at the person we were talking to with indulgent pity if he had made such a remark. But anyone who deals with philosophy or enters into philosophy through meta-theoretical reflection does not have the right to employ everyday gestures. Thus, we cannot simply wag our heads but we must argue and show the falseness in our opponent's reasoning. Herein, lies also, to a considerable degree, the art and the difficulty of philosophizing.

Experience teaches us that in the case of paradoxical statements (and the statement of our respected opponent is precisely paradoxical when transferred from the sphere of remote history to that of everyday life) the key to stumblings in reasoning should be sought in a verbal error, most often connected with the ambiguity of words. If we approach thusly the statements made by Becker which interest us, then it is the word ''directly'' which must give rise, above all, to suspicion.

Becker says that ''we are not dealing *directly* with the fact of Caesar crossing the Rubicon, but we are dealing *directly* with a statement about this fact''. Transferring this trend of reasoning to everyday events we can say similarly: ''we are not dealing *directly* with the fact of X and Y meeting yesterday, but we are dealing *directly* with a statement about this fact.'' What is the meaning of the word ''directly'', twice used here by Becker, and what philosophical consequences are derived therefrom?

This word is connected with the old problem, well known to philosophers which has, at times, given rise to considerable troubles in the history of philosophy. Given a certain interpretation of the meaning of this word we do not perceive or come to know anything *directly*; not only passed events, which is obvious, but also events, things and phenomena which we perceive and come to know actually, even in the very moment of perception itself. After all, that tree which I am perceiving right now exists apart from me objectively (unless in the spirit of extreme idealism I should wish to deny even this) and I experience only an observational impression; hence, I do not receive the tree ''directly'' (in a particular understanding of this word). What then should be said regarding complicated cognitive actions in which no mention could be made of the sensory perception of the object studied in any other way than by means of its effects (for example, in microphysics). In such an interpretation of the problem, and this is true of Becker and the school represented by him, it is only our experiences which are given us "directly"; hence, it is only the position of immanent idealism which is acceptable and rational. This is nothing new for those who are acquainted with the history of empiricism and the wasteland of immanentism, derived from exactly this sort of thinking. On the other hand, proof is provided once more for the thesis that anyone entering into the domain of philosophical reflection (any meta-theoretical reflection is decidedly of this kind) should be acquainted with the history of philosophy; in the contrary case, he faces the peril about which Engels spoke in his time, that the lack of consciousness will lead him into the embraces of the worst possible philosophy, an electic one.

Let us return, however, to the word "directly". If one ascribes such a great significance to this word in reasoning then one should define one's meaning. Becker did not do this and he himself fell into the trap of ambiguity. In saying: "An historical event, since it has already passed is not given us *directly*" with which one has to agree, he put forth the thought, by counterposing, that we come to know the event indirectly, while what we are given directly are only the appropriate sources and the material products of given processes which have lasted up to the present. To our astonishment, however (Carl Becker is, after all, a professional, who knows the historian's metier), we hear that statements, judgements about events and, hence, some spiritual experiences are given us *directly*. This is an error, not only from a factual point of view (for it is difficult to consider the pyramid of Cheops or an authentic copy of the Magna Carta as only a spiritual experience) but primarily from the formal point of view. This second "directly" has, after all, a different meaning from the first and a logical slip-up caused by the ambiguity of the term has obviously occurred. In the first case, when we say "directly" what matters is whether we observe the given object or event *ourselves,* obtaining information about them not by means of other observers (contemporary or those deceased, but who have left their testimony in writing) or of material traces of this object or event (sources, products, effects of actions observable elsewhere) but by means of our own observations. In the second case, when we say "directly" we have in mind the answer to the philosophical problem "what is given in cognition?"; in fact, we are resolving here the dispute between materialism (realism) and immanent idealism. As we have stated, Becker interprets in this case the word "directly" in the spirit of immanent idealism which is not all that extravagant philosophically, considering that scholarly tracts are written in order to prove that not only the objects of the real world, but even sensory impressions are not given us "directly" in cognition.

The trouble rests in that Becker confused these two problems which are linked together, but nonetheless different, and has drawn the conclusion from the banal assertion that we cannot be eyewitnesses of past events, that it is only statements about these events which are given us *directly*. But why? Logically speaking, we are dealing here with a clear "non sequitur"; in fact, it is quite obvious that the sources and the material products of past events, etc., are given us directly (in the first meaning of this word). If an immanentist philosopher denies this he has in mind not historical facts, but the image of the world as a whole. This is, nonetheless, another problem and these two issues should not be confused with each other and, even more, it is impermissible to draw conclusions from one about the other only because in both cases the ambiguous word "directly" is employed.

The issue does not rest, however, only in the ambiguity of words and in logical slips. What matters also is the fetishization of direct observation and thus of cognition (in the first of the meanings of this word outlined above). Is it important for historical cognition (as well as for any other kind) for it to be the action of a single subject and an act of eye-witness participation in all the processes and events being studied? Of course not, such a postulate is nonsense and, if taken literally, would signify a negation of human knowledge. No one can observe and know everything himself as an eye-witness in any field. Considering that science has, by definition, an intersubjective character, this is not only impossible, but also unnecessary. Such vagaries may only enter into the mind of a philosopher of the most outlandish category, those upholding subjective idealism, with a clear tendency to solipsism.

Hence, how do we answer the question posed by Becker, what is an historical fact? An historical fact is an element, a segment of "res gestae", i.e. an objective event in the past (we add the word "past" by pedantry, since if we are not speaking of the future, then all the events about which we can speak belong already, in fact, to the past). The direct or indirect nature of historical cognition, as well as the degree of its exactitude, etc., are problems of another type and do not enter into the definition of an historical fact. On the other hand, a statement regarding historical events may itself become an historical fact if in some fashion it played an historic role and influenced the course of history. To identify the category of an historical event is an erroneous view, contrary to the accepted meaning of this expression and derived from a specific philosophical position erroneously generalized as currently accepted.

It is possible to agree with one of Becker's assertions, although for completely different reasons from those on which he based his own ideas. An historical fact cannot be qualified as true or false, since this is a qualification which pertains to judgements about reality, but not to reality itself. It is also improper, as Becker maintained, to qualify an historical fact as "raw" (he employs the terms "cold" and "hard"), although here too the causes are different from those indicated by Becker (according to him "an historical fact" is a symbol and symbols may be defined only as appropriate or not).

W. Moszczeńska took a position regarding the ontological status of the historical fact which is completely opposite to that of Becker. She distinguishes *a fact in history* (a particle of historical reality which constitutes a relatively isolated system) as a fact which really occurred at some time from an *historical fact* (the object of study) understood as a "particle of this reality separated by the mind through isolating it from a larger totality from which it was, in fact, impossible to isolate it."[12] The historical fact, according to her, is a correspondent of the fact in history but a correspondent which is distorted to a certain degree. She concluded:

It is easiest to grasp the issue from the view of both the concepts. From the aspect of methodological reflection historical facts are those facts which are known or will be known to science, since information regarding them has been preserved in relics of the past, that is, in *historical sources.* . . . Every historical fact is a fact in history, on the other hand, only a minute part of facts in history are historical facts, that is, facts of the historical past about which we know or shall know that they once took place.[13]

Moszczeńka's position shows a number of different aspects. It is possible to agree completely and without reservation with some of them, while others give rise to doubts or even to opposition.

The author's assertion that an historical fact is always a part of objective historical reality, "rerum gestarum", is undoubtedly correct. This is a materialist position counterposed to an idealist conception of facts (for example, C. Becker's).

Nonetheless, a rigid division and even counterposing of facts in history (a particle of historical reality) to historical facts (facts in history known to science) gives rise to doubts for the following reasons:

If we raise every fact in history (that is, some particle of history) which has left a trace (an historical source in the broadest meaning of this word since, according to the author, it includes also living traditions) to the rank of an historical fact, then we devalue thereby this category which thus loses its meaning. The criterion for distinguishing historical facts from among the mass of events, processes and their products which is proposed here is not their particular significance within the framework of a given system of reference, but the fact that they have left a trace. What follows from this? That *every*, literally every, such fact of reality is an historical fact since we cannot speak at all about historical events of which we know nothing (they have left no trace). In this fashion we return to the starting-point: if *all* things in the past are historical facts, then the historical facts which we know from history should be called something different and the criterion for their distinguishing should be questioned anew. In addition, this rigid division into facts in history and historical facts gives rise to an agnostic conclusion: after all, facts in history which have not left a trace do exist. Not only are they not historical facts but, in addition, they constitute a truly Kantian "thing in itself", unknowable, and hence we may assuredly ask how do the authors of such views know at all that such a "think in itself" existed, since by definition, they cannot know anything about it (since no traces of it exist)?

If the intention of the author—to counterpose the materialist position to the subjective-idealist—was undoubtedly praiseworthy, then the fulfilment of this intention followed a false path. It would seem that the solution to the problem troubling the author should be sought not by means of distinguishing two categories of facts, facts in history and historical facts, but by analysing the dual aspects or dual strata of one and the same historical fact which is a particle of objective reality (the second component of the alternative is idealist speculation floating off into the clouds of mysticism) a particle not only known to people but, due to its objective cause and effect links with the historical process, appropriately qualified by the historian.

This leads us in a natural way to a consideration of the fifth version of the question what is an historical fact? It is complementary in reference to the question regarding the structure of the historical fact (simple or complex) but separate, belonging to the domain of gnoseology. The issue here is whether the historical fact is "raw" (that is, does not contain an admixture of the subjective factor) or whether it is the result of the action of the historian and, through him, of a definite theory.

We have mentioned above that similar problems in the domain of the natural sciences were raised much earlier by conventionalism which answered this question in the negative. The conventionalists, Le Roy particularly, in negating the existence of "raw" facts (*le fait brut*) referred to the active role of language (conceptual apparatus), definition and theory, in the constituting of the so-called scientific fact; it was thus, according to their own interpretation, an ultimate point, a result and not a starting-point. The theorist of history acts in a similar fashion although the concrete starting-point of his reasoning is different.

Let us return once again to Becker since, regardless of his idealist trend, his remarks on the subject of the objectivity of historical cognition and on the historical fact are accurate and interesting. His starting-point is the critique of the positivist ideal of history presented as "wie es eigentlich gewesen", which assumes the possibility that an historian does not contribute anything to this cognition, except "the sensitive plate of his mind on which objective facts would register their own, unquestionable meaning" (*op. cit.*, p. 129). In opposing such authorities as Ranke, Fustel de Coulanges and others Becker emphasized that the historian is not only unable to exhaust all the facts in undertaking a selection among them but is also unable to exhaust even a single fact, that is, he is unable to present any particle of reality with all its ramifications. Even within the scope of the so-called historical fact we must carry out a selection of the material of which this fact is composed.

> ... But by no possibility can the historian make affirmations describing all of the facts—all of the acts, thoughts, emotions of all the persons who contribute to the actual event in its entirety. One historian will, therefore, necessarily *choose* certain affirmations about the event, and relate them in a certain way, rejecting other affirmations and other ways of regulating them. Another historian will necessarily make a different choice. Why? What is it that leads one historian to make, out of all the possible two affirmations about the given event, certain affirmations and not others? Why, the purpose he has in mind will determine that. And so, the purpose he has in mind will determine the precise meaning which he derives from the event. *The event itself, the facts do not say anything, do not impose any meaning. It is the historian who speaks, who imposes a meaning.*[14]

The issue of historical events, facts and their mental reflection in the shape of judgements regarding facts is formulated correctly here (in spite of Becker's previous assertions, that a fact is solely a mental symbol). An event, a fact is an objective element of the past, linked by an infinite number of threads with the reality of which it is a fragment. In coming to know this particle of objective reality, that is, the given historical fact we must select from among the infinite number of these links those which interest us within the framework of a given system of reference (from the historian's viewpoint this is his research aim). In this way we endow the historical fact with a specific meaning, thus constituting it as a *scientific fact.*

What is important for us in this exposition is the emphasis placed on the role of the historian as the cognizing subject in historical cognition. This is banal in the light of what has been stated in the first part of this work regarding the cognitive relation and the active role of the cognizing subject (the third model of the cognitive relation). However, when we apply this general formula in a concrete field of research and refer it to the historical fact, its heuristic strength appears anew.

We must distinguish carefully the "fact", as an objective historical event, and the "fact", as its reflection in the human mind, in cognition. The objective historical fact has a definite ontological status, of extreme importance for the entirety of the conception. But is also possesses a definite gnoseological status. From this point of view the historical fact interests us, not as a Kantian "thing in itself", but as a "thing for us". It is precisely from this viewpoint that we speak of raw facts and theoretically interpreted facts, from this viewpoint, as well, it should be clearly stated that "raw facts" are as devoid of meaning as the "thing in itself", that is, as any radical agnosticism. The ontological assertion that something, in this case the historical fact, exists objectively, that is, the rejection of the subjectivist concept which states it to be the creation of the cognizing mind is one thing; the gnoseological assertion that it is an *image* in the human mind is something else. This is exactly what we are talking about in referring to the possibility of the presentation of "raw facts". Since we are dealing with the process of cognition, with a cognitive relation, then, by definition, the cognizing subject and its active role in cognition enters into the picture, which affects the postulated "raw facts", supposedly free of such interference, with an error of "contradiction in adiecto".

Thus, there are no "raw facts"; by definition they cannot exist. The facts with which we deal in science, or even in cognition in general, are always earmarked by the subject and there is no subjectivism in this assertion. Starting with what we recognize as a fact, through its appropriate constitution on the basis of the selection of its appropriate components, the delineation of its temporal, geographical and material limits, up to its interpretation, the cognizing subject constantly interferes, as do its multifold conditionings and, above all, the theory on whose basis this operation takes place.

Let us repeat once more for the sake of caution: the selection of material which goes to constitute an historical fact is not arbitrary. The connections referred to, the mutual interactions, etc., exist objectively and are neither the creation nor the invention of the historian. A conception of this sort, clearly idealist, is anyhow impossible on the basis of the recognized ontological status of the historical fact as a particle of objective reality, a particle of history. The historian contributes to the constituting of a fact a determined *selection* of objectively existing material, objectively present connections and mutual interactions, etc. The criterion of selection, as well as the criterion of endowing the chosen material with an inner structure, differ depending on the theory which rests at their foundation. Some theory must rest at the foundation of this action, if one does not assume that the selection is accidental so reducing such a position to an absurdity. It is clear, of course, that the results of such different selections are also varied.

Thus, in spite of positivist prejudices, it is not so that we first accumulate facts *per se*, "without assumptions", and then let them speak for themselves and, hence, it is necessary solely to beware of the historian's comments which deform reality. On the contrary, it is understandable on the basis of the analysis of cognition, as theorists of history are evermore clearly aware, that the observation and formulation of facts is the result of influence of theory. The theory precedes the determination of facts, although it is in its way based on them.

E. H. Carr, already quoted many times, wrote:

> In the first place, the facts of history never come to us "pure", since they do not and cannot exist in a pure form; they are always refracted through the mind of the recorder. It follows that when we take up a work of history our first concern should be not with the facts which it contains but with the historian who wrote it.[15]

Similarly, we read in Lucien Febvre's work:

> And ultimately the facts . . . what do you call the facts; what meaning do you put into this little word "fact"? Do you think that the facts are given to history as substantial realities, which time has secreted more or less deeply and what matters is simply to excavate, clean and present them to your contemporaries in full light? Or do you recall and use the phrase of Berthelot, exhalting chemistry immediately after its first triumphs, chemistry, *his* chemistry, the only science among all, he said proudly, which *produces its object*. In this Berthelot erred. For all the sciences produce their object.[16]

Theorists of history pose more often and more clearly the question: what is the starting-point in an historian's work, the so-called raw fact or theory? Increasingly they take the second possibility to be the proper answer.

Christopher Blake quotes the following sentence of Oakshot on this subject: ". . . he (the historian) is represented as starting from a 'bare fact' whereas it is safe to say that he never does so, because such a starting place is impossible—he begins with an interpretation which he interprets."[17]

H. J. Marrou wrote: "Logically the process of elaboration of history begins not with the existence of documents but with an original operation—the 'posed question' which impinges on the choice, the delimitation and the concept of the subject."[18]

It is worthwhile noting that Marxist theorists of history currently defend similar positions. Igor Kon, for example, starting with the evolution of the concept "historical fact" (the transition from individual fact to historical processes) simultaneously emphasized the close links between fact and theory.

> Such "facts" as the movement of prices, the differentiation of social classes, the concentration of landed property, primary accumulation, etc., cannot be represented anymore in full as something individual, singular which could be described without resorting to "theoretical generalizations". It has been proved that the dependence between "facts" and "generalizations" is a mutual dependence . . . *the "historical fact" has become in a certain sense not only the premise but also the result of the quest.* [19]

Witold Kula formulated this still more sharply in his beautiful essay "The Historical Fact and the Appraisal of its Significance":

> The historical fact is a scientific construction since, as we have said, it delineates the chronological, geographical and material boundaries of a certain complex of phenomena. The history of historical writing is acquainted with scientific disputes which resulted from a differing delineation of each of these. [20]

In the conclusion of the essay we read:

> Every construction and selection of facts was accomplished on the basis of some knowledge regarding society (or rather some impressions regarding society) and its functioning. . . . The variety of criteria, according to which historians throughout the centuries have constructed and selected facts, testify to the vitality of history. [21]

In this fashion we have come to the end of our analysis of the meanings hidden in the question, what is an historical fact? We have enumerated five of these or we have gained five possible subjects for reflections connected with these questions. They are:

Firstly, in asking what is an historical fact? we ponder as to what such a fact can be; we answer that it may be an event, a process or their products in the field of social life.

Secondly, this question aims at elucidating which fact deserves the qualification "historical": the answer is that the distinguishing criterion rests on the significance of a given fact for social development, which always presupposes a system of reference.

Thirdly, this question pertains to the structure of historical facts, in particular, to the validity of distinguishing between simple and complex facts.

Fourthly, we inquire as to the ontological status of the historical fact; whether it is a segment of "rerum gestarum" or a statement about such a segment.

Fifthly and lastly, we question the gnoseological status of the historical fact, that is, whether historical facts are "raw" or the result of the interference of theory.

An examination of these five versions of the question, what is an historical fact? makes it possible to review a broad scale of problems. At present there remains to be considered the problem which arose in connection with the analysis of the fifth version of the question, that is, the problem of the selection of historical material as carried out by the historian. However, if during the analysis of this last version of the question we were interested primarily in the problem of the selection of material making up an historical fact, then at present it is the problem of the selection of historical fact from among the mass of events, processes and their products which the historian passes by in his consideration, since he did not qualify them to the category of historical facts, which comes to the foreground. This problem arose *en passant* in the course of our reflections up to the present moment but due to its significance it is necessary to pay closer attention to it and to undertake a systematic analysis of it.

This should be done especially, because the problem of the selection of historical facts, thus presented, is strictly bound up with the question discussed above, regarding the constitution of facts through the selection of appropriate historical material. In carrying out such a selection of material in order to determine a given historical fact and thus constituting it in a certain sense gnoseologically, we are, thereby, undertaking a selection of historically important events (historical facts) from amidst a mass of historically indifferent events. Nonetheless, an opposite assertion is equally true: in undertaking a selection of historical facts from amidst historical events—and we accomplish this always on the basis of some theory or hypothesis which constitutes here a system of reference—we also determine the direction of the selection of historical material which constitutes the given fact.

If, in our role as historians, we were to face the past without any conception, any theory or hypothesis (formulated consciously as a scholar usually does, or spontaneously imposed by practice as usually happens in everyday life), then we would be helpless in meeting with the chaos of an infinite quantity of events, processes and their products, each of which could potentially claim the role of an historical fact. When we say: an "historical fact", this pertains not only to the objectivity of the event, etc. (in the sense that each one of them *is* an historical fact), but to a particular qualified objective event, in the sense that we recognize its significance which qualified it as an historical fact, as such a fact which is referred to by history due to the influence it exerts on other events and, by this means, on the course of history. Here once more the complicated nature of the historical fact is revealed which from the point of view of its ontological status is a segment of *history*, of objective reality and from the point of view of its gnoseological status is, just as in all other cases of cognitive relation, a product of a specific mutual interaction of the subject and the object. While remaining a solid element of objective reality, which exists outside of any cognizing mind and independent of it, the historical fact is simultaneously a specific product whose origin is affected by the mind of the historian.

Thus, it is not similar to the positivists' belief that historical facts *themselves* emerge from other events or historical processes because they are important and historically significant and the historian should only register and present them. This is an overly primitive position which cannot be maintained in the light of the achievements of the modern theory of cognition. No event will "emerge" by itself from among others, it will simply remain one of the events. The "importance" or "significance" of an event is an evaluating qualification which calls for the existence not only of the evaluated object but also of the evaluating subject. This is an obvious assertion for anyone who understands what a cognitive relation is and what role the subjective factor plays in it (this was already discussed in the first part of this work and we refer back to these concepts only for the sake of caution); this pertains *a fortiori* to the relation of evaluation. It is not odd in the least and not a negation of materialism in the theory of cognition, or of the theory of reflection (at least in its specific interpretation) to state, as we do, that the historical fact is a result and a creation of theory. It is on the basis of a determinate theory that the historian undertakes the *selection* of objective events and historical processes, choosing those which he "promotes" to the dignity of historical facts. This is the source of the notorious fact that historians often differ in this respect (that is their selection is not accepted by all), or that what in certain periods or by the historians of a certain school was by-passed as an event of no historical significance, becomes raised to the dignity of an historical fact in other periods or by historians of another school.

Why does this occur? In answering this we shall refer to the opinion of E. H. Carr, whose merit is that with a true English sense of humour he said what should have been said in this case.

> When you read a work of history, always listen out for the buzzing. If you can detect none, either you are tone deaf or your historian is a dull dog. The facts are really not at all like fish on the fishmonger's slab. They are like fish swimming about in a vast and sometimes inaccessible ocean; and what the historian catches will depend, partly on chance, but mainly on what part of the ocean he choses to fish and what tackle he choses to use—these two factors being, of course, determined by the kind of fish he wants to catch. By and large, the historian will get the kind of facts he wants. History means interpretation. Indeed, if, standing Sir George Clark on his head, I were to call history "a hard core of interpretation surrounded by a pulp of disputable facts", my statement would, no doubt, be one-sided and misleading, but no more so, I venture to think, than the original dictum.[22]

The eminent French historian, Lucien Febvre supplemented this statement of Carr's in a specific fashion:

> Have you not heard your elders repeat: "the historian has no right to chose facts". What right? In the name of what principle? To chose, in striking against "reality", hence against the "truth". Always the same idea; the facts, the little cubes of mosaic, quite distinct, quite homogeneous, beautifully polished. An earthquake has scattered the mosaic; the cubes have been buried in the ground; let us excavate them and, above all, let us remember not to lose a single one. Let us gather them all. Let us not chose ... they have said this, our masters, as if due to the accident which has destroyed one trace and preserved another (we do not speak here of the human fact) all history were not a choice. And if there had been no accidents there? In effect, history is choice. Arbitrary, no. Preconceived, yes. ...
>
> Hence, without a preceding theory, a preconceived theory, no scientific work is possible. Theory, the construction of the spirit which corresponds to our needs to comprehend, is the experience itself of science. . . . An historian who refuses to consider the human fact, an historian who professes a pure and simple submission to these facts, as if the facts were not in the least his own fabrication, as if they had not been chosen by him to start with, in all the meanings of the word chose (and they cannot avoid being chosen by him) is a technical assistant. He may be excellent. But he is not an historian.[23]

These quotations are overlong but it was worthwhile to give them. These are, after all, statements by "pur sang" historians engaged, in addition, in meta-theoretical reflection with a consciousness of its implications. "Quae est mutatio rerum" one is inclined to say in the name of positivist historians, when one listens to these words. Nonetheless, it is impossible not to admit the correctness of the innovators. At most it seems desirable to add some warnings to their words against the dangers which threaten if, following them, one crosses certain boundaries. But this does not undermine the correctness of their words.

The problem rests, above all, on the subsequent, undoubtedly objective dilemma: in the process of the life of mankind in infinite quantity of events, processes and their products appear which could be historical facts; in addition, connections, mutual dependencies and interactions between them also appear. Only an insignificant part of these attain the dignity of historical fact, while others do not. Why does this happen?

The answer emerges spontaneously that these are precisely those important facts which played some role in the development of society. This is all right. But how do we know this? After all, these facts in themselves bear no special identifying marks. In addition, historians and in particular historians belonging to various epochs, differ, sometimes very seriously, in the appraisal of these facts. The promotions of heretofore unnoted facts to the role of historical facts and, in turn, the decline of others, once upon a time considered to be significant, to the category of everyday facts, deprived of historical importance, must strengthen our scepticism.

It is, of course, the man who examines the historical process, the historian who decides that some facts, and not others, are ascribed historical importance. But this is not, in the least, an act of individual self-will, of pure subjectivism and individual arbitrariness. The historian himself is a social "product", he himself has been shaped in the spirit of some theory and is its exponent.[24] Thus, it is the historian's historical background, the theory applied by him, in itself a social fact, which determines the selection of facts. It is precisely in this sense that the theory *precedes* the facts.

Thus it is interpretation which promotes ordinary facts to the rank of historical facts or which casts them down from this pedestal. In an arbitrary fashion?—we repeat Febvre's question. Of course not. Firstly, because the events, processes, etc., themselves have an objective character; they are not the product of the historian's mind.

Secondly, because the historian's decisions are determined by the theory which he embraces. Thirdly, because he is conditioned socially by the interests of his epoch, the class to which he belongs, etc. Nonetheless, bearing in mind this social correction, he brings the subjective factor into historical cognition. Since this sounds perilous, let us repeat once more that in embracing such views one does not sin against materialism or against the theory of reflection. On the other hand, one gains the fact that it is possible to be in accord with the modern theory of cognition and with the attainments of those particular sciences, which, such as linguistics, psychology, the sociology of knowledge, etc., expand by their concrete research the horizons of our knowledge about man and the process of cognition.

Hence, it is the historian who undertakes selection, although this is not an arbitrary selection. He undertakes a selection of material which composes the content of the fact (constituting it in this meaning); he undertakes a selection of historical facts from amidst everyday facts of life. Therefore, it is correct to assert that there are no "raw" facts; the so-called "raw" facts are also the result of some theoretical elaboration and, in addition, their "promotion" to the category of historical fact is not a starting-point but the result, the point of arrival. Even if we deal with such a simple sentence as "The battle of Grunwald took place in 1410" which is either true or false, depending on whether the judgement is in accord or not with reality, the recognition of this fact as historical is, nonetheless, the result of the acceptance of a definite system of reference (political history) and of a definite theory. Nothing is changed here by the circumstances that certain facts (as, for example, the fact of the battle of Grunwald) will be recognized as historical on the basis of all theoretical systems; nonetheless, these are not "raw" facts, that is, historical "in themselves", without the undertaking of an appropriate selection on the basis of a definite theoretical reflection.

In the light of what has been said above we may conclude our reflections with an eloquent quotation from Carr's work:

> The historian and the facts of history are necessary to one another. The historian without his facts is rootless and futile; the facts without their historian are dead and meaningless. My first answer therefore to the question What is History? is that it is a continuous process of interaction between the historian and his facts, an unending dialogue between the present and the past.[25]

Notes

1. The comparison and reasoning is taken from Lucien Febvre who criticized the positivist conception of "histoire historisante" (cf. L. Febvre, *Combats pour l'histoire*, pp. 114 ff., Paris, 1953).
2. C. L. Becker, "What are historical facts?" in the *Western Political Quarterly*, no. 3, 1955, as quoted by H. Meyerhoff (ed.), *The Philosophy of History in our Times*, pp. 120–121, New York, 1959.
3. The reader may find more precise data on this subject in A. Schaff's *Z Zagadnień Marksistowskiej Teorii prawdy* ("On Problems of the Marxist Theory of Truth"), Warsaw, 1951, Chap. 6, "Conventionalism". This chapter contains much factual material which may be useful for examining the problems concerning us here, although the author does not sustain any longer either the aggressive tone of the criticism or still more the one-sided critical evaluation of conventionalism (also of so-called radical conventionalism). This one-sidedness caused the disappearance of the interesting problem raised by conventionalism as well as its original contribution to the problem of the role of the subjective factor in cognition and, in particular, to the problem of the active role of language in this respect.
4. See C. Bobińska, *Historyk, fakt, metoda* ("The Historian, Fact and Method"), pp. 24–25, Warsaw, 1964. M. Bloch, *Apologie pour l'histoire ou mêtier de l'historien*, Paris, 1967. I. Kon, *Idealizm filozoficzny i kryzys burżuazyjnej myśli historycznej* ("Philosophical Idealism and the Crisis of Bourgeois Historical Thought"), pp. 316 ff., Warsaw, 1967.
5. H. Lévy-Brühl, "Qu'est-ce que le fait historique?", in *Revue de Synthèses Philosophique*, vol. XLII, p. 55, Paris, 1926.
6. C. L. Becker, "What are historical facts?", *ed. cit.*, pp. 121-122. (Emphasis—A.S.)
7. *Ibid.*, pp. 122-123.
8. For example, C. Bobińska (*op. cit.*, pp. 22-23) writes that "Formerly science made use of particular internally non-contradictory events" which is a misunderstanding since an event is neither internally contradictory or non-contradictory. W. Kula in his *Rozważania o Historii* ("Reflections on History"), p. 66, Warsaw, 1958, spoke of "physical facts" (birth, death, execution, etc.) as the simplest elements of an historical fact, followed this same path and, in addition, contradicted his own correct observation that physical events become an historical fact only "through the social location of this phenomenon (*ibid.*, p. 62). Thereby, the appearance of "simplicity" vanishes.
9. W. Moszczeńska, *Metodologii historii zarys krytyczny* ("A Critical Outline of the Methodology of History"), p. 102. Warsaw, 1968.
10. S. Czarnowski, *Definicja i klasyfikacja faktów społecznych* ("The Definition and Classification of Social Facts"), vol. II, pp. 231–232, Dziela, Warsaw, 1956.
11. C. L. Becker, "What are historical facts?", *ed. cit.*, pp. 124-125.
12. W. Moszczeńska, *Metodologii historii zarys krytyczny, ed cit.*, p. 47.
13. *Ibid.*
14. C. L. Becker, *op. cit.*, pp. 130–131. (Emphasis—A.S.)
15. E. H. Carr, *What is History?* pp. 16–17, London, 1962.
16. L. Febvre, *Combat pour l'histoire, op cit.*, pp. 115-116.
17. As quoted by C. Blake, "Can history be objective?", in P. Gardiner (ed.), *Theories of History*, pp. 330-331, Glencoe, Ill., 1959.
18. H. J. Marrou, "De la connaissance historique", *op. cit.*, p. 61.

19. I. Kon, *Idealizm filozoficzny i kryzys burżuazyjnej myśli historycznej* ("Philosophical Idealism and the Crisis of Bourgeois Historical Thought"), p. 316, Warsaw, 1967. (Emphasis—A.S.)
20. W. Kula, *Rozważania o Historii, op. cit.,* pp. 63-64.
21. *Ibid.,* pp. 72-73.
22. E. H. Carr, *op. cit.,* p. 18.
23. L. Febvre, *Combats pour l'histoire, op. cit.,* pp. 116-117.
24. Various reviews of my anthropological works have criticized me for the ugly word "product" utilized in this context; this is undoubtedly Marxist jargon, but the word corresponds exceedingly well to the thought it is to transmit and I am unable to find a better one. Anyone who knows Marxism will understand that a vulgarized and simplified usage of this word is not involved and, therefore, the whole problem is only apparent.
25. E. H. Carr, *op. cit.,* p. 24.

CHAPTER 6

Description—Explanation—Evaluation

> Vous recueillez les faits. Pour cela vous allez dans les Archives. Ces greniers à
> faits. Là, il n'y a qu'a se baisser pour en récolter. De pleines panerées. Vous les
> posez sur votre table. Vous faites ce que font les enfants quand ils s'amusent avec
> des 'cubes' et travaillent à reconstituer la belle image qu'on a brouillées pour eux.
> . . . Le tour est joue, l'histoire est faite. Que voullez-vous de plus? Rein. Sinon:
> savoir pourquoi. Pourquoi faire de l'histoire? Et donc, qu'est-ce que l'histoire?
>
> Lucien Febvre, *Combats pour l'histoire*

The eminent French historian Lucien Febvre ended with the above
words one of his polemical essays directed against the conception of
factographic history, "histoire historisante".

The questions are significant. Does history, as a science, limit itself,
and can it limit itself to a "pure" presentation of facts, to a "pure"
description? And, if not, what should and can history deal with, what,
in effect, is it?

A negative answer to the first question is implicitly contained (apart
from the sporadic explicit statements in the course of other reflections)
in our considerations up to this moment. No, history is not, and
cannot be, "pure" description and the postulate of history presenting
the past "wie es eigentlich gewesen", in the interpretation of this
programme in the spirit of its creators, is a scientifically harmful
fiction. Firstly, because the historian cannot erase his active role as the
cognizing subject from the cognitive relation of which historical
cognition is also a form; hence, he cannot avoid an introduction of the
subjective factor into cognition which is always, almost by definition,
"partial", "partisan", in the sense of the conditioning of the
historian's cognitive perspective by the social relations and interests
marked out by the epoch and social milieu in which he lives (not to
speak of the conditioning of this perspective by his individual

psychosomatic structure). Secondly, because the basic category of the postulate of "purely descriptive" history, of "histoire historisante", the category of the historical fact, introduces into cognition a complicated system of interactions of the subjective factor; it is not a guarantee of "pure" objectivity of cognition, of the "eradication" from it of the subjective factor, as the creators of the positivist trend in historical thought erroneously assumed but, on the contrary, the historical fact, as a scientific category, brings into the foundations of historical writing (if one may employ a metaphorical expression here) the subjective factor with its entire cognitively complex character.

We have dealt with these matters in our earlier reflections. Nonetheless, in preparing a synthetic answer on the subject of the objectivity of cognition we cannot be satisfied and rest with this; the aim, after all, is to achieve a possibly all-sided analysis of the interactions of the subjective factor on historical cognition. Does this problem culminate with an analysis of the historical fact and its selection? Of course not. After all, the historian does not only present facts but explains and evaluates them. Thus, we face at least two new problems: explanation and evaluation in history.

The problems which we shall raise here in connection with the question whether history can limit itself to "pure" description belong traditionally to the domain of dispute regarding idiographic or nomothetic character of this science. However, this dispute does not enter into the sphere of our present interests.[1] Firstly, because we are concentrating here on the influence of the subjective factor on historical cognition. Secondly, because the tendency to defend extreme idiographism is exceedingly rare at present among historians. They are inclined to accept the thesis of moderate nomothetism proclaiming that the historian may refer to laws of historical development, although the formulation of such laws is not the specific task of the science of history. Hence, let us continue to concentrate our attention on the problem of explanation and evaluation in history.

Both of the above-mentioned problems are methodologically and theoretically important and complicated. Thus, it should be remarked at the outset that we do not intend to subject them to a detailed and comprehensive analysis. In the case of the first problem, an analysis would call for recourse to a more broadly conceived theory of explanation in science which would imply the necessity of an analysis of the problem of scientific laws in general and the laws of history in particular. In the second case, it would be unavoidable to refer to a broadly conceived axiology, with its concrete application to evaluation in history. It is clear that each one of these subjects would require a monographic study and, in any case, if dealt with more broadly, it would explode any sensible construction of our present reflections. Therefore, it is necessary to limit our concern to a certain segment of the problem, that is, to the role of the subjective factor, both in explanation and in evaluation in history. The aim clearly is to obtain additional knowledge about the role of the subjective factor in historical cognition; it is a limited aim, but of considerable significance for an ultimate synthesis within the framework of the subject of interest to us.

Let us return to Lucien Febvre's statement. History, according to him, does not consist only in the assembling of particular facts into one entity, but also in elucidating *why* things happen in one way and not another. It is this "savoir pourquoi", postulated by Febvre, which turns history into a science.

In taking a similar position we bear in mind the counterposing of history to chronicles. This is an old problem which Benedetto Croce exploited on the basis of his spiritualist metaphysics. We cannot utilize his conception precisely because of this connection. Nonetheless, the counterposing of history to chronicles contains certain fertile thoughts which make it possible to understand better and more vividly the meaning of history as a science and the role played by historical explanation in it. Let us utilize another, more neutral source of analysis of this problem. I have in mind a passage from Morton White's introduction to a symposium on problems of philosophy and history.

> A chronicle of a subject, I shall say, is a conjunction of non-explanatory empirical statements which expressly mention that subject and which report things that have been true of it at different times. By a non-explanatory statement I mean one that does not connect two statements of fact with a word like "because". The stipulation that the chronicle's conjuncts be non-explanatory is imposed in order to remain faithful to the idea that a chronical merely reports "facts" in a narrow sense. [2]

In contrast to a chronicle, a history explains the phenomena about which it speaks. In this fashion explanation is contained, by definition, in the concept of history. An historian, as distinct from a chronicler, asks not only what happened but also why it happened.[3]

I believe this differentiation of the chronicle and history to be correct and significant. The importance of explanation in history becomes understandable precisely on the basis of this differentiation.

To know why means to be able to answer the question why. The explanation of phenomena rests exactly on this ability. However, difficulties connected with the role of the subjective factor appear here from the very outset. Explanations on the basis of one and the same set of facts can be and are, after all, different, as we know from the practice of historical writing. The significant meaning of the differences between theoretical systems and schools in history rests precisely here; it is they which, directly or indirectly, cause historians, taking their stand, having the same factual knowledge at their disposal understand, to evaluate and elucidate these facts differently and at times contradictorily.

Another eminent French theorist of history wrote the following on this subject:

> ... All interpretation is reconstruction ... in accord with the aim towards which he strives, the historian determines the various links between elements, applies different conceptions; *this aim he sets himself.*
> ... The plurality of interpretations is obvious when one considers the historian's work. As many interpretations arise as there are systems, which means, speaking generally, as there are *psychological conceptions and original logics.* What is more, it may be said that *theory preceeds history,* if by theory one is to understand both the determination of a certain system and the value ascribed to a certain type of an interpretation.[4]

Thus, on the basis of a certain sum of facts universally acknowledged by historians, due to their determination in sources (the word "source" is taken here in its broad meaning), different historians interpret and present the historical process in various ways. This is so not only because they undertake a different selection of the facts which they consider to be important, to be historical but also because they link them together and elucidate them in varying ways.

Since we have stated above that explanation enters, by definition, into the concept of history (if we distinguish history from chronicles) then we should state at present, event in a most general form, what we mean by the word "explanation".

At the outset of present reflections we have made the reservation that we do not intend to undertake a detailed analysis of the problems of explanation and evaluation in history. However, we should at least draw attention to what knowledge in this field we consider indispensable for taking up the aspect of the problem which concerns us.

Various authors who deal with the problem of explanation in science have grasped this problem in reference to history in different ways, beginning with a typology of the kinds of explanation present in it, up to an interpretation and evaluation of the role of these particular kinds.

R. B. Braithwaite, whom I consider to be the most eminent authority in this field, distinguishes causal and purposive explanation. In both cases what matters is the answer to the question, Why?, but in each of them the nature of the answer, both formal and substantial is different. In the first case, the answer of "because of g", in the second: "in order that g".[5]

If, in accord with Braithwaite's intention, we take the question regarding the cause of a phenomenon as a question relating to events preceding it, or appearing simultaneously with it, and these events together with unspecified special constant conditions are sufficient to determine—in line with some causal law—the phenomenon which is to be elucidated, then we must, at the same time, add the author's reservation, which is of immense significance from the viewpoint of the aspect of the problem which concerns us. It is precisely due to the significance of this statement that we quote it verbatim:

> The "Why?" question is not expected to be answered by detailing all the events which together make up a total cause, that is, a set of events which collectively determine the explicandum event; all that is usually expected is the *part-cause which is of most interest to the questioner*—which presumably is that of which he is ignorant. One sense of giving a *complete* explanation would be that of specifying a total cause; in this sense, as indeed in most sense of complete explanation, a *"complete explanation" will not be unique, since* (in almost all senses of "cause") . . . *the same event can perfectly well have many different total causes.*[6]

In the course of our further reflections we shall return once more to this statement in the context of a generalization pertaining to the role of the subjective factor in historical explanation. Nonetheless, it is obvious at first glance that Braithwaite has introduced the subjective factor (that which is most interesting for the inquirer) as an organic component of his reflections.

However, causal explanation becomes complicated not only due to its incompleteness but also because it can be taken either as the search for sufficient conditions (the stronger meaning) or only for necessary conditions (the weaker meaning). Quite often the question: Why?, embraces both aspects of the problem; it is a question pertaining to the sufficient conditions, as well as to a specification of the necessary conditions of a given event.

According to Braithwaite, the second type of explanation is a teleological elucidation. In this case we answer the question: Why? by pointing to the aim while the event or activity being elucidated serves as a means to its realization. An example of this type of explanation, which the author considers to be fully satisfactory from a scientific point of view is, an answer, for instance, to the question: "Why do you spend the summer at home", which indicates the purpose of spending the summer at home, for example, "In order to finish writing my book". [7]

Let us quote the author's further explanation which throws a certain light on the problem with which we are concerned and to which it will be worthwhile to return in the further course of our considerations. "The explanation consists in stating a goal to be attained: it describes the action as one directed towards a certain goal—as a "goal-directed activity" . . . the word 'directed' being used . . . *to imply a direction but not to imply a director.*" [8]

In this case, the author clearly strives to eliminate the subjective factor. Has he succeeded in this? Is it really possible to recognize the existence of purposive activity without the subject who determines this purpose?

Braithwaite's typology, however, is not the only typology.

Hempel, the author of a splendid essay, exemplary in the precision with which he expresses his thoughts on the subject of elucidation in history, recognizes, in fact, only one type of explanation—causal elucidation. It depends always on subordinating a concrete event to some general law. Here is Hempel's classical definition of explanation:

> The explanation of the occurrence of an event of some specific kind "E" at a certain place and time consists, as it is usually expressed, in indicating the causes or determining factors of "E". Now the assertion that a set of events—say, of the kinds $C_1, C_2 . . . C_n$—have caused the event to be explained, amounts to the statement that, according to certain general laws, a set of events of the kinds mentioned is regularly accompanied by an event of the kind "E". Thus, the

scientific explanation of the event in question consists of (1) a set of statements asserting the occurrence of certain events $C_1 \ldots C_n$ at certain times and places, (2) a set of universal hypotheses, such that (a) the statements of both groups are reasonably well confirmed by empirical evidence, (b) from the two groups of statements the sentence asserting the occurrence of event "E" can be logically deduced. [9]

This is by no means an original position or formulation. In the neo-positivist school, from which Hempel also comes, Karl Popper had much earlier stated in his *Logik der Forschung* an analogous formulation of explanation in science and a number of other theorists in history defended this position at the same time as Hempel (for example, Patrick Gardiner, who in the conclusion of similar reasoning wrote: ". . . an event is explained when it has been brought under a generalization or law.")[10]

Nonetheless, Hempel, although so categorical in his definition of explanation (which according to him always presumes the existence of some general laws), maintained, when coming to deal with the practice of historical writing, that these demands of explanation are not observed. This is the case both when the general laws (hypotheses) are not stated *expressis verbis* since they pertain to individual psychology and seem banal, as well as when (this case is particularly interesting) they cannot be strictly formulated due to their statistical and thus—in relation to particular events—only probabilist nature. Hempel concluded:

Many an explanation offered in history seems to admit of an analysis of this kind: if fully and explicitly formulated, it would state certain initial conditions, and certain probability hypotheses, such that the occurrence of the event to be explained is to be made highly probable by the initial conditions in view of the probability hypotheses. But no matter whether explanations in history be construed as "casual" or as "probabilistic" in character, it remains true that in general the initial conditions and especially the universal hypotheses involved are not clearly indicated and cannot unambiguously be supplemented. [11]

Thus, and this is worth emphasizing, the lack of sharpness of the starting-point (both of starting conditions as well as of the presumed hypotheses) which determines the probabalistic nature of explanation is neither haphazard nor subject to elimination. Thus, however, the problem of the possibility of *various* explanations and the problem of decision regarding the selection of one of them comes to the fore in full force. Why do we chose one and not another version? On what basis do we undertake such a decision?

This aspect of the problem appears still more acutely in the work of Ernest Nagel. He also maintains that the historical explanation of human activities is probabilistic since generalizations pertaining to human behaviour, which enter into the sum of assumptions of this explanation, have a statistical character.[12] Nevertheless, in analysing this concept he delves deeper:

> The incompleteness of the premises when measured by the standards of valid deductive reasoning, and their formulation of necessary rather than sufficient conditions for the occurrence of events, are two generally acknowledged traits that explicate in part the sense in which historical explanations are "probabilistic".[13]

The "probability" of an event, Nagel continued, always contains a subjective element which cannot be eliminated since individuals, assuming the same initial data and hypotheses, will ascribe different degrees of probability to the same events.

In aiming to eliminate the element of subjectivity in explanation, Nagel proposed a revision of the concept of probability, which he called "personalistic probability".[14] It is the individual decision which is decisive and this individual, with definite initial data, is inclined to ascribe greater or smaller chances of a given possibility as compared to others. Thus, in fact, the subjective element is not removed from explanation, it is only the form of the statement on the subject which is changed.

The incompleteness of historical explanation, emphasized by the majority of authors, and its probabilist character connected therewith have inclined Hempel to maintain that in reality it is not an explanation *senso stricto* but only an "explanation sketch".

> What the explanatory analyses of historical events offer is, then, in most cases not an explanation in one of the meanings developed above, but something that might be called an *explanation sketch*. Such a sketch consists of a more or less vague indication of the laws and initial conditions considered as relevant and in needs "filling out" in order to turn into a full-fledged explanation.[15]

While Hempel defends the empirical character of these "explanation sketches" (they are verified in the process of their ensuing concretization, in contrast to the "nonsenses", taken in the neo-positivist spirit as sentences devoid of empirical sense) which contain, according to him the directives of their concretization, nonetheless, he does not eliminate thereby the situation in which the cognizing subject plays an active role in providing concrete content to the explanation scheme.

A much more important problem, however, of which a number of authors are aware, lies at the foundations of these troubles with the subjective factor in explanation. It is a *par excellence* philosophical problem, well known in connection with philosophical reflection on causality.

When we say that one event was the cause of another (for example, the casting of a stone against the window was the cause of the breaking of the pane) we *always* make a selection of some event from among a mass of others, which we call the condition of the event we are concerned with. For the casting of the stone against the window to have broken the pane, various other events must have preceded or coexisted with that event which we call the effect: the earth had to gravitate around its orbit, a specific gravitation field had to exist, the pane had to be of glass of a given consistency, etc. We do not negate this, but these are conditions of the events which we tacitly assume; on the other hand, we are interested in the event which *directly* brought about the effect and without which this effect would not have occurred. What matters then is the necessary condition of the event and not the sufficient condition. Every philosopher knows, however, the problems and difficulties which emerge here. Beginning with what should be recognized as the necessary condition, including the impossibility of exhausting the sufficient condition, up to the fictitiousness in the distinguishing of events which "directly" bring about others, and a relativity of the choice of the cause of the event from among its other conditions, from the point of view of the "importance" of this cause. In the given context it is the last question which is particularly interesting and this has inclined the advocates of conditionalism to reject totally the concept of "cause" in favour of conditions of the event of equal rank and value.

In pointing to the problems connected with the question of causality we do not intend to elaborate on them or to resolve them in the spirit of one of the many parties engaged in this long-standing dispute. Nonetheless, there is one thing to which we cannot avoid paying attention and which in this context cannot be passed over in silence; this is the fact that if we distinguish the causes of some events we are always undertaking a *selection*; we do so due to a certain system of reference and guiding ourselves by a certain system of values which determines the greater or lesser "importance" of events from among which we undertake this selection.

In addition, still another circumstance should be taken into consideration. In illustrating above the problem of causality we have utilized a simplified example: the striking of the stone shatters the pane in the window. In history such banal situations and examples do not appear, or, in any case they are of no interest. Every "historical fact" is a complicated condensation of relations and mutual interactions—contemporary and past—it is also in a certain sense a "montage" of events, in the shaping of which the historian participates actively. An analysis of even a so-called simple historical fact shows its complicated character and its connections with literally all of social reality, present and past. Therefore, the indication of causes and laws is always a question of choice; even the choice of the aspect of the problem to be studied and, hence, also of the system of reference in which the studied historical fact is placed.

As has already been mentioned, historical explanation is always incomplete. Hempel speaks of an "explanation sketch" which should be continuously and endlessly concretized. Gibson maintained that explanation makes use only of certain selected factors and never gives (and cannot give) a full set of the factors making up the sufficient condition of an event.[16] One feels impelled to pose the question—on what principle, from amid the infinite quantity of events and relations preceding a given event or contemporary with it, does one undertake a selection of factors and recognize then as the explanatory causes of a given event? What is the criterion of their importance?

Gibson replied that this criterion rested in the effects brought about by given factors.[17] But, after all, the issue rests exactly in how to decide which factors brought into being the effects regarded as particularly important. Hence, a vicious circle in reasoning clearly arises.

Ernest Nagel is much more careful in the interpretation of this problem and, in fact, leaves it unanswered, noting only the various difficulties and question marks.[18] In distinguishing endogenic factors (lying within the historian's sphere of competence) from exogenic ones (not lying within it) Nagel concentrated his attention on the former while not denying, in the least, that biological, geographical, etc., factors can play an immense role in the unfolding of historical events. Nonetheless, even this conscious limitation of the field of interest does not eliminate all the complications. The question remains open: what does "important" signify in reference to historical events? Even the elimination of the ambiguity of this expression does not resolve the issue.

An interesting point of view pertaining to the subjective factor in historical explanation was introduced by McIver. Every history generalizes, but, McIver maintained, various levels of this generalization exist, from an individual description to very general interpretations of history. The mingling of these levels gives rise to errors in reasoning and to verbal discussion. This leads, as well, to consequences in the field of historical explanations; various types of historical explanations, adapted to different levels of generalization, exist. Nevertheless, it is precisely in connection with this and due to the choice made by the historian of the level of generalization on which he wants to regard a given phenomenon that the subjective factor enters into the picture.

> In historical explanation at all levels above the purely individual, whatever is unimportant is disregarded. This sounds subjective, but in fact there is no subjectivity in it, apart from the subjectivity of the motive dictating choice of a particular level.[19]

Historical explanation taken as causal explanation has still another aspect which is of interest to us. We consciously refrain here from entering into the dispute regarding the differences between explanation in history and explanation in the natural sciences which is linked with the dispute regarding the status of these domains of knowledge. In accepting the concept that history examines concrete events we reject, however, the extreme thesis of Ranke's school about limiting it to the presentation of "pure" facts. If history is to explain historical events (in the contrary case it would not be history), it must take recourse to the most varied laws, which in different fields really do speak of the regularities in the life of individuals and societies. It is only under this condition that the causal explanation of given events by means of the past or present events can come forth. The historian, however, undertakes also another form of reflection and reasoning which is akin to explanation. If, knowing the starting-point and the laws governing the development of a given field or reality we are able to *foresee* the events of the future, then we can also do the opposite: on the basis of this same knowledge, starting with the existing present state, we may draw inferences about what the past was like. In Anglo-American literature this conduct has been called *retrodiction* (introduced by G. Ryle) which may be considered a "pendant" to the term prediction. Here is what W. H. Walsh had to say regarding this problem.

> It has been said that whilst it certainly is not the business of historians to predict the future, it is very much their business to "retrodict" the past: to establish, on the basis of present evidence, what the past must have been like. And it is argued that the procedure of the historian in retrodicting is exactly parallel to that of the scientist in predicting, since in each case the argument proceeds from the conjunction of particular premises (that so-and-so is the case now) with general truths, in the case of science laws of nature, in that of history laws governing human behaviour in situations of this *kind or that*. [20]

Hence what is at stake here is a type of recursive reasoning which occupies an important place in the historian's arsenal when he formulates his hypothesis pertaining to the history he examines, something similar to prognostication projected backwards, into history: on the basis of known facts and certain general laws one arrives from effects to the possible causes of given events. A situation arises similar to that which faces the astronomer who, after having made his calculation, maintains that in such and such a place an astral body of such and such magnitude should exist. This constitutes a valuable heuristic indication for him, which permits him to search in a planned fashion: if this search produces a result, then the hypothesis will be verified. A similar situation faces the historian who, on the basis of such retroduction, obtains a fertile hypothesis in reference to searching for the material traces of ancient cultures, institutions, and economic bases of certain customs and habits, etc. More than one example from the history of historical writing could serve to illustrate this.

Nevertheless, the problem of the active role of the historian in formulating hypotheses regarding the past, in research, verification and so forth, appears here once again. It is clear that the results depend, to an immense degree, on the historian's individuality, on his knowledge, his theoretical and philosophical background, his personal convictions conditioned by his social situation, etc. Thus, we have a new element and a new problem in our search for the content of the concept relating to the objectivity of historical truth.

In concluding these reflections it should be noted that some authors speak not about a causal explanation, but about a genetic one stressing that the issue rests on the explanation of phenomena by means of their history. However, they assume in this that what matters is not a simple sequence of events, but a cause-effect series and thus, in reality, they are engaged in causal explanation, and being conscious of the fact that in reporting only the necessary but not the sufficient condition of events, they are undertaking a probabilistic explanation (for example, Ernest Nagel).

Causal explanation has been the main subject of our interest up to this moment. On its basis we have sought to bring out the role of the subjective factor in order to prepare more fully our reflections on the objectivity of historical cognition. Nevertheless, as we shall seek to show further on, causal explanation in history always goes hand in hand with teleological explanation. Thereby, however, the problem of the subjective factor in historical cognition arises anew.

Let us return to Braithwaite's typology in which he differentiates causal and teleological, purposive explanation. To explain some event signifies simply an answer to the question: why did this and this happen? One can answer this question either by pointing to the causes which have brought it about, in accord with a given law, or to the aim which motivated people acting in a specific fashion. Thus, in the first case, the question "why?" is taken as tantamount to the question "for what reason?", in the second, as tantamount to the question "for what purpose?".

It is clear that purposive explanation and thus the question "for what purpose?" are appropriate only then when we are dealing with *conscious* action and its effects, when the aim is to explain the actions of beings who consciously set themselves specific aims and adapt to them action directed at the fulfilment of these aims. This is precisely why teleologism, taken as a philosophical trend, extends purposive explanation to *all* events, thus also to nature, and must assume therefore the existence of a supernatural being, whose conscious and purposive action gives rise to everything which occurs. In accepting such a stand it is also necessary to accept the religious premises and thus its philosophical consequence, spiritualism. An acceptance of philosophical positions opposed to the premises of religion and spiritualism leads, as a result, to a rejection of teleologism.

A decided negation of the validity of teleogism is a universal principle for the explanation of the events of reality, a negation which is characteristic primarily to all varieties of materialism, does not, by any means, imply the rejection in every case of the validity of purposive explanation. On the contrary, where we are dealing with purposive action and thus with rational beings who consciously strive towards the fulfilment of definite aims, teleological explanation is not only permissible, but in certain cases simply necessary if we desire really to understand what has taken place.

Let us take as an example some fact of undoubted historical significance. Lenin agreed in 1917 to return to Russia with a group of his colleagues in a sealed German train. The fact was not trite and the decision not an everyday one, not to mention the effects of this event which led to the October Revolution.

We state that an historian cannot limit himself to ascertaining this fact, to registering it, but should explain it, should answer the question: "Why?". In this case which of the two possible interpretations of the meaning of this question are we concerned with: the causal or the teleological? It may be maintained that the historian is always concerned with both and in one sense this is undoubtedly true. Taking this position we recognize the validity and need for teleological explanation. Thus, it is not only valid but even indispensable for an understanding of events. What will we gain from the demonstration of cause-effect connections shaping a chain of events at the end of which there is to be found concretely the event interesting us (Lenin's decision to return to Russia in a German train) if we do not explain the purpose towards which Lenin was striving, since only this makes it possible to explain the sources of the motivation of his action?

This is the crux of the issue: where we are dealing with intended, purposive action, in order to explain (that is, to answer the question: "why?") it is necessary to have recourse to the motivation of the people undertaking the action, to the aims which they have consciously

marked out; it is only this which makes it possible to understand and—
an essential thing for an historian—to evaluate their action. It is this
possibility and necessity of utilizing teleological explanation, without
the danger of falling into mysticism and spiritualism—which is
inevitable if one accepts the stand of teleologism as a method for
explaining *all* events in reality—which constitutes one of the important
differences between the social and the natural sciences. Everywhere
where the subject of our studies is man, acting socially (and thus far the
Homo sapiens is the only species about whom we can state that it acts
consciously, or strives consciously towards the fulfilment of
previously set aims, both in his individual as well as his social life), we
must undertake purposive explanation of his action in order to avoid
the failure *to understand* them. This is obvious because the word
"understand" has been employed in the meaning that if one
understands someone's action then one is able to recreate their
motivations and thus, above all, become aware of the aim towards
which the acting person was striving.[21] We have said "above all" in
order to emphasize that we do not eliminate here the action of other
factors and thus also of the causal conditioning of the stands and
behaviour of people; however, it is impossible to make do here without
purposive explanation. In the domain of the natural sciences
(including the study of man as a particle of nature) not only is it
possible to make do without such an explanation, but it would be a
nonsense to engage in teleological explanation.

This ascertaining of one of the specific traits of the social sciences
(understood here in a special way, as embracing all the humanities)
implies, however, further consequences. If, without purposive
explanation, it is impossible to understand events in the domain
embracing conscious and purposive human action, then it is also
impossible to provide a purposive explanation without understanding
these actions (that is, without recreating the motivations and aims of
the persons involved). How can one answer the question: "for what
purpose did so and so act in such and such a way?" if we have not
understood the motives of his actions. Here we discover the sound idea
of the concept of an "understanding science", although not in that
tradition which Dilthey and Max Weber had left behind them. If one
casts away all the increments, there remains a significant remnant of

this concept, which is linked with the bringing out of the specific traits of the social sciences derived from their studying of purposive human actions (which, it would be noted, remain conscious and purposive even then, when the consciousness is false and the person acting is not aware of the true, deeper causes of his actions).

It is extremely important to be aware of the significance of "understanding", interpreted in this way, for purposive explanation in the field of the social sciences in general and history in particular. Does a more objective and, therefore, a more infallible in its inter-subjectivity, method exist in this scope? For instance, the recourse to sources, to speeches, memoirs, historical works written by statesmen who participated directly in given events, explaining the motives and aims of certain actions (for example, a declaration of war, the conquest of other nations, the signing of a peace treaty, etc.).

It suffices to ponder for a moment in order to reach the conviction that the utilization of source material research, necessary in historical reflection, does not free the historian from the employment of "reasoning" and hence from empathy, from the attempt to reconstruct the experiences and the purposive actions of historical personalities. On the contrary, it renders this imperative and, we would add, assumes it. What do even the most personal historical sources, mentioned above, reveal? In the best case, they will reveal that which the authors of the given memoirs, letters, speeches, etc., thought about themselves and the events; in the worse case, that which they wanted to have others think about them and the events. Thus, we are faced always with ideology—in Mannheim's usage of the word—from self-deception to the conscious deceiving of others.

Marx had stated once that one should not evaluate social classes, just like individuals, according to what they themselves think and speak about themselves. Every historian must anyhow be a sceptic in this respect, must, in his everyday work, confront similar sources originating with the representatives of parties engaged in the dispute. These sources are, after all, quite contrary, as a rule, not only in their evaluation but even in the description of facts, thus revealing in this singular fashion the partisanship and involvement of the people participating in the contentious events, even if they do desire to be objective. It is only important for the biography of a given personality whether we are dealing—in the case of something obvious to the historian—with a conscious lie or with auto-mystification. Psychologically speaking the latter is probably the most common case, since if the authors of these falsehoods were not really convinced of the correctness of the views voiced by them—most often that such actions were needed precisely by the interest of humanity or, at least, of their own nation—they would not have been capable of such exuberant zeal, or even fanaticism, in actions which were often quite criminal.

The historian appears here in the role of a super-arbiter, as a metatheorist, engaged in critical reflection on these auto-reports dealing with conscious human actions (which does not free him from meta-meta-criticism, since he too, as we know, is not free from "partisanship" and partiality). How does he do this?

The techniques of a critical evaluation of sources and the information contained therein are numerous, beginning with the ascertaining of the origin of these sources and their authenticity, then the comparison of the information which they provide; finally the verification of the data obtained on the basis of previously known and verified data, other statements by these same people, etc. Nonetheless, at the foundations of all these techniques and professional manipulations of the historian there lies most often the tacit assumption that he understands the events he studies in that he is able to recreate the motivations and the purposive actions of individuals or groups guided by the same ideas and purposes, that he is able to recreate them (thus experience them anew in a singular fashion) both when he evaluates them from the point of view of the judgements they contain as true, as well as then when he considers them to be false.

The significance of this concept can be best grasped when we examine the possibility, no longer so fictitious today, of coming into contact on other planets with rational beings whose psychosomatic structure would be totally different from ours and who would have developed, in connection with this, a totally different culture. Not possessing a key for the purpose of "translating" the language of their culture into our language, the historian, faced even with an abundance of the varied sources pertaining to the past of this culture, would remain completely helpless, since he would be unable to understand the motivations and the aims of the actions of these beings, although he would at the same time have proofs of the fact that they acted consciously and purposively. If here the absence of a common biological fate, which automatically creates a plateau of contact for even the most distant rational beings on our planet, were to occur, then one could imagine a situation in which the "languages" of those cultures and of our culture would be mutually exclusive; that is, they would not have one single common element. (Applying in this fashion K. Hajdukiewicz's concept of so-called open and closed languages.) This would make impossible not only mutual communication, but also mutual *understanding*. In such a situation an historian, having at his disposal even the most sophisticated and subtle apparatus for the critical appraisal of sources, would have to give up the struggle: if one does not understand events, one cannot explain them. Without understanding human action it is thus impossible to explain the past. Formulating this differently, understanding constitutes a component part of historical explanation.

This is an undeniable fact, but a fact which, in addition, gives rise to dangerous situations for the objectivity of historical cognition and the truth attained in this cognition. This could be put differently, by stating that it introduces an additional portion of the subjective factor into historical cognition. Understanding is always a subject-object relation, and everything which has already been said regarding cognitive relation and, in particular, the role of the subjective factor in this relation, pertains to this as well. Understanding as an act, and without this act there is no product, is always *someone's* act, linked with the definite subject who experiences this understanding. In the given case, it is the historian who is the subject seeking to explain events. How he perceives certain facts, understands them and thus explains them, depends on his knowledge and talent, on the nature of his social conditioning, connected with the epoch in which he lives, the nation of which he is a member, the class to which he belongs, the professional group to which he adheres, etc. The stamp of the historian's individuality is impressed upon every historical work: this is his view of history, his understanding of the historical process or, otherwise, he is a failure as an historian. This stamp is inevitable, but it does not negate the objectivity of historical cognition; it makes it possible only to understand properly the nature and the limits of this objectivity and, in consequence, to overcome and do away with these limits in the continuous process of perfecting our knowledge.

Participation and understanding in historical explanation are connected, however, with real dangers of cognitive deformation, when the subjective factor exceeds the necessary measure of the active role of the subject in the cognitive relation, without which this relation itself would have to disappear. The error of modernization in explaining the past, when past events taken out of their proper cultural context are explained as if they were a component part of the culture contemporaneous to the historian, with its proper political, economic mechanisms, etc., may be such an example (for instance, when events of the Middle Ages were interpreted and explained in categories of the modern nation and patriotism, although neither one nor the other had then taken shape). An analogous error is archaization, when Medieval or Modern history is thrust into the Procrustean bed, not only of the categories but also of the social relations proper to ancient times, although often these ancient times are, in turn, interpreted in terms of contemporary politics projected on to the past in the spirit of presentism. These are examples of an indubitable cognitive deformation, whose danger lies in the subjective factor. There is only one remedy for this: since it is impossible to do away with the subjective factor, without "doing away" simultaneously with cognition and understanding of events, one should be aware of the danger which exists here and by controlling the results of cognition, overcome the deformations in the process of perfecting knowledge.

The question of evaluation and appraisal in history still remains to be considered.

The representative of so-called objective history, that is, of the positivist trend of Ranke's school, postulate the elimination of evaluation and appraisal in history. This postulate, regardless of the possibilities of its fulfilment, is comprehensible on the basis of the premises and the model of history accepted by this school; if this is to be a purely descriptive history, presenting only facts, "wie es eigentlich gewesen", without any admixtures of a subjective character, then evaluation and appraisal are impermissible within the framework of a science thus conceived. This is simply because any evaluation inevitably introduces the subjective factor into the image of reality.

In accord with what we have stated, we shall not indulge here in reflections on the subject of the theory of value and shall concern ourselves only with the actions of the theorist engaged in evaluating reflections and this from the aspect of subjective implications. Without entering into the solution of the dispute on the subject of the essence of value, it should be noted, however, that everyone who engages in evaluating events or human behaviour does so on the basis of some system of values, which he accepts consciously or spontaneously. It is this system which provides models and measures by means of which a given event or behaviour is evaluated. However, regardless of whether we assume that the origin of the system of values is social or connected only with the individual employing it, its concrete application is always individual, both in the sense of the choice of a given system of values, and in the sense of all the individual additions and variants which always appear in the process of evaluation. The subjective factor which acts here in a similar manner to that in the cognitive relation, but in a much sharper and clearer form, is inevitably connected precisely with this. The attempt to escape from this influence of the subjective factor on the process of evaluation, and from the danger of relativism connected with this (the appraisal that something is good or evil, noble or vile, beautiful or ugly, etc., is always connected with the appraising subject, which we gladly acknowledge in relation to taste, but not in relation to moral appraisals) is a concept of absolute and thus unchanging value. This is a concept which it is difficult to accept; firstly, because it can be consistently carried out only on the basis of an ontology in which values appear as ideal real existences (platonism) and hence, a decided idealistic and even a purely mystic ideology; secondly, because even this absolutist concept relating to the essence of values does not eliminate the difficulties connected with the individual application of values in the process of evaluation which cannot be, after all, conceived of without the evaluating subject. Thereby, however, the problem of the subjective factor remains open. Hence, it is understandable why the advocates of a positivist, exclusively descriptive, concept of historical writing disengage themselves so decidedly from all evaluating and appraising activities in history. However, is it possible to realize this postulate?

The negative answer to this question rests on a number of arguments.

In proclaiming the postulate of the elimination of evaluation in history, the advocates of Ranke's trend overlook the unusually significant fact that evaluation and appraisal are not a function which the historian undertakes only on the basis of certain factual material, "raw" as they maintain, and free from any admixture of the subjective factor, but rests at the foundations of this material, in the historical facts themselves. This is so in a twofold sense.

As we already know from the preceding considerations, the historical fact is not a spontaneously appearing brick, which remains unchangeable and the same regardless of who subsequently utilizes it, but is a specific segment of reality, simultaneously constituting a collage of various narratives of a given event with others. As to which narratives enter into the picture to constitute that what we call an historical fact, this a matter not only of objective reality, but also of the cognizing subject who undertakes the selection.

The historical fact which, according to Ranke's school, is the simplest atom in the construction of history, is in reality, a complex structure in which the subjective factor plays a distinct role, mainly by means of evaluation. For in undertaking selection—and the historian undertakes such a selection from among objective narratives, shaping the historical fact as an objective-subjective product, just as any other product of the process of cognition—he does so by *evaluating*. It is only the criteria of evaluation, provided by a definite system of values, which make possible a conscious selection which matters. Thus, it can be seen that evaluation, along with the entire ballast of the subjective factor contained therein, is not a function developed by an historian on the basis of facts (although this also takes place and we shall revert to this issue in further reflections), but is inherent already in the facts themselves.

And if this is so, if these facts are in a certain sense the product of an historian, then, when he postulates a refraining from an evaluation and appraisal of events and human behaviour, a limiting only to the reporting of given facts, his self-defence against evaluation proves to be illusory.

Evaluation impinges itself on the historian's work by still another route, which also by-passes the barriers erected on the postulate of a description of "naked" facts without any additions. What are the facts which the historian is to narrate? If we identify, by definition, the historical fact with all events of the past then, of course, there is an infinite number of them and no one will be able to narrate them all. On the other hand, if the historical fact is an event of special importance from the point of view of some system of reference—and this is the way in which historians see the problem—then it is an event which has been selected with regard to certain criteria. This is tantamount to stating that the historian, in determining the historical facts which go to make up his presentation of the historical process, evaluates and appraises the events of the past in order to carry out a proper selection among them.

Finally, evaluation and appraisal often act as the factor which constitutes the fact by the interpretation itself of this fact. William H. Dray has pointed out correctly that historical facts are often *value constituted*; as for example, when we speak of such facts as religious persecution during the Thirty Years War or the bestialities of the soldiers in that period. The issue is not to refrain from an appraisal of such facts, since they contain this appraisal in themselves, in the very formulation of the fact. Dray concluded: "Facts and values are always clearly distinct for objectivists. But if we are to call persecution and cruelty 'facts'—and historians are generally inclined to do so—it is easy to understand why evaluation is considered to be logically contained in the historian's subject." [22]

There still remains the question of evaluation and appraisal in the historian's work, as a component part of his narration of the historical process. This question is not as obvious as in the case of historical explanation which is an indispensable condition for history. However, can the historian refrain from all evaluations and appraisals of historical events if we leave aside the evaluation which, as pointed out above, is inherent in the facts themselves?

If an historian were to undertake the appropriate efforts in order to conceal his evaluating and this "engagé" and partisan stand under a mask of formulations, neutral in relation to evaluation, then, obviously, he can achieve this aim. Ranke is an example of this. It does not follow, however, that this is so in reality. Ranke can serve as an example once more, as shown by the previously quoted presentist critiques of his position. Evaluation does not appear necessarily in the shape of appropriately expanded sentences, that is, *explicitly*. It also appears, most often, *implicitly* through the appropriate interpretation and selection of facts and mainly through a diverse presentation of events which do not in the least have to be accompanied by *explicitly* formulated appraisal.

In any case, it can be stated with full conviction that evaluation enters into the historian's work in many ways, often escaping his control or even his consciousness. It is a necessity of which one must be aware in order to be able to control it consciously, to avoid extremes which lead to a deformation of cognition.

In conclusion, let us try to sum up the results of our reflections.

We have ascertained that history is composed not only of a description of events, but also of their explanation and evaluation. Both explanation and evaluation introduce the subjective factor into historical cognition.

The following reasons argue in favour of this concept in reference to causal explanation:

In causal explanation we limit ourselves to presenting a partial cause (we do not give a full explanation) and the choice of this fragment is dictated by the interests of the questioner.

If we take causal explanation as falling under a general law, then, in view of the imprecision of the premises of historical explanation (the starting condition and the assumed hypotheses), it has of necessity a probabilistic character which makes various explanations of one and the same fact possible and we are faced with the choice of one of these.

Historical explanation is always incomplete and hence can be treated only as an "explanation sketch" which has to be "filled out" by the historian, something which different authors can accomplish to varying degrees.

Historical explanation may be carried out on different levels of generalization; the decision connected with the choice of an appropriate level is of a subjective nature, since it is connected with the historian's interests and research needs.

A second type of explanation of history is teleological explanation which is necessary in history in view of the fact that it deals with human actions which are conscious and purposive. This explanation also introduces the subjective factor into historical cognition and for the following reasons:

In order to recreate the aim which marked the human action being studied, we must understand the motivation of the people who were acting; this comprehension, which is a subject-object relation, assumes the active role of the subject and thereby introduces the subjective factor into cognition.

As far as evaluation and appraisal in history are concerned we have ascertained the possibility of eliminating them, since they appear here not only *explicitly* but also *implicitly*: in the very facts themselves, whose cognitive constituting calls for a selection of the material composing them; in the selection of facts considered by the author as historically important within the framework of a given system of reference; in the interpretation and presentation of facts.

What general conclusions follow from this?

Above all, that by means of explanation and evaluation the subjective factor enters into historical cognition and its role and degree of influence must be taken into consideration in reflections on the subject of the objectivity of historical truth. In any case, we have obtained, as a result of these reflections, an additional viewpoint regarding this problem and we have added one more aspect to the panorama of the manifold facets of the influence of the subjective factor on historical cognition.

Notes

1. I have dealt with this problem more extensively in my work *Obiektywny charakter praw historii* ("The Objective Character of the Laws of History"), Warsaw, 1955.
2. M. White, "Philosophy and history", in *Philosophy and History*, p. 5, New York, 1963.
3. *Ibid.*, p. 6.
4. R. Aron, *Introduction à la philosophie de l'histoiré. Essai sur les limites de l'objectivité historique,* ed. Gallimard, p. 111, Paris, 1968.
5. R. B. Braithwaite, *Scientific Explanation,* p. 320, Cambridge, 1953.
6. *Ibid.,* p. 320. (Emphasis—A.S.)
7. *Ibid.,* pp. 322-323.
8. *Ibid.,* p. 323. (Emphasis—A.S.)
9. C. G. Hempel, "The function of general laws in history", in H. Feigl and W. Sellars (eds.), *Readings in Philosophical Analysis,* pp. 459-560, New York, 1949.

10. P. Gardiner, *The Nature of Historical Explanation,* p. 1, Oxford, 1952.
11. C. G. Hempel, *op. cit.,* p. 465.
12. E. Nagel, *The Structure of Science,* p. 558, New York, 1961.
13. *Ibid.,* p. 561.
14. *Ibid.,* p. 561.
15. C. G. Hempel, *op. cit.,* p. 465.
16. Q. Gibson, *The Logic of Social Inquiry,* p. 187, London, 1960.
17. *Ibid.,* p. 191.
18. E. Nagel, "Relativism and some problems of working historians", in S. Hook (ed.), *Philosophy and History,* pp. 90-91, New York, 1963.
19. A. M. McIver, "The character of historical explanation", in A. M. McIver, W. H. Walsh and M. Ginsberg, *Aristotelian Society,* Supplementary vol. XXI, p. 42, London, 1947.
20. W. H. Walsh, *An Introduction to Philosophy of History,* p. 41, London, 1951.
21. The problem of understanding history was approached from a different aspect and, as a result, interpreted differently by Leszek Kołakowski in his sketch "Rozumienie historyczne i zrozumiałiść zdarzenia historycznego" ("Historical reasoning and the intelligibility of historical events") in L. Kołakowski, *Kultura i fetysze* ("Culture and Fetishes"), Warsaw, 1967.
22. William H. Dray, *Philosophy of History,* p. 25, Englewood Cliffs, Prentice-Hall, 1964.

CHAPTER 7

Why is History Continuously Written Anew?

"There is no doubt at present that the world's history must be from time to time written anew. Nonetheless, such a necessity is not derived in the least from the fact that many heretofore unknown events have been discovered but from the fact that new views have arisen that the one who accompanies the forward flow of time arrives at viewpoints from which he can look at the past anew and evaluate it. . . ."

J. W. Goethe, *Geschichte der Farbeniehre*

". . . the anatomy of man is the key to the anatomy of the monkey. In lower animal species one cannot comprehend the signs forecasting higher forms unless these higher forms are already known."

K. Marx, *Introduction to the Critique of Political Economy*

E. H. Carr began his book *What is History?* from a stimulating juxtaposition of two statements regarding historical cognition in two editions of the large synthesis of history composed by the Cambridge scholars, which came out sixty years apart. These statements are not only symptomatic and suggestive but also instructive. Since they are an excellent introduction to the subject which interests us, we shall, following E. H. Carr's footsteps, also begin with them.

In 1896 the eminent British historian Lord Acton, in characterizing the aims of the *Cambridge Modern History,* wrote the following words in his report to the Syndics of the Cambridge University Press:

> It is a unique opportunity of recording, in the way most useful to the greatest number, the fullness of the knowledge which the 19th century is about to bequeath. . . . By the judicious division of labour we should be able to do it, and to bring home to every man the last document, and the ripest conclusions of international research.
>
> Ultimate history we cannot have in this generation: but we can dispose of conventional history and show the point we have reached on the road from one to the other, now that all information is within reach, and every problem has been capable of solution.[1]

Sixty years after this optimistic statement, unconcernedly assured regarding history's cognitive value, George Clark referred to it in the following fashion in his general introduction to *The New Cambridge Modern History*.

> Historians of a later generation do not look forward to any such prospect. They expect their work to be superseded again and again. They consider that knowledge of the past has come down through one or more human minds, has been "processed" by them, and therefore cannot consist of elemental and impersonal atoms which nothing can alter. . . . The exploration seems to be endless, and some impatient scholars take refuge in scepticism, or at least in the doctrine that, since all historical judgement involve persons and points of view, one is as good as another and there is no "objective" historical truth.[2]

The change of positions here is clear and striking: the positivist faith in the cumulative power of historical knowledge, which can attain the status of an ultimately grounded and finished knowledge, gives place to a conviction that historical cognition is an infinite process and, since the human mind plays an active role in it, the historian's work must be continuously undertaken anew. This is a change whose basis and reasons are known to us from preceding conclusions. It faces us with a new aspect of an interesting problem: why does the interpretation of the historical process change unceasingly, why do historians continuously write history anew and differently?

That this is so, in reality, is an indisputable fact. It may be illustrated by means of the history of the historical writing of any important historical event. We do not take into consideration here the difference in viewing historical reality, the differences of interpretation and explanation of the historical process, which are the results of the social conditioning of the historian's views. Apart from these class, national and other differences—and even in spite of their existence—there emerges, after all, something which is common to the works of a given period, as distinct from the works of other periods, something which, in spite of the differences, joins them together within the framework of a way of looking at history and a style of its interpretation which is specific to a given epoch. This is precisely what interests us: why does practically every generation have, and, according to some, even should have its own vision of the historical process? Where does this come from and what influences this?

This problem has fascinated many theorists of history in the twentieth century, who have dealt with the undoubted fact of the changeability of the vision of the historical process in the broader context of reflections regarding the manifold conditionings of the process of historical cognition. The various views expressed on the subject may be placed within the framework of two typological groups which, although they impinge upon each other, explain this phenomenon differently:

1. That the reinterpretation of history is a function of the varying needs of the present.
2. That the reinterpretation of history is a function of the emerging effects of the events of the past.

It is clear that this delimitation is neither a sharp one, as has been stated already, nor does it constitute counterposed methods of expounding the phenomenon which interests us here; on the contrary, they both often appear simultaneously and alongside each other as complementary factors of explanation. The distinct examination of these methods is justified by the facilitating of the analysis of a complex phenomenon and the clarity in the exposition of the results obtained in this fashion. In the further course of our considerations we shall thus present our arguments in the sequence referred to above, with the assumption that these factors are complementary, and that a need to treat them separately arises for didactic reasons.

The first type of explanation of the constant reinterpretation of history is bound up with the position of presentism and is represented mainly by its advocates. As we know, presentism in its extreme form leads to a negation of objective historical truth and thus, in consequence, to a negation of history as a science. Nonetheless, that which constitutes the rational core of presentism, the genetic-psychological concept that the historian's stands and views are linked with the social conditions of contemporary life and its associated needs, is not a subjectivist concept and does not lead to negative consequences with respect to the scientific character of history. However, even on the basis of this moderate interpretation of presentism, the conclusion regarding the need, and even the necessity, of a constant reinterpretation of history, is inevitable. If the stands and views of historians are shaped as a function of the contemporary conditions of social life and its needs, then it is understandable that in step with a change of these conditions and needs, the stands and views of the historians, as well as the product of their creative activity—history—must also change. If, as Carl L. Becker had stated metaphorically, the past is a screen on which the present projects a vision of the past,[3] then history is, in consequence, not only functional but also necessarily changeable.

Nonetheless, let us attempt to analyse this concept more closely by posing a few additional questions in connection with it.

First of all, let us inquire about the mechanism of this projection of the interests of the present day on to the screen of the past. It takes place by means of an appropriate selection of historical facts, which is changeable, since it is a function of present-day interests.

John Dewey, who from this viewpoint may be regarded as a representative figure, in stressing that all historical construction is selective and everything in this domain depends on the criteria of selection, reached the conclusion that history is necessarily written from the position of the present which decides, after all, what is to be regarded as important, and thus determines the criteria for selection.[4] Here also we meet an explanation of the constant reinterpretation of history: "There is no material available for leading principles and hypotheses save that of the historical present. As culture changes, the conceptions that are dominant in a culture change. Of necessity new standpoints for viewing, appraising and ordering data arise. History is then rewritten."[5]

In this interpretation history is a function of present-day interests or—as M. N. Pokrovsky had it—contemporary politics projected into the past. The view that a vision of the *past* is a function of the aims which we set for the *future* is a variant of this position.[6] This does not change the essence, since our vision of the future is also just as much a function of the present-day as our vision of the past.

As postulated above, let us reject the extreme version of presentism, and what is left is a concept whose correctness cannot be denied: we rewrite history continuously anew, since the criteria of the appraisal of importance of past events change in time, and along with them the perception and selection of historical facts; hence, the historical image itself also changes. It is worth emphasizing that this concept, in one verbal formulation or another, is accepted by various students of the problem, totally unconnected with presentism, or even completely opposed to this world outlook. M. N. Pokrovsky, as we have mentioned, starting from the Marxist concept regarding the class conditioning of views on social problems, saw history as the politics of the present projected onto the past. K. R. Popper, connected, after all, with neo-positivism, postulated the reinterpretation of history by each new generation as a duty derived from new deeds.[7] In Polish literature on the subject W. Kula speaks of the translation by each epoch of the heritage of the past into a contemporary language with the addition that the richer a culture becomes the more able it is to draw from the past.[8] As we can note, the verbal formulation differs, as does the argumentation, but the idea remains the same: the changeability of the historical image is a function of the changeability of the criteria for the selection of historical material.

The second question, which arises in this context, pertains to the psychological aspect of the process of the reinterpretation of history; when are historians inclined to undertake new appraisals and new interpretations of history? An extremely suggestive and common-sensical reply to this question is to be found in C. L. Becker's previously quoted work. Periods of stabilization which favour a feeling of satisfaction with the present also favour the acceptance of a traditional image of the past. On the other hand, in periods of storm and stress, when stabilization has been upset, people dissatisfied with the present are inclined to be dissatisfied also with the past. History is then subjected to reinterpretation in the light of contemporary problems and difficulties.[9]

Nevertheless, another type of argument in favour of the need of a constant reinterpretation of history, which explains the fact of the changeability of the historical image in almost every generation, appears as well. It takes as its basis the changeability of the vision as a result of the constant emergence of new effects caused by the events of the past.

Marx's position, as expressed in the aphorism "Human anatomy is a key to the anatomy of the monkey", is classical in this respect.

Marx developed his stand on the basis of an analysis of economic categories. Since bourgeois society is the most highly developed organization of production, then the categories which make it possible to understand the structure of this society make it possible simultaneously to understand the structure of past social forms. Why? Since it is only a higher stage of development of a given segment of reality which, by revealing the effects of past events, makes possible their proper vision and appraisal. This is the meaning of the metaphorical saying that human anatomy is a key to the anatomy of the monkey.

In order to explain this position better let us resort to another comparison. If we find ourselves on a plateau we can note only the immediate surroundings, while other details of the formation of the terrain, as well as their mutual interconnections into a given entirety, escape us. But it is enough to climb one of the mountains to have the landscape change its character and reveal heretofore unknown and unnoticed lowland features. The higher we climb the broader is our horizon, the better our grasp of the whole.

This is, of course, only a comparison but it makes it possible to comprehend better the problem of interest to us. It is only necessary to change the spatial parameters into temporal ones. The further away we are in time from a given event, the more profoundly and comprehensively we perceive it and are able to evaluate it, just as a landscape looked at from an ever greater altitude. Why? Because we are always dealing with processes and it is very difficult, if not impossible, to foresee in advance not only the details but even the general trend of events. Hegel's colourful saying about Minerva's owl, which flies out at twilight, is fully applicable here. It is only after the results of events-causes have appeared that they can be evaluated. Here again, however, this is not a static judgement, but a judgement-process. When dealing with a continuing process, the effects of events appear constantly, without end, and history is precisely such a process. New effects impel one to look at the events in a new fashion, to interpret them differently, to place them differently in the context of the whole. It often happens, then, that what was originally not appreciated or perhaps even completely disregarded, now appears to be historically significant and vice versa. As a result, the image of the whole also becomes different in form. This is precisely why we see history better from a certain time perspective, when the effects of events, having been already revealed, make possible a fuller and more profound appraisal of them; this is why it is so difficult to write modern and especially contemporary history. The point is not only that it is difficult to achieve objectivity, in the sense of interpreting events "sine era et studio", although this is also undoubtedly important, but, above all, that it is most difficult to comprehend the meaning of events which are contemporary to us. They have not yet revealed their effects and the significance of historical events rests in the effects which they bring about in reality.

This position, which is in accord with the principles of historicism, is adhered to by scholars belonging to different schools of thought.

We have already become acquainted with Marx's remark on the subject which served as the epigraph for this chapter. Here are some statements by authors representing different views in the domain of the theory of history.

Sidney Hook wrote on this subject in the following fashion:

> . . . history will be rewritten whenever new perspectives arise that enable us to see the significance of some past events which escaped their contemporaries. These events fall into patterns of continuity which embrace events that were future to those who lived in the past. . . .
> . . . Similarly, those who live after us in some ways will understand our age better than we do ourselves, because they will be in a position to see what came out of events which we presently ignore and which are unsuspected beginnings of important trends that will reach fruition after we are gone.[10]

This is a statement maintained in the spirit of the classical position: it is only the effects of events, only the fulfilment of the future which makes possible a comprehension of the past, but further effects and the new future bring with them a new image of the past.

The Belgian historian M. J. Dhont, although approaching the problem differently, presents it in a similar fashion:

> The historian never sees the facts in the way that the *contemporaries* saw them. He sees their development as an infallible prophet; what distinguishes the historian completely from any category of people who were contemporaries to the facts about which he speaks rests precisely in that the historian knows the future. This deprives him completely of the possibility of looking at the facts with the eyes of the contemporaries. . . . It follows from this remark that the historian always writes history as a function of the point of arrival of development. This will incline him to interpret as important those events which constitute a line of development towards that result, events, which in a majority of cases, did not make the least impression on their contemporaries.[11]

Karl Heussi took up the same thought from the aspect of the new relations of the given events with others as they emerged in the historical process. In conclusion he wrote:

The past greatnesses which we may possibly not regard as particularly significant may, in the time which is the future for us, lead under certain circumstances, to significant results. From this point of view, the past is not something immobile, but something which is alive, constantly changing and growing.[12]

It is, however, in the works of J. H. Randall Jr. that we find this thought in its most expanded form.[13] In illustrating, on the basis of the example of the evaluation of World War I, the concept regarding the changeability of the historical image in line with the appearance of new effects of past events, Randall concluded:

New consequences flowing from past events change the significance of the past, of what has happened. Events which before had been overlooked, because they did not seem "basic" to anything that followed, now come to be selected as highly significant; other events that used to seem "basic" recede into the limbo of mere details. In this sense, a history-that-happens is not and in the nature of the case cannot be fully understood by the actors in it. They cannot realize the "significance" or consequences of what they are doing, since they cannot foresee the future. We understand that history only when it has become a part of our own past; and if it continues to have consequences, our children will understand it still differently. In this sense, the historian, as Hegel proclaimed, is like the owl of Minerva, who takes his flight only when the shades of night are gathering. . . . The significance of any history-that-happens is not completely grasped until all its consequences have been discerned. The "meaning" of any historical fact is what it does, how it continues to behave and operate, what consequences follow from it.[14]

Thus, two factors function together towards a constant reinterpretation of history: the emergence in the historical process of the effects of past events, which constitute their "significance", and the change in the criteria for the selection of historical facts as a result of a different conditioning of the stands and views of historians. Both these factors are, as already mentioned, bound up with the present which is the future in relation to past events. The rational core of the conception of presentism rests in this.

Nonetheless, does not this changeability of the image of the past which, using Heussi's suggestive formulation, is not taken as something immobile, but as something living, continuously changing, negate the objectivity of historical cognition, negate the possibility of obtaining the objective truth in this cognition? It does not, if we do not commit the previously discussed error of identifying the objectivity of truth with its absoluteness. Partial, fragmentary truths are not a falsehood, but an objective, although incomplete truth. It follows only from the fact that history (in the meaning of "historiae rerum gestarum") is never ultimately finished, that it undergoes constant reinterpretation that it is a process, an image which is not ultimately complete, that it is not an absolute truth. But this is a platitude if one understands the process-like character of cognition. Historical truths have an additative, cumulative character and historical cognition has the character of a process. In comprehending this, we understand thereby the regularity of the phenomenon of the constant reinterpretation of history, a changeability which not only does not negate the objectivity of truth but, on the contrary, is its substantiation in a process-like interpretation of historical cognition.

Notes

1. "The Cambridge Modern History: its origin, authorship and production" (1907), pp. 10-12; quoted in E. H. Carr, *What is History?* p. 1.
2. *Ibid.,* pp. 1-2.
3. C. L. Becker, "Mr. Wells and the New History", in *Everyman His Own Historian, Essays on History and Politics,* pp. 169-170, New York, 1935.
4. J. Dewey, *Logic, the Theory of Inquiry,* p. 235, New York, 1949.
5. *Ibid.,* p. 233.
6. E. H. Carr, *What is History?,* p. 118.
7. K. R. Popper, *Die offene Gesellschaft und ihre Feinde,* p. 332, Bd. II, Bern, 1958.
8. W. Kula, *Rozważania o Historii,* pp. 104-105, Warsaw, 1958.
9. C. L. Becker, *op. cit.,* p. 170.
10. S. Hook, "Objectivity and reconstruction in history", in S. Hook (ed.), *Philosophy and History,* p. 256, New York, 1963.
11. M. J. Dhont, "Histoire et reconstitution du passé", in C. Perelman (éd.), *Raissonnement et demarches de l'historien,* pp. 87-88, Brussels, 1963.
12. K. Heussi, *Die Krisis des Historismus,* p. 69, Tübingen, 1922.
13. See J. H. Randall, Jr., *Nature and Historical Experience,* New York, 1958, and "On understanding the history of philosophy", the *Journal of Philosophy,* no. 17 (1939).
14. J. H. Randall and G. Haines, "Controlling assumptions in the practice of American historians", in *Theory and Practice in Historical Study. A Report of the Committee on Historiography, Social Science Research Council,* Bulletin 54, p. 20, 1946.

CHAPTER 8

The Objectivity of Historical Truth

"Even the usual average historian who believes in maintaining that his stand is purely receptive and that he only follows the facts is not passive in his thinking but contributes his own categories through which he regards that which exists."

Hegel, *Lectures on the Philosophy of History*

"The poet creates his world arbitrarily in accord with his own idea and, therefore, can present it in a perfect and finished fashion; the historian is cramped since he must build his world in such a fashion as to have all the fragments which history has preserved for us fit into it. This is why he will never be able to bring forth a perfect work and the effort of his searchings, collecting, seeking and assembling will always remain apparent."

Goethes *Gespräche;* Gespräch mit H. Luden

At the beginning of the present work, in the chapter devoted to the gnoseological premises of considerations regarding historical truth, we distinguished three meanings of the word "objective" when it is employed as an adjective in the expression "objective cognition":

1. "objective" is tantamount to that which is derived from an object, which exists outside of the cognizing mind and independent of it: "objective cognition" is a cognition which reflects (in a special meaning of this word) that object;
2. "objective" is tantamount to "cognitively significant for all";
3. "objective" signifies "free from emotional coloration and partiality linked therewith".

The word "subjective" means correspondingly:

1. a creation of the subject;
2. having a cognitive value not for all;
3. colored emotionally and thus, in connection with this, partial.

Let us begin with the first of the meanings of the word "objective" listed above. As we have noted, objective cognition is the same as cognition derived from an object, a cognition constituting a special reflection of this object. When one takes the stand of materialism there is in this interpretation a banal aspect, to the effect that human cognition is the cognition of an objective object, existing apart and independent of the human mind. Nonetheless, besides this, there stretches a field of immense complications both for the materialist, and perhaps even, above all, for the materialist (for subjective idealism *this* problem does not exist at all). What is at issue here is the role of the subject in the process of cognition or, to put it differently, the role of the subjective factor in cognition.

In discussing the gnoseological premises of the problem we are concerned with, we drew attention to the danger of a mechanistic interpretation of the process of cognition, when in the subject-object relation its first component is taken as a passive element. The entire course of our further analysis of the factors which socially condition historical cognition has provided additional proofs of the erroneousness of such an interpretation. The subject plays an active role in historical cognition and the objectivity of this cognition always contains a subjective admixture. Otherwise, it would be a non-human or superhuman cognition.

Objective cognition, in spite of the suggestions emanating from the word "objective", always contains contents which cannot be reduced exclusively to the object but are bound up with the quality of the given, historically (thus concretely socially) shaped object. Given a proper interpretation of the process of cognition, this is a trite observation. But in the light of such a conception it is unnecessary either to be frightened of this role of the subject or to seek artificially to eliminate it. This is simply impossible since there can be no cognition without the cognizing subject; it has to be involved in the process of cognition. What matters is to comprehend its proper role since only then can one counteract effectively the deformations which threaten and overcome excrescences of the subjective factor in cognition. It is only this which is a real task in the striving towards what we qualify as objective cognition. As H. M. Lynd has noted correctly in his essay on the objectivity of historical cognition, the more precisely we are able to define what the subject contributes to a cognition of an object, the more exactly can we become aware of what this object really is.

Any order inherent in the external world may be presented more clearly the more conscious we are of the order inherent in our method of observation. *Any accuracy obtained by us is accessible solely under the condition of being aware of the observer's role as a part of the process of observation, not by means of disregarding this observer but by taking him into account.* Even in physics it is necessary to take into consideration the fact that the thing measured is effected by the instrument which measures it and vice versa. *There is no greater obstacle on the path towards the obtaining of objectivity than the confusion of "subjectivity" with the fact of taking into account the position of the observer.* [1]

This thought has been developed and concretized by Paul Ricoeur in his *Histoire et Verité*. After analysing the main forms of the subjective factor in historical cognition: evaluating judgements in connection with the selection of historical material, causal explanation and the hierarchization of the various types of historical causes, the historical imagination and finally the human factor as an object in history, Ricoeur presented in a more concrete form the concept that the historian constitutes a part of history. Does this signify an undermining of the objectivity of historical truth? Not in the least. So-called pure objectivity is, after all, a fiction, the subjective factor is introduced into historical cognition by the very fact of the existence of the cognizing subject. On the other hand, different types of this subjectivity may appear: A "good" one, that is, one which is derived from the essence of cognition as a subject-object relation and from the active role of the subjective in the process of cognition, and a "bad" one, that is, one which deforms cognition as a result of the actions of the factor of interest, partiality, etc. "Objectivity" is thus the name for the difference between this good and bad subjectivity and not its complete elimination. ". . . Objectivity appeared first as the *scientific* intention of history; at present, it signifies the divergence between an historian's good and bad subjectivity; the definition of objectivity has been transformed from a 'logical' into an 'ethical' one." [2]

This concept, so simple and simultaneously so profound, leads us to the principle problem: how to attain the objectivity of historical cognition, by overcoming "bad" subjectivity.

The issue here pertains, above all, to objectivity in the second and third meanings of this word listed above: objectivity in the sense of impartiality and the general value of judgement.

Let us commence with the trite, but nonetheless not always fully realized truth that the identification of the objectivity of cognition with full impartiality, with an absolute uniformity of appraisals of the historical process, rests on a misunderstanding. One of the most eminent Polish historians Michal Bobrzyński expressed this thought very clearly and convincingly.

What is the historian's impartiality, which is spoken of so often?

One can never really demand impartiality in the precise meaning of this word from the historian. It is only the historical fact, which is the historian's object of study, which can be impartial. The historian desiring to appraise this fact must take a certain position in respect to it. . . . The historian's stand can and should be scientific, can be high and ever higher, but it must always be a certain stand and viewpoint. His successor, who will ascend to a higher stand, will see more broadly, will appraise more impartially and better, will also find someone else who will surpass him in this respect. The historian who would strive towards an impossibility, that is, who would desire to be completely impartial and not take any stand, would be similar to a man who wanders through a forest, rubs against trees, smells their fragrances, sees their roots and trunks, but does not embrace one thing—the forest itself.

The historian's impartiality, in the good and advantageous meaning of this word, can be only denoted as his effort to free himself, in his judgement from all aims which, in his conviction, are foreign and alien to historical and scientific truth. This is for him the most difficult task. . . . We have defined the historian's impartiality only as his sincere effort, which has brought with it a greater or smaller result. Profound knowledge, an excellent research method, and arduous work aid in this effort, but the result of this effort is never complete, for the historian always remains a human being.[3]

As we have stated above, there are two kinds of subjectivity: the one which, in natural fashion, is bound up with the active role of the subject in cognition and therefore cannot be completely eliminated, although its particular manifestation may be overcome in the infinite process of the perfection of cognition, and the one derived from extra-scientific sources, such as personal interests, distaste for a given person, prejudice towards certain groups of people on the basis of nationality or class, etc. While it is true that the boundary between these two types of subjectivity is not sharp, and that they interpenetrate each other, it is possible and necessary, however, to distinguish every day, extra-scientific, "bad", subjectivity by putting forth, as Ricoeur does, the postulate that the historian should approach historical events *sine ira et studio*. This postulate is clear and simple, although its realization is by no means easy and, in practice, it appears only as a process. The problem of "good" subjectivity, connected in a natural fashion with the active role of the subject in cognition, is much more complicated.

The historian—the cognizing subject—is a man, like every other, and cannot cast off human traits. He is unable to think in isolation from the categories of a given language, he has a personality shaped socially within the framework of a concrete historical reality, he belongs to a definite nation, a definite class, stratum, professional group, etc., with all the consequences flowing therefrom in the field of the stereotypes accepted by him (most often unconsciously), of whose culture he is a product, while simultaneously being its creator, etc. If one adds to this the biological and psychosomatic factors which, in spite of their social links, constitute a factor of personal differentiation transmitted by heredity, then we obtain an immense number of parameters which, in addition, have a complicated structure whose resultant defines the individual as the subject in the process of cognition. It is obvious that, as a result, we arrive at the specificity of an individual, as well as the specificity of certain classes of individuals which, in addition to individual differences, show certain common traits which may be extrapolated as group traits.

If objectivity of cognition were to signify the elimination of all such individual traits of the human personality, if impartiality were to rest in the fact that appraisals are to be made by rejecting one's own stand and system of values, if a universal value of judgement were to rest in the fact that all individual and group differences therein were to be eliminated, then objectivity would be simply a fiction, since it would assume that man is a superhuman being. Man, in knowing, always remains, to use a simile, in boots of some sort; he may, it is true, jump out, although with difficulty, from one pair (in spite of the saying) but only under the condition that he puts on another pair. In this case, one can simply not do without "boots" and corresponding postulates are based on a misunderstanding.

But objectivity of historical cognition in the meaning of its impartiality and hence of its universal value is not to be reduced, as Bobrzyński has it, only to the efforts of the historian "to free himself in his judgement from all aims which, in his conviction, are foreign and alien to historical and scientific truth". This is an exaggerated scepticism bound up, as it happens, with the state of the theory of cognition in the period when this opinion was formulated. Today we know that the subjective factor in the historian's cognition does not consist solely of the intervention of extra-scientific aims, but rests in scientific cognition itself, in its manifold social conditioning. The proper problem, or at least the most interesting problem, lies precisely in the examination of the conditions and forms of overcoming this feature of subjectivity (this is a *par excellence* process-like activity).

The work of the historian, as Pirenne has stated,[4] is simultaneously a synthesis and a hypothesis: a synthesis, in so far as it strives towards a total recreation of an image on the basis of a knowledge of individual facts; a hypothesis, in so far as the relations determined between these facts are never ultimately obvious or provable. It would be better perhaps to say that what arises as a result of the historian's work is a synthesis of a hypothetical character, since these two aspects of the historian's work, synthesis and hypothesis, can be isolated only by means of abstraction, while in fact they constitute a unity. The emphasizing of the hypothetical nature of the results of the historian's work is only another way of interpreting the role which the subjective factor plays in this work.

Pirenne illustrated this hypothetical nature in the determination of relations between facts with various cases; all of them express the influence of the subjective factor on historical cognition: the theoretical background, knowledge about social reality and its laws, creative imagination, a comprehension of human actions, etc., all this causes different historians to interpret the same material in various ways. Is it thus possible to overcome the influence of the subjective factor? The answer is a positive one, if one takes into consideration the cumulative nature of knowledge which becomes enriched in gathering partial truths.

> Each author throws light on some part, brings certain features into relief, considers certain aspects. The more these accounts multiply, the more the infinite reality is freed from its veils. All these accounts are incomplete, all imperfect, but all contribute to the advancement of knowledge.[5]

Hence, the solution here lies in a transition from a platform of individual cognition to the platform of cognition as a social process; individual cognition is always limited, burdened by the influence of the subjective factor, having the nature of a partial, and in this sense a relative truth, but cognition taken in the scale of humanity, understood as an infinite process of overcoming the limitations of relative truths by means of the formulation of more complete truths, is a process advancing towards full cognition. This prescription for overcoming the subjective factor in an infinite process of social perfection of knowledge corresponds to Engels' concepts regarding relative and absolute truth which he set forth in *Anti-Dühring*. We may find a similar trend of thought in the work of K. R. Popper. He also emphasized the necessity of a transition to the social platform, if one desired to solve the problem of objectivity of cognition: it can be assured by the co-operation of many scholars (objectivity of cognition is tantamount to the intersubjectivity of the scientific method) and consistent scientific criticism which makes possible the constant progress of cognition.[6]

Thus, the overcoming of the influence of the subjective factor, which deforms cognition, takes place in the social process of the progress of knowledge, by the accumulation of partial truths. This does not signify, however, that the overcoming of the limitations of cognition is impossible on an individual scale, as a process of the scientific ontogenesis of the individual scholar. Mannheim dealt with this problem, amongst others, in his sociology of knowledge.

The influence of the subject on cognition is inevitable, since one could eliminate the subject from the cognitive relation only together with this relation itself. An understanding of this state of affairs gives rise to the conclusion that the striving for objectivity of cognition cannot depend on the total elimination of the subjective factor in cognition—such a postulate is fictitious—but on the overcoming of the concrete manifestations of the deforming influence of the subjective factor, which clearly endows the process of such overcoming with an infinite nature. Hence, the dissatisfaction of those who sought to obtain the results in the form of absolute truth, not being aware of the fact that it is attainable in this field solely in the shape of an infinite process. Hence, simultaneously, a cause for satisfaction of those who, taking progress of knowledge as the accumulation of partial truths, correctly envisage in each overcoming of one of the limitations of the degree of cognition already achieved, a new stage in the progress of human knowledge. The path towards overcoming the deforming influence of the subjective factor lies in the awareness of its character and influence. The more we know about what and how the active role of the subject contributes to the process of cognition, the better and more profoundly we come to know the features of the object. In analogy to the situation in which, when, being aware of the mutual interactions in the physical dimensions of the object studied and the instrument with which we conduct these studies, we are able to introduce appropriate corrections, eliminate or minimize the errors.

The above thought constituted the core of Mannheim's concept of "recalculating perspectives". This comparison is a striking one and exceedingly well chosen. Similarly, when knowing the laws of geometric perspective we are always able to transpose an image into another perspective, to look at an object from another point of view— although it is always a *certain* perspective and a *certain* point of view —and as a result by multiplying these perspectives and points of view we attain an ever fuller, an ever more global vision of the object; we can similarly attain progress in other domains of knowledge as well. However, it is necessary to have knowledge regarding the perspectives and the method of "recalculating" them, of passing over from one point of view, which reveals to us one aspect, one vision of the object, to another point of view which reveals to us another aspect of it and thus another vision of it. This knowledge, objective in nature, is based on a familiarity with the traits of the cognizing subject, of the way in which he undertakes the act of cognition and what he contributes to this act by his cognitive activity. In other words, what is necessary here is knowledge about the cognitive instrument, a familiarity with its parameters and methods of reacting to the subject under examination. This is a relatively simple task in the case of the instrument which serves for physical measurements; it is much more complicated in the case of calculating the influence of the human perceptual apparatus on the image of the object perceived, on the perspective of the perception; it is infinitely more complicated when seeking to be aware of the active role of the cognizing subject, of the influence of the so-called subjective factor on the cognition of changing social reality.

The complicated nature of this task derives, above all, from the fact that the number of parameters is much greater than in the case of physical measurements or visual perception and, in addition, one is concerned here with an object undergoing changes in the course of cognition. This is why, amongst others, it is impossible to codify in this field any prescriptions for "recalculating perspectives", to state in advance how one should overcome particular manifestations of cognitive deformation, connected with the functioning of the subjective factor. After all, one does not know in advance what this factor is, what will be its influence in given conditions, and hence how one should act in order to overcome it. On the other hand, it is possible to put forth the general concept that one should, in the first place, become *aware* of the deforming situation and discover its connection with the functioning of a given factor. This general concept can serve as a basis for an appropriate methodological doctrine relating to the cognitive conduct which is to vitiate this evil. This is precisely what the sociology of knowledge had in mind in its doctrine "recalculating perspectives", and in its theory of the intelligentsia as the bearer of the appropriate cognitive function. Herein also rested one of the main theoretical merits of the sociology of knowledge, in spite of all its stumblings and difficulties in this field which we have already dealt with in detail elsewhere.

The directive: "become aware of the subjective factor which you bring into cognition and of the danger of cognitive deformation bound up therewith" appears to be naïve. Is this not a pious wish? How can one, by oneself, arrive at one's own cognitive limitations and subsequently even overcome them, if the corresponding point of view seems to be a "natural" one, as a result of social conditioning? Nonetheless, this is only an appearance of *naïveté,* since the directive has a content which is not in the least trite and its fulfilment in cognitive practice is not merely a pious wish doomed to failure in advance. Precisely because it is not so, the sociology of knowledge and its directives have a considerable cognitive value, and the formulation of its theses, signifying the comprehension of certain regularities of the cognitive process was of quite revolutionary significance with respect to the process of knowledge regarding social problems.

The awareness that cognition is affected by factors which deform it, is of long standing; Bacon had already endowed this with a theoretical shape with his conception of the "idol". Nevertheless, as we have already stated above, the bringing out of the theoretical implications, in the shape of the theory of the basis and the superstructure and in the theory of ideology, was the achievement of Marxism. Modern sociology of knowledge concretizes and develops this set of ideas. It is precisely this theoretical fact—that recognition of the social conditioning of human cognition and of the influence of the subjective factor in deforming cognition, as a regularity, and not as only a haphazard event—which is the starting-point for activity which will make possible the steady overcoming of subsequent, concrete forms of limitations and deformations of cognition.

The starting-point here cannot be the individual but the social aspect of the process of cognition. The semblance of *naïveté* of the directives of the sociology of knowledge is bound up precisely with the erroneous shifting of the problem to a purely individual platform. In such cases, the following question may seem justified: "In what fashion can one become aware of the influence of the subjective factor if its functioning on the basis of the social conditioning of individual cognition is such, that it is experienced as an objective factor?" The fact is that the starting-point of the question thus posed is erroneous.

The cognizing subject, socially conditioned and introducing the subjective factor into the process of cognition, is, after all, not an isolated atom, not Leibnitz's "monad without windows". On the contrary, he is shaped by its own environment and also shaped by contemporary science, of course, on the condition that he is sufficiently educated. It is precisely by means of this path that knowledge about the subjective factor in cognition and the role of this factor in deforming cognition reaches his consciousness. In our opinion, the significance, the role of the sociology of knowledge which revolutionizes cognition rests precisely in this.

The sum of knowledge of contemporary man which gives rise to the fact that many revolutionary discoveries and inventions seem to him to be obvious, is not an individual but a social product. This is a trite assertion. Nevertheless, it pertains also to the ever more general awareness that our cognition is conditioned manifoldly, that these conditionings, if they do not deform cognition outright, then they cause at least its limitations and one-sidedness; that as a result, the truths attained in our cognition do not possess a full, ultimate and absolute nature (with the exception of the relatively narrow scope of cognition in which partial absolute truths are attainable), but are always limited, partial, relative truths (not including so-called partial absolute truths, when these are placed in the context of broader fields of cognition). The psychological effects of this knowledge are significant. A vigilance in respect to claims to absolute, "purely" objective cognition, may be either by oneself or by others; to desire to analyse this cognition in order to reveal its limitations and the interfering subjective factor; in connection with this, a growing tolerance towards the views of the opponent which are not in accord with one's own, a tolerance not in the meaning of resigning from a consistent defence of ones own position, but in the sense of a readiness to recognize the relative truths which the views of the opponent contain. It is this, precisely, which constitutes the "equipment" of modern man and especially of the intelligentsia which is professionally trained for this, an "equipment" which makes it possible to undertake the overcoming of the subjective factor with full optimism as to the results of these activities. This is so, of course, always in a non-absolute sense, always in the sense of overcoming this concrete manifestation of the subjective factor, this concrete limitation or one-sidedness of cognition, and not the overcoming of the influence of the subjective factor in general, or of all the limitations and one-sidednesses of cognition.

The process of overcoming the deforming influence of the subjective factor is a social process: both in the meaning that the awareness by the cognizing subject of the limited and socially conditioned nature of his cognition has a social origin, since the theoretical awareness of this state of affairs is brought in "from the outside", as socially constituted knowledge which the subject acquires in the process of education, as well as in the fact that the very process itself of overcoming the influence of the subjective factor on the process of cognition has a social nature in the meaning of co-operation of scholars and, above all, in the form of scientific criticism. The point does not rest, however, in that someone else, the critic, perceives and overcomes the limitations of the views of the person criticized. This does frequently happen, but the ascertainment of this factor is banal. What we are interested in here, above all, is *self-criticism, self-reflection* on the limitations of one's own cognition, the ability for *self-correction* of this cognition by means of overcoming the deforming influence of the subjective factor. The theory of "recalculating perspectives" and the directive of Mannheim's sociology of knowledge linked therewith pertains primarily to this process. This problem is particularly interesting from the point of view of striving towards objectivity of cognition.

The cognizing subject, in this case the historian, is, as we know, conditioned socially in many ways and introduces into cognition a correspondingly shaped subjective factor: prejudices, bias, predilections and phobias which mark his cognitive stand, as well as a corresponding vision of social reality, bound up with the theory accepted by him and the system of values utilized; a tendency to a corresponding articulation of this reality, an articulation which leads to the construction, out of fragments, of facts which are significant in a given system of reference; a readiness to accept a given selection of historical facts, that is, those considered to be significant from the viewpoint of the historical process, etc. The cognizing subject cannot rid himself of this property—social conditioning with respect to cognition—simply because he is a man and a human personality cannot be shaped in any other fashion than socially, by means of an appropriately understood education. Nonetheless, being unable to rid himself of this property, which belongs to his "essence", the cognizing subject *can* be aware of it, be conscious of the fact that this is an inseparable trait of all cognition. He is not only able to do this but, in certain conditions, when appropriate knowledge has been gained and socially universalized, he *should* do so in order to avoid the disqualification of the level of his scientific reflection. This, in turn, leads to far-reaching results.

The scholar may be—and most often is—infected in his views and stands by those phobias, prejudices, tendencies to interpret and evaluate events, which are characteristic of his epoch, class, social and professional milieu, etc. This affects his view of the world, his position and viewpoints regarding social problems in an extremely essential way and this, in turn, must influence his vision of the historical process, the construction and selection of historical facts, not to mention their interpretation when taking up historical syntheses. It is precisely this content which is to be found under the cryptonym "the subjective factor in historical cognition".

It can be agreed that the emergence of this factor in historical cognition is inevitable, although its shape can and even must be variable. But does some *fatum* bear down on the historian who has been correspondingly shaped, as a result of a given historical conditioning? Does the personality of the historian, once it has been shaped *have* to remain changeless, be deprived of all elasticity and dynamics? Can the limitation of his views, derived from the given nature of the subjective factor, hence, be overcome by means of scientific criticism only by *other* thinkers; above all, those who represent other views, derived from different social conditioning, either connected with a change of a general condition of the epoch, or evolved from a different class interest of the milieu to which the given historian belongs?

All these questions are rhetorical in nature and the answer to them is, of course, negative. We know from experience that man is a malleable being, capable of change and adaptation. Herein rests, among other things, man's superiority to the rest of the animal world. This pertains also to the psychic aspect of human life. We know from experience that the theoretical views of scholars are malleable and susceptible to change, and that they are often able not only to undertake superficial modifications of their positions, which is normal in the creativeness of every scholar, even if simply as the function of knowledge and experience accumulated with age, but also profound changes, profound scientific self-criticism which leads outright to the rejection of previously accepted views.

One of the powerful motors of self-criticism which should constantly feature the creativeness of the scholar, being the guarantee of its vitality, is the *self-awareness* of the socially conditioned and subjectively limited nature of this creativeness. When a scholar becomes aware of this fact in its general theoretical shape, the result is a concentration of attention in this respect also on his own creativeness, an inclination to reflect on the social conditioning of his own position, on the limited nature and the possibility of cognitive deformation of his own views, due to the functioning of the subjective factor. This is, of course, not a panacea, and this theoretical self-awareness in respect to the sociology of knowledge does not, by any means, guarantee that the influence of the subjective factor will be overcome completely in the creativeness of the scholar who engages in this reflection. This would be too simple and such a belief would border on *naïveté*. In such circumstances it would be sufficient to disseminate data regarding the sociology of knowledge among scholars in order to have "pure" objective truth prevail in science, which, as we know, is impossible. The aim here is not to achieve miracles but real effects in the progress of knowledge as expressed in the postulate of the progress of objectivity of cognition. This progress is not only possible, but in effect does appear in the practice of scientific work, in a practice aided by the influence of methodological auto-reflection, instigated by the sociology of knowledge.

Thus, the postulate of striving towards objectivity of cognition, in the meaning of a process of overcoming the influences of the subjective factor which limits and deforms this cognition, both in the primitive interpretation(when the postulate of writing history *sine ira et studio* is taken as an appeal to "suspend", in the field of science, those animosities and extra-scientific interests which block the road to historical truth), and in the more subtle and complicated interpretation (when one asks that the historian undertake autoreflection on the social conditioning of his views as the means of overcoming the influence of the subjective factor which limits and deforms cognition), can be addressed to the scholar in general and to the historian in particular.

Nevertheless, how can we reconcile this postulate of overcoming the influence of the subjective factor in the social process of cognition with the postulate of consciously adopting class positions in the study of social phenomena?

The issue is completely clear and simple when the postulate of overcoming the influence of the subjective factor is accompanied by the assertion that the cognition of social phenomena is always conditioned on a class basis. The class conditioning of cognition is after all, one of the manifestations of the subjective factor and it is precisely because, amongst others, this conditioning does take place, that the postulate of overcoming the influence of the subjective factor in striving towards higher degrees of objective cognition is justified. On the other hand, the simultaneous postulating of overcoming the subjective factor in an infinite process of the progress of knowledge and the adopting of class positions in the study of social phenomena, that is, the conscious postulating of permitting the subjective factor to emerge, calls for an explanation. Does this theoretical position of the Marxists—for it is precisely they who join together these two postulates—not contain a contradiction? In my opinion this is an apparent contradiction, derived from an insufficiently concrete and precise form of the statements dealing with the need to adopt consciously class and party positions in the study of social questions.

It is undoubted that progress in the domain of cognition, which can be presented also as the growth of its objectivity, is a function of the overcoming of the factors which limit this objectivity, cause a one-sidedness of cognition or even deform it. One should accept that objective cognition can emerge only as an amalgam of that which is objective with that which is subjective, since cognition is always cognition undertaken by some subject. But one should also accept the fact that *progress* in the domain of cognition and the development of knowledge obtained as its result is possible only by means of overcoming concrete, although constantly different, forms of the subjective factor. The class conditioning of cognition is subject to this same regularity: the concrete forms of deformation, one-sidedness, limitation of cognition, etc., bound up with it, should be *overcome* in the process of progress of knowledge, so as to avoid stagnation and petrification.

Such is the starting-point of our reflections and such it must be, if one does not wish to assert—coming into contradiction with the foundations of Marxist gnoseology—that any cognition, and thus also that which is socially conditioned by the class interest of the proletariat, is perfect cognition, is absolute truth. Hence, in the face of this, what does the postulate of taking class and party positions in research mean, how can this postulate be reconciled with the struggle for the objectivity of cognition? Let us note. above all, that we are dealing here with an elliptic statement, which does not contain all the necessary definitions and parameters and thus leads, as a result of its apparently universalistic, supra-temporal form, to possible misunderstandings.

What does the directive, which is of interest to us, sound like? We say to the students of social phenomena: "If you wish to attain objective truth in your studies, then consciously adopt class and party positions which are in accord with the interests of the proletariat." What does this signify, what are we trying to say by it, and what do we not intend to say by it?

Firstly, we are stating here a directive which is not universalistic nor supra-temporal, but only concretely historical, although this has not been noted *expressis verbis,* and follows only indirectly from the statement. We have here the following line of reasoning: all cognition is socially conditioned; in a class society cognition is necessarily conditioned classwise. The possibility of avoiding social conditioning is a fiction, since the cognizing subject is a social product (in a special meaning of the word "product") and hence in class society, a class-determined product. In this situation there remains only the choice of one of the possible types of social conditionings, and not emancipation from them in general. From the point of view of the objectivity of cognition (in its only real interpretation as relative and not absolute objectivity) the optimum solution is to take the positions conditioned by the class interests of the proletariat. Conditioning by the interests of a *revolutionary* class does not lead to conservative deformations but, on the contrary, shapes a student's position so as to be accessible to social progress and changes. Thus, we are concerned here with a directive bound up with a concrete, historical social situation, with a class society of the capitalist type and not with a universalistic, supra-temporal directive. We are concerned with a directive which takes into account the degree of truthfulness of cognition conditioned by the position of a given class, and thus derived from the assumption that truth is relative and not absolute.

Secondly, it does not follow in the least from the directive recommending the acceptance in studies of the class and party positions of the proletariat, as the cognitively optimum position, that one considers the cognition attained in this fashion to be perfect and complete and the truth contained therein to be absolute. We know that the contrary is so. Cognition conditioned by class and obviously containing the subjective factor, although it has constituted the highest achievement of the human mind in *given* conditions (we are referring to the model and not to the realization which often diverges very far from it) is only a relative truth which in further development, when cognition achieves a higher level, must be overcome. The road which leads to this is the constant overcoming of those objective limitations which the subjective factor, among others, entails. Let us repeat once again: the assuming of the class position of the proletariat provides in one sense a superiority over the cognition conditioned by the interests of other classes but does not, by any means, provide perfect cognition, absolute truth. This is precisely why it is necessary to strive, here also, towards fuller, richer and, in this sense, superior cognition.

Therefore, there is no contradiction between the two directives mentioned above. Whence the appearance of this contradiction and of this misunderstanding? It was derived primarily from the fact that due to the misleading form of expression a directive of an authentically universalistic and supra-temporal nature was placed on the same platform and compared with a directive of a concrete historical nature, referring to a specific type of social relation. The directive of perfecting cognition, of striving to a greater objectivity by means of overcoming the subjective factor, is a universalistic, supra-temporal directive; the process of cognition is, after all, an infinite process in which it is possible to overcome its concrete limitations, as they appear at a given stage, but in which it is impossible to overcome completely all limitations, since this would signify the attainment of the end of something which by its very essence is infinite. On the other hand, the directive of accepting in study the class positions of the proletariat is a concrete historical directive bound up with a given system of social relations. It is only as a result of the general form in which it has been expressed, and of the vicinity of a universalistic directive, pertaining to the fundamental condition of the progress of cognition in all social conditions, that it gives rise to an impression of a universalistic directive, thus suggesting a contradiction.

When we say to a scholar: "If you wish to attain objective truth while studying social problems under the conditions of capitalism, you must consciously accept the class position of the proletariat" we do not maintain, in the least, that this is the road leading to the attainment of absolute truth, but only that it creates a better position for the attainment of objective truth, relative it is true, but the fullest and richest on a given level of the development of human knowledge. Thus, we do not provide the scholar with a guarantee; we only indicate the possibility of success: we do not assure him that he will gain absolute truth, but only relative truth. This is precisely why we do not tell him to consider the cognition attained to be perfect and ideal, but only to be a degree in development which should be exceeded by means, amongst others, of being aware of this necessity and, in consequence, by eliminating its limitations.

When Lenin in his polemics with Struve, praised the class and party nature of historical cognition, stating, *inter alia,* that the materialist who accepts the position of a definite class (that is, a party position) realizes more fully the objectivism of cognition than the so-called objectivist, this did not negate, in the least, the directive of striving in research towards objective truth and of overcoming the limitations blocking its achievement, including those bound up with the class limitation of cognitive perspectives. In spite of appearances, Lenin did not identify here the "partyness" of the accepted position (which he recommended) with the objectivity of cognition as such. He simply stated, as is clear from the context, that a "party" position, which takes into consideration the class structure of society, leads to an objective truth (with the assumption that what one is dealing with are always relative truths which are different from the point of view of the adequacy of reflecting social reality) superior to the position which ignores this structure and its influence on cognition and for this reason claims to be called "objectivist".

Two issues arise here, which should be clearly distinguished. One has a verbal, terminological character and should be explained to counteract the arising of possible verbal misunderstanding. Why does Lenin employ, referring to Struve, the word "objectivist" in a pejorative sense, although he considers objectivity as something positive, proclaiming that it is precisely the materialists who apply objectivism more fully than others? The misunderstanding arises from the fact that Lenin employs the term "objectivist", not in referring to those who really carried out cognitive objectivism, but to those who, due to the rejection of the principle of the class nature of cognition, improperly claim the fulfilment of this objectivism when, in fact, by ignoring the class structure of society which constitutes objective reality, they introduce subjectivism into cognition and deform the objectivity of cognition. Hence, Lenin's usage of a pejorative version of the term "objectivist" is derived not from the fact that he castigates the striving towards the objectivity of cognition (on the contrary, he praises this striving), but from the fact that he criticizes the attempts to disguise class-based cognitive subjectivism with the use of phrases about objective truth, only on the basis that, in a declarative fashion, one rejects in cognition the subjective factor bound up with the objective structure of society. The misunderstanding is heightened by the presence of the expressions "objectivist" and "objectivism" which, in spite of their common root, function here in a different meaning.

After explaining the terminological aspect of Lenin's statement let us pass over to its intrinsic content.

When criticizing Struve, Lenin undertook a differentiation between the position of a Marxist and that of an objectivist of Struve's kind. The objectivist limits himself to ascertaining a given process and its necessity, risking that he will deviate to the position of an apologist of the facts ascertained. The materialist of the Marxist type, on the other hand, examines concretely the given formation and the class forces acting in it; he does not speak simply about "historical tendencies", but about the class which rules in the given order. Lenin concluded:

> In this way the materialist is, on the one hand, more consistent than the objectivist and applies his objectivism more fully and profoundly. ... On the other hand, materialism contains within itself, if I may say so, partyness, makes it obligatory to take a direct and clear stand of a determinate social group in any evaluation of events.[7]

Lenin emphasized in his elucidation that there is no contradiction between the directive of "partyness" in social studies and the directive of striving towards objectivity of cognition. This was already referred to above.

However, in Lenin's reasoning one more motive appears which throws additional light on the problem concerning us here: this refers to the negative appraisal of the "objectivists" or those who represent the view that a negation of the class nature of cognition enhances its objectivity. We have already mentioned above one reason for this negative appraisal: the smoke screen of words about the objectivity of cognition, allegedly deformed by the recognition of the class conditioning of this cognition, serves to disguise, in fact, a cognitive subjectivism which negates dogmatically social reality and deforms the understanding of social phenomena.

This negative appraisal contains one more thought which it is worthwhile to bring into the open. As we know, the objectivity of cognition is realized in the process of overcoming its limitations, connected with the influence of the subjective factor in its multitudinous shapes and manifestations. An important path leading towards this is cognitive auto-reflection which permits the scholar to become aware of which shapes of the subjective factor are active in his particular case and, subsequently, to overcome their influences. It is precisely in this respect that an immense difference exists between the scholar who understands the influence of the class structure of society on cognition and the so-called objectivist who, negating reality, shuts off the road towards an understanding of the mechanism of their functioning. The former is, of course, closer to that possibility of self-realization of his own cognitive position and, thereby, of overcoming it, than the so-called objectivist. The advocate of the concept regarding the class nature of cognition does not only come to know social reality better and more fully (and in this sense "applies his objectivism more fully"), but also possesses better potential conditions for a further development of understanding.

In concluding, we may state that not only is there no contradiction in Marxist theory between the directive of perfecting the objectivity of cognition and the directive of assuming a class, party position in research but, on the contrary, the Marxist scholar, having objective truth as his ultimate aim, fulfils this aim by overcoming his own cognitive limitations, including those which are bound up with his class point of view. Although this may appear like a paradox, the directive of partyness of his research position accepted by him, not only does not hinder but, on the contrary, aids him in this. In any case, the dominant force for the Marxist scholar, his ultimate aim, is always objective truth and everything else is only the means of serving for the achievement of this aim. In accordance with Marx's words:

> Is it not the first duty of a searcher for the truth to strive for it on a straight path, looking neither to the right nor to the left? Will I not forget the very essence of the thing, if I must remember, above all, to discuss it in a prescribed form? [8]

The truth attained in historical cognition is a relative objective truth.

The entire course of our considerations up to this moment bears witness to it. Subjectivism speculates on this relativity of the truths gained in historical cognition, confusing the problem of the objectivity of truth with the problem of its absoluteness. This was already referred to in general at the beginning of the present work, but in view of the importance of the problem it should be taken up once again in a new context.

Let us begin with a general thesis: the conception of relative objective truth, as presented in our considerations, is different and in a sense contrary to the conception of objective relativity defended in the methodology of history by the advocates of presentism.

Of what does the conception of the objective relativity of historical understanding consist? The answer can best be provided by J. H. Randall, one of its principal representatives.

> The historian *must* make a selection. From the infinite variety of relatedness that past events disclose, he must select what is important or "basic" for his particular history. If that selection is not to be merely what *seems* important *for him*, if it is not to be "subjective" and "arbitrary", the selection must have an "objective" focus in something to be done, something he sees forced and imposed on men, some *Aufgabe* or *faciendum,* some job to be accomplished. The history of what is important *for* and relevant *to that problem* . . . will then be perfectly objective, in a sense in which no mere recording of arbitrarily selected "facts" could ever be.
>
> This is the "objective relativism" that is characteristic of historical knowledge as it is of all types of knowledge. Knowledge is "objective" only *for* some determinate context; it is always a knowledge of *the* structure and relations essential *for* that context. [9]

In continuing this line of thought Randall concluded with a particularly expressive formulation: "'Objectivity' means always being *objective* for something, just as 'necessity' means always being *necessary for* something. There can be no 'objectivity' without relation to an objective. . . ." [10]

Let us analyse Randall's position in order to bring out what distinguishes it from the conception of relative objective truth.

Randall's starting-point is the ascertainment of the "partyness" of the historian who undertakes the selection of historical material. In undertaking this selection and in making appropriate evaluations, the historian is conditioned by the interests of the epoch contemporary to him and partial in this sense. However, this does not affect negatively the objectivity of his understanding, on the contrary, it is a guarantee of this objectivity: ". . . Only by definitely taking sides, at least intellectually, can we hope to understand or write the history of anything 'objectively'." [11]

Why is this so? What, according to Randall, does the "objectivity" obtained in this way signify?

The argument of presentism, already known to us, provides the answer to the first question. The historian must undertake a selection of historical material, hence, he must undertake an appraisal of its importance. Thus it is assumed that there exists some system of reference in relation to which the given criterion of importance is of value. This system of reference is the determinate aim or task which the historian puts forth as a social task. When it organizes the historian's work, then the danger of arbitrariness and subjectivity in the selection of material is eliminated and the historian's work becomes objective. This is a relativism which guarantees the objectivity of historical inquiry by referring it to a chosen research aim; hence, its name— Objective relativism.

What does "objectivity", according to Randall, signify? It can be seen from the reflection quoted above that he endowed this expression with some special meaning.

Randall interpreted the objectivity of knowledge in the spirit of extreme relativism. "Knowledge is 'objective' only for a certain determinate context", Randall maintained. Thus, everything depends on the chosen point of view or system of reference: the same cognition will be objective in one case and will not be so in another. Randall explained further that "'Objectivity' cannot exist without relation to a determinate objective", thus employing a play on the words "objectivity" and "objective". Hence, for Randall, "objectivity" signifies the "application to a determinate objective". In accepting such a meaning of the word "objectivity" Randall was able to maintain further with full justification that it is possible to write history "objectively" only when one adopts a "partisan", "partial" stance. When we understand the meaning with which he endows the corresponding expression, then the appearance of a paradox vanishes.

How then can we regard this conception of "objective relativism" from our position of relative objective truth?

In juxtaposing the concept of the theory of relative objective truth

with those of the theory of objective realtivity in historical understanding, we must take note of the similarities as well as of the differences.

Let us commence with the similarities. Both theories take up the
problem of truth in history with the question pertaining to its relative
or absolute character; both recognize that historical truths are relative
in nature. This emphasis on the relativity of historical truth is what
links them and constitutes their similarity.

Both theories speak of the relativity of historical truth, but each one
of them takes up this problem from a different aspect and, as a result,
speaks of it in another way. It is here too that the differences begin.

According to the theory of relative objective truth the problem lies
in the counterposing of historical truth as a partial, incomplete, and in
this sense relative truth with ideal cognition which provides a full,
exhaustive, and in this sense absolute knowledge about the object. In
ascertaining that historical cognition strives toward absolute truth as
the ''limes'', one assumes as the starting-point the thesis that historical
truth, although relative, is always objective truth in the sense of
reflecting objective reality.

The theory of objective reality is concerned with the problem of
relativity of historical truth from another aspect and does not
formulate the initial premise mentioned above. It is not interested in
the qualification of truth, whether one deals with partial or full and
exhaustive truth, but only with whether our cognition is related to
some aim, takes place within the framework of some system of
reference and is relative in this sense, or whether it is independent of
any system of reference, remote from any aim and in this sense
absolute. This is an important question although, from one point of
view, trite. As voiced by an advocate of presentism, or for that matter
an advocate of any of the theories of the social conditioning of social
cognition, this is a rhetorical question. Historical truth in this understanding of the word is, of course, relative since historical cognition is
always dependent on certain conditionings and, hence, is related to
certain aims. Randall incorporates the entire ballast of presentism into
this obvious concept but this does not alter the validity of the initial
thesis on the relativity of historical cognition (in the sense of its
relation to . . .) nor the validity of the paradoxically sounding
conclusion drawn from it, that only relative cognition can be

objective; when a certain system of reference and a certain aim of inquiry have been determined, a criterion is thus obtained for the selection of historical material which hence cannot be arbitrary, subjectivist, but is objective due to the given system of reference. This is what Randall had in mind when he stated in the passage quoted above that: "'Objectivity' cannot exist without relation to a determinate objective." This is an undoubted truth which could in any case be inferred from the negation of the absoluteness of historical cognition.

We have spoken thus far only about the differences between the theory of relative objective truth and the theory of objective relativity in reference to the interpretation of the problem of relativity of historical truth. These were, however, differences arising from the divergence of the question posed pertaining to this problem, differences which did not counterpose both the theories to each other, but made it possible to grasp their results in a complementary fashion, as mutually supplementary. Nevertheless, differences in both conceptions also appear which counterpose both these theories and it is these differences, above all, which should be discussed.

We have already stated above that the starting-point, the premise in one sense, of the theory of relative objective truth in historical cognition is the thesis that relative truth, and not only absolute, also has an objective nature and that the problem of the objectivity and the problem of the absoluteness of truth differ, although they are linked with each other. It is clear that this starting-point is bound up with a corresponding philosophical background and is its consequence; this background rests in a materialist philosophy according to which true cognition is a reflection, in a special meaning of this word, of objective reality. The theory of relative objective truth thus possesses clear world outlook implications and is connected with a materialist stand in the theory of cognition. How does the theory of objective relativity appear in this respect? It passes this problem over in silence but, as follows from the context, not because it considers it as understandable, but because it defends the positions of idealism.

The theory of objective relativity places an emphasis on the justification of cognitive relativism; when it employs the expression "objective" it is concerned solely with the adequacy of the selection of historical material from the point of view of the aim of the inquiry. "Objective" in this case means the same as "related to given needs" and in this sense "not arbitrary". Nothing at all is said about the relation of cognition to reality; this problem is completely ignored.

This is not an accident: as we know, presentism consciously followed in the footsteps of Benedetto Croce and was also influenced by his idealism.

Hence, it appears that while both the theories have a certain point of contact as expressed in their names, in which the words "relative" and "objective" appear, they are simultaneously—and this is of the utmost importance—separated by a fundamental difference in the understanding of objectivity. In one case (the theory of relative objective truth), the issue is objectivity in the sense of recognizing the objective existence of reality which cognition reflects. In the second case (the theory of objective relativity), "Objective" signifies "adapted to given needs", "adapted to a given aim" with an avoidance of the problem of the relation cognition-reality. The issue rests thus in an error-creating homonim which conceals different meanings under an identical sonar cover.

We have taken up this comparison of two theories of relativity of historical cognition not only for the purpose of abstract comparative interests or concern with a semantic analysis of certain expressions. What is at stake is a concrete and significant issue in the context of our reflections. In introducing the subjective factor into the analysis of historical cognition and in undertaking this analysis with consideration of the anthropological factor, the duty of the Marxist is to oppose sharply subjectivism which, after all, traditionally arose from speculation on the role of the subjective factor in cognition, to defend decidedly the thesis of the objectivity of cognition. In saying "duty" we have in mind the consequences derived from an accepted position and philosophy: when, on the basis of determinate reasons, one accepts a materialist stand, one must also, in consequence, accept the theory of objectivity of cognition and truth. It is precisely in the name of this "duty", which extends also to a struggle with the views of philosophical opponents, that we have undertaken the task of "enriching" the theory of objective truth with the subjective factor, with an understanding of the active role of the subject in cognition.

However, one should not lose sight of the dangers which threaten on this road, and this also enters into the scope of this "duty". What we have wanted to achieve on this road rests, as we have already stated, in the "enriching" of the theory of objective truth with such elements which will make possible a better awareness of the true process of cognition and increase thereby the attractiveness of the theory for a perceptive recipient. In no case, however, is it our task to make concessions to the idealist opponent, who, after all, often employs the argument of the active role of the subject in order to negate the thesis regarding its objectivity. The solution of this controversy depends ultimately, of course, on the general philosophical position which a given scholar holds; here theory clearly supersedes history. If a decidedly diverse selection of this starting position is present, then, at a given moment, one can only ascertain a difference of opinions. Nonetheless, this too is important for theoretical self-consciousness and constitutes an indispensable step towards possible progress in this domain.

In concluding these reflections let us pose the question with which we began this work: "Do historians lie when, having at their disposal the same stock of historical materials known in a given period, they write different history? Are they certifying the non-scientific nature of history when, in line with a change of the conditions of a period and not only due to having richer factual material at their disposal, they write history not only anew, but also differently in every period?"

A negative answer to both these questions at the present moment— the end of our reflections—is better grounded by considerations of the social conditioning of historical cognition and the role which the activity of the subject plays in this cognition. It is not worthwhile to revert to these issues here. One would like to add only to what has already been stated within the framework of detailed reflections on various aspects of this subject a few remarks of a more general character.

The apparently striking problem of the variability of the historical vision of particular historians living in the same period and more so of those in diverse periods is, in reality, a banal problem; the appearance of theoretical complications is derived from an erroneous starting-point accepted in reasoning.

It is usually taken for granted that the historian begins with facts and it is precisely the historical facts which are the object of his inquiry and cognition; the word "fact" is taken to be the name of a concrete occurrence in the past. But it is not true that the historian begins his mental work with facts, nor that it is precisely such facts which are the object of his inquiry and cognition. Such convictions are a remnant of the positivist belief in the model of history written "wei es eigentlich gewesen" from a compilation of facts which an historian only presents. It is in this erroneous premise that we find the key to deciphering the problem which concerns us.

The historian commences his work not with facts, but with historical materials, with sources in the broadest meaning of this word, from which he constructs that what we call historical facts. He constructs them both in the sense that he appropriately selects the material which he has at his disposal, employing some criterion of importance, as well as in the sense that he articulates the source material endowing it with the appropriate shape of historical events. In spite of appearances, historical facts are thus not the starting-point, but the end, the result. On the other hand, it is not odd at all that this same source material can serve, and in fact does serve, as raw material for various constructions. A broad span of the manifestations of the subjective factor enters into the picture here; beginning with the effective knowledge about society up to various forms of social conditioning.

The issue becomes additionally complicated when we realize that the subject of historical inquiry and cognition is not, and cannot be, a number of facts grasped in isolation, but only complete historical processes. What we call "fact", in the sense of some concrete historical event, is the product of speculative abstraction, is treated in isolation, separated from multitudinous links and mutual dependencies within the framework of the historical process which makes possible the understanding of the particular fragments, the "facts". When the historian assures that he starts with facts, then this is only an illusion; even if he thinks so subjectively then, being a good historian, he acts differently. The subject of historical inquiry and cognition is always the complete historical process, although we realize this aim by studying fragments of the whole. It is impossible to do otherwise; this is only an illustration of the broader problem of the relation of the whole and the part, when the part becomes understandable only within the framework of the whole, and the whole is attainable in cognition only through its parts. The better the historian, the more perfectly he will be able to fulfil those tasks and methodological self-awareness will undoubtedly be of use to him in this project.

However, this state of affairs implies also far-reaching consequences in the practice of historical writing. If it is the process of history as a whole which is the subject of historical cognition, and if it is precisely this process which is the starting-point of the historian's inquiries, although he may not be always aware of this, then a variability of historical vision is a necessity. A whole, and especially a process-like, variable whole cannot be comprehended otherwise than by fragments. Even if we are aware of the necessity of arranging these fragments within the framework of the entirety of the process, then this will always remain an imperfect deed, due to its partiality. Cognition here must take on the nature of an infinite process which, in perfecting knowledge from various sides, in accumulating partial truths, leads not only to the simple addition of information, to quantitative changes of our knowledge, but also necessarily to qualitative changes of our vision of history.

The fact that historians perceive the image of history diversely, although they have the same source material at their disposal and, even more, the fact that this perception varies when the stock of material changes in step with time and—what is more important—the ability of posing questions and noting the problems lurking in this material also differs. All this is valid and understandable, if one comprehends the process of historical cognition.

Do historians lie? This does happen at times when they are guided by extra-scientific aims and regard history only as an instrument for the current needs of practice. There has been a multitude of infamous deeds of this kind in the history of historiography, but in spite of the social weight of this problem it is trite and theoretically of no interest. What is theoretically interesting, on the other hand, are those cases when the variable historical vision is accompanied by scientific honesty and a fully competent striving towards objective truth. Under such circumstances historians, of course, do not lie, although they may speak about the same matters diversely, or even contradictorily. This is simply the result of the specific nature of cognition which strives constantly towards absolute truth, but does so in an eternal process of accumulating relative truths.

Is this a proof of the inferiority of historical cognition as compared, for instance, with mathematics? We have touched here upon the core of the old controversy regarding the value of the social sciences and, more broadly, the controversy regarding the evaluation of the humanities as against the strict sciences. It is possible to answer this question by means of an apparent banality which, nonetheless, embodies a profound content: everything that we have said on the subject of historical cognition, the conclusions pertaining to historical truth imbued with scepticism, shows only that we are dealing with another type of cognition than is the case with the strict sciences. All attempts to weigh the value of the social sciences, which have led in the history of this problem to efforts to endow them with the shape of deductive sciences, are doomed, as shown by experience, to failure and only damage the domains of knowledge "perfected" in this fashion. As regards the claims of one domain or another, and the methods applied in it, to "superiority", everything depends on the system of reference, on the aims and tasks set in cognition and the criteria of evaluation connected therewith. In any case, there is no unambiguous answer or any unambiguous appraisal in this respect. Given a determinate system of reference, definite aims of inquiry and the application of set criteria, historical cognition, as more complicated and bound up with societal life is "superior". But, assuredly, this is not what matters and the attempts to engage in such emulation are not only not serious, but show that scientific communities also sometimes suffer from complexes. On the other hand, the assertion that historical cognition is different, peculiar, is important, although banal. What is most important is the postulate that this cognition should be arrived at competently; that is, with full awareness of its specific nature. Only such scientific self-awareness is the best guarantee of progress.

Notes

1. H. M. Lynd, "The nature of historical objectivity", the *Journal of Philosophy,* no. 2, p. 35, 1950. (Emphasis—A.S.)
2. P. Ricoeur, *Histoire et Verité,* p. 34, Paris, 1955.

3. M. Bobrzynski, "W imie prawdy dziejowej", ("In the name of historical truth"), in M. H. Serejski (ed.), *Historycy o historii* ("Historians on History"), vol. I, pp. 190-191, Warsaw, 1963.
4. H. Pirenne, "What are historians trying to do?", in H. Meyerhoff (ed.), *The Philosophy of History in Our Time*, pp. 87-100, New York, 1959.
5. *Ibid.*, p. 98.
6. K. R. Popper, *Die offene Geselschaft und ihre Feinde*, vol. II, p. 267, Bern, 1958.
7. V. I. Lenin, "Treść ekonomiczna narodnictwa i jej krytyka w książce P. Struwego" ("The economic contents of Narodism and its criticism in P. Struve's book"), *Collected Works*, Polish edition, vol. I, pp. 433-434, Warsaw, 1950.
8. K. Marx, "Remarks pertaining to the new Prussian instruction on censorship"), in Marx and Engels, *Collected Works*, Polish edition, vol. I, p. 6, Warsaw, 1960.
9. J. H. Randall, Jr., *Nature and Historical Experience*, p. 60, New York, 1958. This author presents similar views in his "Understanding the history of philosophy", in the *Journal of Philosophy*, vol. XXXVI, no. 17, p. 472 (1939).
10. J. H. Randall, *Nature and Historical Experience, ed. cit.*, p. 61.
11. J. H. Randall, "Understanding the history of philosophy", *ed. cit.*, p. 472.

Bibliography

Aron, R., *Introduction à la philosophie de l'histoire—essai sur les limites de l'objectivité historique*, Paris, Gallimard, 1948.

Aron, R., *Dimensions de la conscience historique*, Paris, Plan, 1961.

Aron, R., *Essai sur la théorie de l'histoire dans l'Allemagne Contemporaine La philosophie critique de l'histoire*, Paris, Voin, 1938.

Baczko, B., "Wiedza historyczna i pouczenia moralne" ("Historical knowledge and moral instructions"), in *Księga Pamiątkowa ku czci prof. T. Kotarbińskiego, Fragmenty filozoficzne*, Third Series, Warsaw, 1967.

Barnes, H. E., *History and Social Intelligence*, New York, 1926.

Barnes, H. E., *History of Historical Writing*, New York, Dover Publ., 1962.

Barnes, H. E., *The New History and the Social Studies*, New York, The Century, 1925.

Barth, H., *Wahrheit und Ideologie*, Zurich, 1945.

Bauer, W., *Einführung in das Stadium der Geschichte*, Tübingen, Verlag J. C. B. Mohr, 1928.

Beale, H. K., "What historians have said about the causes of the civil war", in *Theory and Practice in Historical Study . . .*, Social Science Research Council, Bull. 54, 1946.

Beard, Ch. A., "Written history as an act of faith", in the *American Historical Review*, vol. XXXIX, no. 2 (1934).

Beard, Ch. A., "That noble dream", in the *American Historical Review*, vol. XLI, no. 1 (1935).

Beard, Ch. A. and Vogts, Alfred, "Currents of thought in historiography", in the *American Historical Review*, vol. XLII, no. 3 (1937).

Becker, C. L., "Everyman his own historian", in the *American Historical Review*, vol. XXXVII, no. 2 (1932).

Becker, C. L., "Der Wandel im geschichtlichen Bewusstein", *Die Neue Rundschau*, XXXVIII Jahrgang, zweites Heft (1927).

Becker, C. L., "Mr. Wells and the new history", in *Everyman His Own Historian. Essays on History and Politics*, New York, Appleton, 1935.

Berlin, I., *Historical Inevitability*, Oxford, 1954.

Bernheim, E., *Lehrbuch der historischen Methode und der Geschichtsphilosophie*, Leipzig, Duncker, 1903.

Blake, Ch., "Can history be objective?", in P. Gardiner (ed.), *Theories of History*, Glencoe, 1959.

Bloch, M., *Apologie pour l'histoire*, Paris, 1967.

Bobińska, C., *Historyk, fakt, metoda* ("The Historian, Fact and Method"), Warsaw, 1964.

Bobrzyński, M., "W imię prawdy dziejowej" ("In the name of historical truth"), in M. H. Serejski (ed.), *Historycy o historii* ("Historians on History"), vol. I, Warsaw, 1963.

Carr, E. H., *What is History?*, London, Macmillan, 1962.

Collingwood, R. G., *The Idea of History*, Oxford, 1946.

Croce, B., *My Philosophy*, London, Allen & Unwin, 1951.

Croce, B., *History as the Story of Liberty*, New York, Meridian Books, 1955.

Croce, B., *Die Geschichte als Gedanke und als Tat*, Bern, A. Francke, 1944.

Croce, B., *Zur Theorie und Geschichte der Historiographie*, Tübingen, 1915.

Croce, B., "Antihistoricisme", *Revue de Métaphysique et de Morale*, janvier-mars 1931.

Czarnowski, St., *Definicja i klasyfikacja faktów społecznych* ("The Definition and Classification of Social Facts"), *Works*, vol. II, Warsaw, 1956.

Danto, A. C., "Mere chronicle and history proper", in the *Journal of Philosophy*, vol. L, no. 6 (1953).

Dardel, E., *L'Histoire science du concret*, Paris, Presse Universitaires de France, 1946.

Destler, Ch. A., "Some observations on contemporary historical theory", in the *American Historical Review*, vol. LV, no. 3 (1950).

Dewey, J., *Logic, the Theory of Inquiry*, New York, 1949.

Dhont, J., "Histoire et reconstitution du passé", in Ch. Perelman (ed.), *Raisonnement et démarches de l'histoire*, Bruxelles, 1963.

Dovring, F., *History as a Social Science*, The Hague, Martinus Nijhoff, 1960.

Dray, W. H., *Laws and Explanation in History*, Oxford Univ. Press, 1957.

Dray, W. H., *Philosophy of History*, Prentice-Hall, Engelwood, New York, 1964.

Dunning, W. A., *Truth in History*, New York, Columbia Univ. Press, 1937.

Engels, F., *Ludwig Feuerbach*, New York, International Publishers, 1935.

Engels, F., *Anti-Dühring*, New York, International Publishers, 1934.

Fales, W., "Historical facts", in the *Journal of Philosophy*, vol. XLVIII, no. 4 (1951).

Febvre, L., *Combats pour l'histoire*, Paris, Armand Colin, 1953.

Flechtheim, O. K., *History and Futurology*, Meisenheim and Glan, 1966.

Folkierska, A., "O pojęciu ideologii" ("Regarding the concept of ideology"), in *Studia Filozoficzne*, no. 1, 1968.

Frankel, Ch., *The Case for Modern Man*, Boston, Beacon Press, 1959.

Gardiner, P. (ed.), *Theories of History*, Glencoe, Ill., The Free Press, 1959.

Geiger, L. B., "Métaphysique et Relativité Historique", in *Revue de Métaphysique et de Morale*, Oct.-Dec., 1952.

Geyl, P., *Debates with Historians*, New York, Meridian Books, 1958.

Goethe, J. W., "Geschichte der Farbenlehre", in *Auswahl in drei Bänden dritter Band*, Leipzig, Bibliographisches Institut.

Goethe, J. W., *Goethes Gespräche*, Erster Band, Leipzig Biedermann, 1909.

Gibson, Q., *The Logic of Social Inquiry*, London, Routledge and Kegan Paul, 1960.

De Gré, G., "The sociology of knowledge and the problem of truth", in *Journal of the History of Ideas*, vol. II, no. 1 (1941).

Grünwald, E., *Das Problem der Soziologie des Wissens*, Wien-Leipzig, W. Braumüller, 1934.

Haldane, R. B., *The Meaning of Truth in History*, Coulighton Lecture, London, 1914.

Harnack, A., *Über die Sicherheit und die Grenzen geschichtlicher Erkenntnis*, Münich, 1919.

Hayek, F. A., *The Counter-Revolution of Science. Studies on the Abuse of Reason,* Glencoe, Ill., 1952.

Hegel, G. W. F., *Wykłady z filozofii dziejów* ("Lectures on the Philosophy of History"), vols. I and II, Warsaw, 1958.

Heussi, K., *Die Krisis des Historismus,* Tübingen, Verlag J. C. B. Mohr, 1932.

Hexter, J. H., *Reappraisals in History,* London, Longmans, 1961.

Hofer, W., *Geschichtschreibung und Weltanschauung,* Munich, 1950.

Hood, S. (ed.), *Philosophy and History,* New York Univ. Press, 1963.

Ingarden, R., "Betrachtungen zum Problem der Objectivität", *Zeitschrift für Philosophische Forschung,* Band 21, Heft 1, u. 2, 1967.

Kahler, E., *Der Sinn der Geschichte,* Stuttgart, Kohlhammer, 1964.

Kaufmann, F., *Methodology of the Social Sciences,* London, Thames & Hudson, 1958.

Klibansky, R. and Paton, H. J. (ed.), *Philosophy and History,* New York, Harper & Row, 1963.

Klibansky, R. and Paton, H. J. (eds.), *Philosophy and History,* New York, Harper & Oxford, 1936.

Kon, I., *Idealizm filozoficzny i kryzys burżuazyjnej myśli historycznej* ("Philosophical idealism and the Crisis of Bourgeois Historical Thought"), Warsaw, 1967.

Kozyr-Kowalski, S., *Max Weber a Karl Marx,* Warsaw, 1967.

Kula, W., *Rozważania o historii* ("Reflections on History"), Warsaw, 1958.

Lee, D. E. and Beck, H. R., "The meaning of historicism", in the *American Historical Review,* vol. LIX, no. 3 (1954).

Lessing, T., *Geschichte als Sinngebung des Sinnlosen,* Munich, 1919.

Lewis, H. D., *Freedom and History,* London, Allen & Unwin, 1962.

Levy-Brühl, "Qu'est-ce que le fait historique?", *Revue de Synthese Historique,* vol. XXVI, 1926.

Lieber, H. J., *Wissen und Gesellschaft. Die Probleme der Wissenssoziologie,* Tübingen, Max Miemeyer, 1952.

Lovejoy, A. O., "Present standpoints and past history", in the *Journal of Philosophy,* vol. XXXVI, no. 18 (1939).

Lukacs, G., *Geschichte und Klassenbewusstsein,* Berlin, Malik Verlag, 1923.

Lutman, R., "Zagadnienie prawdy w historii" ("The problem of truth in history"), in M. H. Serejski (ed.), *Historycy o historii* ("Historians on History"), vol. 2, Warsaw, 1966.

Lynd, H. M., "The nature of historical objectivity", in the *Journal of Philosophy,* vol. XLVII, no. 2 (1950).

Malewski, A. and Topolski, J., *Studia z metodologii historii* ("Studies on the Methodology of History"), Warsaw, 1960.

Mandelbaum, M., *The Problem of Historical Knowledge. An Answer to Relativism,* New York, Liveright Publ. Corp., 1938.

Mandelbaum, M., "Causal analysis in history", in *Journal of the History of Ideas,* vol. III, no. 1 (1942).

Mannheim, K., *Ideology and Utopia,* London, 1968.

Mannheim, K., *Essays on Sociology and Social Psychology* (ed. by Paul Kecskemeti), London, Routledge & Kegan, 1953.

Mannheim, K., "Historismus", in *Archiv für Sozialwissenschaft und Socialpolitik,* Band 52, Tübingen, 1924.

Mannheim, K., "Das Problem einer Soziologie des Wissens", in *Archiv für Sozialwissenschaft und Sozialpolitik,* Band 53, Tübingen, 1925.

Marx, K. and Engels, F., "The Communist Manifesto", *Selected Works*, vol. I, Moscow, 1951.

Marx, K. and Engels, F., *The German Ideology*, New York, International Publ., 1939.

Marx, K., *The Eighteenth Brumaire of Louis Bonaparte*, New York, International Publ., 1938

Marx, K., *Introduction to the Critique of Political Economy, Collected Works*, vol. 13, Warsaw, 1966.

Marrou, H. I., *De la connaissance historique*, Paris, Editions du Seuil, 1959.

May, E., *Am Abrund des Relativismus*, Berlin, Lüttke Verlag, 1942.

McIlwain, C. H., "The historian's part in a changing world", in the *American Historical Review*, vol. XLII, no. 2 (1937).

Mead, G. H., "The Philosophy of the Present".

Meinecke, F., *Die Entstehung des Historismus*, Bands I and II, Munich, Verlag Oldenburg, 1936.

Merton, R. K., *Social Theory and Social Structure*, Part III, *The Sociology of Knowledge and Mass Communication*, Glencoe, Ill., The Free Press, 1957.

Mises, L., *Theory and History*, Yale Univ. Press, 1957.

Moszczeńska, W., *Metodologii historii zarys krytyczny* ("A Critical Outline of the Methodology of History"), Warsaw, 1968.

Nagel, E., "The logic of historical analysis", in H. Meyerhoff (ed.), *The Philosophy of History in Our Time*, New York, 1959.

Nowell-Smith, P. H., "Are historical events unique?", in *Proceedings of the Aristotelian Society*, New Series, vol. LVII, 1957.

Ortega y Gasset, J., "History as a system", in H. Meyerhoff (ed.), *The Philosophy of History in Our Time*, New York, 1959.

Perelman, Ch. (ed.), *Raisonnement et démarches de l'historien*, Bruxelles, Edit. de l'Institut de Sociologie, 1963.

Pirenne, H., "What are historians trying to do?", in H. Meyerhoff (ed.), *The Philosophy of History...*, New York, 1959.

Popper, K. R., *The Poverty of Historicism*, London, Routledge & Kegan Paul, 1957.

Popper, K. R., *Die offene Gesellschaft und ihre Feinde*, Bands I and II, Bern, Francke Verlag, 1957.

Randall, J. H., *Nature and Historical Explanation*, New York, Columbia Univ. Press, 1958.

Randall, J. H., "On understanding the history of philosophy", in the *Journal of Philosophy*, vol. XXXVI, no. 17 (1939).

Randall, J. H. and Haines, G., "Controlling assumptions in the practice of American historians", in *Theory and Practice in Historical Study. A Report of the Committee on Historiography*, Social Science Research Council, Bulletin 54, 1946.

Ranke, L., *Geschichten der romanischen und germanischen Völker von 1494 bis 1514*, Leipzig, Duncker und Humboldt, 1885.

Read, C., "The social responsibilities of the historian", in the *American Historical Review*, vol. LV, no. 2 (1950).

Ricoeur, P. *Histoire et verité*, Paris, Edit. du Seuil, 1955.

Riezler, K., "The historian and truth", in the *Journal of Philosophy*, vol. XLV, no. 14 (1948).

Rotenstreich, N., *Between Past and Present*, New Haven, Yale Univ. Press, 1958.

Rothacker, E., *Einleitung in die Geisteswissenschaften*, Tübingen, Mohr, 1930.

Rowse, A. L., *The Use of History*, London, 1946.

Salomon, G., "Historischer Materialismus und Ideologienlehre", *Jahrbuch für Soziologie,* zweiter Band, 1926.

Schaff, A., "La définition fonctionnelle de l'ideologie et le probleme de la 'fin des siècle de l' idéologie", *L 'Homme et la sociéte,* no. 4, 1967.

Schaff, A., *Z zagadnień marksistowskiej teorii prawdy* ("On Problems of the Marxist Theory of Truth"), Warsaw, 1959.

Scheler, M., *Die Wissensformen und die Gesellschaft,* Leipzig, 1926.

Simmel, G., *Die Probleme der Geschichtsphilosophie. Eine Erkenntnistheoretische Studie,* Munich and Liepzig, Verlag von Duncker, 1923.

Social Science Research Council (USA) (ed.), *Theory and Practice in Historical Study: A Report of the Committee on Historiography,* Bulletin 54, 1946.

Stark, W., *The Sociology of Knowledge,* London, 1958.

Szacki, J., "Uwagi o marksowskim pojęciu 'świadomości fałszywej'" ("Remarks concerning the Marxian concept of 'False Consciousness'"), in *Studia Socjologiczne,* no. 2, 1966.

Teggart, F. J., *Theory and Processes of History,* USA, 1941.

Thyssen, J., *Der philosophische Relativismus,* Bonn, 1947.

Toynbee, A. J., "L'histoire insaissiable", *La Table Ronde,* no. 86 (1955).

Troeltsch, E., *Der Historismus und seine Probleme,* Tübingen, J. C. B. Nohr, 1922.

Walsh, W. H., *Philosophy of History. Introduction,* New York, Harper Tarchbooks, 1960.

White, M., "Can history be objective?", in H. Meyerhoff (ed.), *The Philosophy of History. . .,* New York, 1959.

Witar, J. J., *Czy zmierzch ery ideologii?* ("The End of the Era of Ideology?"), Warsaw, 1966.

Williams, W. A., "A note of Charles A. Beard's search for a general theory of causation", in the *American Historical Review,* vol. LXII, no. 1 (1956).

Zagorin, P., "Carl Becker on history", in the *American Historical Review,* vol. LXII, no. 1 (1956).

Żywczyński, W., *Narodziny i dzieje pojęcia historyzmu* ("The Origin and History of the Concept of Historicism"), *Historyka,* vol. I, Warsaw, 1967.

Bibliography of Works Consulted Regarding the Causes of the French Revolution

Aulard, A., *Histoire politique de la Révolution française,* Paris, Armand Colin, 1921.

Barnave, J., *Introduction á la révolution française,* Cahier des Annales 15, Paris, Armand Colin, 1960.

Barruel, A., *Mémoires pour servir a l'histoire du Jacobinisme,* Hamburg, cher P. Fauche, 1803.

Blanc, L., *Histoire de la révolution française,* nouvelle edition, Paris, Flammarion, 1878.

Burke, E., *Reflexions su la révolution française,* Paris, chez Laurent fils.

Funck-Brentano, F., *L'Ancien régime,* Paris, Fayard, 1926.

Gaxotte, P., *La Révolution française,* Paris, Fayard, 1962.

Godechot, J., *Les révolutions (1770-1799),* Paris, Presses Universitaires de France, 1963.

Jaures, J., *Histoire socialiste de la révolution française,* Paris, Ed. de l'Humanité, 1922.

Labrousse, C. E., *Esquisse du mouvement des prix et des revenus en France au XVIII siècle,* Paris, Dalloz, 1932.

Labrousse, C. E., *La Crise de l'économie française à la fin de l'ancien régime et au debut de la révolution,* Paris, Presses Universitaires, 1944.

Laponneray, *Histoire de la révolution française,* Paris, 1838.

Lefebvre, G., *Etudes sur las revolution française,* Paris, 1954.

Lefebvre, G., *La Révolution française,* Paris, Presses Univ. de France, 1957.

De Maistre, J., *Considérations sur la France,* Paris, chez Petey, nouvelle edition, 1871.

Mallet du Pan, *Correspondance inédite avec la cour de Vienne,* Paris, Libr-Plan, 1884.

Mallet du Pan, *Correspondance politique pour servit à l'histoire du republicanisme français,* Hambourg, PP. Fauche, 1798.

Mathiez, A., *La Révolution française,* Paris, Armand Colin, 1937.

Michelet, J., *Histoire de la révolution française,* Paris, Bibl. de la Pleiade, 1952.

Qunet, E., *La Christianisme et la révolution française,* Oeuvres completes, tom. 3, Paris, Pagnerre, 1857.

Rabaut, M. J. P., *Almanach historique de la révolution française pour l'année 1792,* Paris, chez Onfroy.

See, H., *La Vie économique et les classes sociales en France au XVII siècle,* Paris, Felix Alcan, 1924.

Soboul, A., *La Révolution française 1789-1799,* Paris, Ed. Sociales, 1948.

De Staël Holstein, *Considérations sur les principaux événements de la révolution française,* Liège, J. A. Latour, 1818.

Taine, H., *Les Origines de la France Contemporaine,* Paris, Libr. Hachette, 31 edition.

Thiers, A., *Histoire de la révolution française,* Paris, chez Lecointe, 1834.

De Tocqueville, A., *L'Ancien règime et la révolution,* Paris, Michel Levy Freves, 1857.

Author Index

Subject Index